Men of the Pentagon

From Forrestal to McNamara

C. W. BORKLUND

Within the vast labyrinth of the Pentagon—the concrete cobweb of the military hierarchy—Room 3E880 has special significance. As the office of the Secretary of Defense, it is the headquarters of the key U.S. official responsible for national security. Since 1947, when the armed forces were combined under one department, eight men—drawn from the diverse fields of finance, politics, industry, and the military—have sat in this office. Through cold wars and hot, through periods of domestic and international political strife, Room 3E880 has been witness to military rivalries, personal and organizational triumphs, advance and retreat, misunderstanding and frustration and breakthrough, and at least one tragedy.

MEN OF THE PENTAGON is a study of the men who have occupied Room 3E880—from James Forrestal to Robert McNamara—and of how they met, or failed to meet, the multiple crises of national security that have beset the United States since the end of World War II. Against a background of conflict in Korea, Latin America, and Vietnam, C. W. Borklund draws sharply defined portraits of each of the defense leaders, examining the pressures, problems, and personal politics that challenged them as they struggled with the larger and more deadly questions of national defense. Here are probing, behind-the-scenes analyses of Forrestal's abortive attempt to bring about a cooperative interservice spirit; Louis Johnson's entanglement in the "Revolt of the Admirals"; George Marshall and the

(*continued on back flap*)

the Armed Forces Management Association's National Literary Award.

Men of the Pentagon

Men of the Pentagon

FROM FORRESTAL TO McNAMARA

CARL W. BORKLUND

FREDERICK A. PRAEGER, *Publishers*
New York • Washington • London

FREDERICK A. PRAEGER, *Publishers*
111 Fourth Avenue, New York, N.Y. 10003, U.S.A.
77–79 Charlotte Street, London W. 1, England

Published in the United States of America in 1966
by Frederick A. Praeger, Inc., Publishers

Library of Congress Catalog Card Number: 66-18890

Printed in the United States of America

To the man in the Pentagon's room 3E880—
whoever he may be

Acknowledgments

To me, the most pleasing aspect of researching for and writing this book was the full, frank disclosure of information and opinion I received from dozens of persons who still are, or once were, closely tied to operations at the highest Pentagon levels. Regrettably, I am permitted to thank very few of them by name, rank, and job title.

Since the beginning, in 1947, there has been an unwritten but clearly understood rule that the Pentagon's spokesman is the Secretary of Defense, not one of his staff—no matter how important that staff man's contribution to the Secretary's work may be. (That rule has been broken only once, by McNamara's so-called Whiz Kids in the early 1960's, to the considerable aggravation of Pentagon veterans.)

Even though many of the men who have held Pentagon staff positions of great importance are now producing movies in Hollywood, practicing law in Miami, financing businesses on Wall Street, or engaging in other careers in and out of Washington, it is surprising how consistently they still stick by that rule. Thus, the price they all insisted I pay for free access to their invaluable experience was my promise to preserve their anonymity. I broke that promise only where their views, stated to me, were also part of some printed record that anyone could find who followed the same trail I took. The former Defense Secretaries still living when this work began—Louis Johnson (who has since died), Robert Lovett, Neil McElroy, and Thomas Gates—spoke to me openly, and I have quoted them often in these pages. The present Secretary, Robert McNamara, has been generous, indeed, with time and with comment.

Anonymous or not, all who helped me know my deep debt. To each of them I say, "Without your contribution, this book would not have been possible."

C. W. Borklund

Preface

IN THE PAST TWENTY YEARS, there has been little theoretical disagreement on the need for unification of the U.S. military forces. But there has been bitter argument on how to achieve it. Unification in the national defense organization has meant lots of different things to lots of different people—and still does. In 1947, U.S. leadership agreed to cross off outdated outfits, merge old ones into new ones, and pull the power of top command up from separate, largely autonomous Army, Navy, and Air Force services into a single Office of the Secretary of Defense. Over a decade later, in 1959, an Air Force Lieutenant General summed up the frustration over the plodding progress toward achieving unification when he said, "Halfway measures are not enough. The only way unification will be achieved is through a hard-hitting free press informing and educating Americans in the actions necessary for survival."

The milestones in the building of a stronger Department of Defense have been well marked. What has been only sketchily detailed is the human tug-of-war. People make decisions, rightly or wrongly. People change organizations, shift power, cause progress, or wreck it. In the midst of the swirling military turmoil, the prime target for psychological power plays, is, has been, and by design will continue to be the Secretary of Defense.

His personal plans, hopes, perceptions, frustrations, interests, abilities, strengths, and weaknesses have, in the final analysis, decided how well, if not *how*, U.S. military strength has been built and used. To understand best what goes on in the Department of Defense requires knowing the trials of the man who runs it. The trials of the men of Defense are what this book is all about.

C. W. B.

June, 1966

Contents

Men of the Pentagon

I

The Concrete Cobweb

TWENTY-FIVE YEARS AGO, on the west bank of the Potomac River in Washington, D.C., on a stretch of swampy bottomland running, roughly, from the Memorial Bridge on the north to U.S. Highway 1 on the south, there was a collection of shacks, dump grounds, and rendering works, known locally as "Hell's Bottom." Sprawled along the foot of the Arlington National Cemetery, just across the river from both the Lincoln and Jefferson Memorials, the area was an eyesore the U.S. Congress, and the annual avalanche of Washington tourists, could do without.

Another thing the Congress of those days could do without was the way the U.S. Army's Washington headquarters was set up. Then known as the War Department, it actually amounted to little pockets of people spread all over town wasting a lot of time, energy, and money running back and forth from office to satellite office. In 1941, just prior to U.S. entry into World War II, the Congress ended several months of bombastic debate by deciding to take care of both problems at once. It ordered construction of what amounted to the world's largest office building. It was to (1) replace the architectural junk yard on the Potomac; (2) house "in one place to increase management efficiency" all those people working for the Army. In fine farsighted fashion, Congress ordered the building designed so that it could be turned into a veteran's hospital when "peace is restored, and the Army no longer needs the room."

"Hell's Bottom" did become a softly rolling, tree-filled landscape laced with wide, clover-leaf commuter highways. But, what with one thing and another, the Washington-based Army was never quite able to pull all of itself together under that one roof. And, even though wide ramps still climb from the basement to the top floor, so that an ambulance could drive almost to the door of any room, there is precious little chance that this office building will ever become a hospital.

What it has become, instead, is a five-sided, five-story-high concrete cobweb; five concentric buildings, actually, labeled the A, B, C, D, and E rings, tied together with covered crosswalks; seventeen and a half miles of corridors running into and around eighty-three acres of offices, drafting rooms, tabulating sections, store rooms, laboratories, libraries, restaurants, auditoriums, dispensaries—even a shopping center. It is known all over the world as the Pentagon, command post and corporate headquarters for the most powerful military machine and largest single business in the world—the United States Department of Defense.

To run the Pentagon each year takes a donation equal to nearly $275 from every man, woman, and child in the country. The Defense Department buys some of just about every kind of goods and services produced in the United States, as well as spending incomprehensible billions for products of its own unique design. The Department's plans, decisions, cost, success, and failure all directly affect the lives of more than 180 million persons; indirectly, they affect, if not the well-being, at least the peace of mind of hundreds of millions more.

What the Defense Department's leaders do, or want to do, consumes over half the undivided attention of the U.S. Congress, changes the texture and strength of whole blocks of the economy, creates or destroys entire industries, weakens or cements relations with foreign countries, prevents or propagates wars. The Pentagon is a complex, curious contradiction of waste and efficiency, brilliance and stupidity, patriotism and pork-barrel politics, courageous vision and reactionary caution. It directs an arsenal fully capable, given the order, of obliterating all the world's major cities in something less than half a day.

Since 1947, this organizational maze has been run, in theory at least, by one man—a sort of Deputy President of the United States for National Security, who is officially titled the Secretary of Defense. There are many things worth knowing about this man. He worries about his family, his health, how well he's doing his job. He faces the same hazards of daily living as anybody else. (The first Secretary of Defense frequently took his morning shower in a bathroom adjacent to his Pentagon office; once, he found himself trapped there without a towel.)

The Secretary worries about whether he has enough bright people around him who can and will analyze soundly and unemotionally—and help him solve—the problems, or at least the military problems, of keeping the nation from being pulverized. With so many of these bright people disagreeing all the time, he worries about whether they know what they're doing.

He worries about whether he is delivering what his boss, the President, wants—and whether what "the Boss" wants is what he really ought to have. He worries about whether the people who work for him understand his decisions, about whether they will perform efficiently, economically, and effectively. He has literally thousands of critics eager to tell him what's wrong with his decisions. Yet, to run the organization well, he must have an intense conviction about the correctness of what he alone is trying to do. If he does not, the organization will run him.

In the past fifty years, there has been a barrage of studies—good, bad, and inconsequential—on what makes U.S. military forces tick and how they ought to be led. From 1920 to 1944, the Federal government alone averaged better than one study a year, almost all of them without comprehensive result. The "right defense organization" is a favorite subject of military command and general staff colleges. It is a favorite subject of retired and active-duty Pentagon professionals, and of the Congress, and of that amorphous mass known as "informed observers."

These analysts discourse in maddening detail on procedural panaceas, organizational utopias, and "the best way" to run the outfit. It's a favorite Pentagon subject. The truth is, as the eighth Secretary of Defense, Robert S. McNamara, has pointed out, "There is no 'best' way."

Since James Forrestal took the oath of office as the first Secretary of Defense on September 17, 1947, the job has been held by eight different men: Forrestal, Louis Johnson, General George Marshall, Robert Lovett, Charles Wilson, Neil McElroy, Thomas Gates, Robert McNamara. No single feature distinguishes how well each has done his work as compared with the others. What each accomplished, or failed to, has been largely a result of the environment in which he had to operate, his human ability to deal with it, and the power tools he was given to use. While earning their individual accolades and criticisms on the job, the men themselves have been, variously, leaders and followers, arbiters, prophets, scapegoats, circumstantially successful, haunted by tragedy, amenable, disputatious, unimpressive, dynamic, and dull.

As with any organization, control of the Defense Department is determined by how tightly the Secretary is able to control three things: the money, the people, and the communications. The first is the fuel that runs the second, the third the steering gear that gives direction to the other two. (As former Strategic Air Command General Thomas Power once said, "Without communications, I don't control anything except my desk. I can't throw it very far, and it won't kill anybody.")

With money, people, and communications under control, the Secretary has in harness an organization with the generally recognized ability, as past wars have proved, to do whatever is demanded of it. Not having control of these elements helped destroy Forrestal's life and made a scapegoat out of Johnson. Marshall lent his name to the job for a year to restore its prestige, fought the Korean War, and let the rest of the organization control itself. Lovett, too, was "preoccupied" with Korea. When he got back to refighting the same battles Forrestal had fought, he had only enough time left in office to suggest some guidelines for the next Secretary to follow. Wilson ignored a lot of Lovett's guidelines, made some of the same mistakes Forrestal had made about what he could expect of Defense people, and lost control of the organization.

McElroy never really had much chance to establish control. Russian missile-satellite launchings had frightened the nation into giving the Department of Defense money faster than even the Pentagon could spend it. (With enough money, military people aren't much of a problem, and communications becomes almost an academic afterthought.) McElroy let his people have their way —a course that turned out to be something of a mistake. His successor, Tom Gates, trapped by a lame-duck political situation, wasn't in office long enough to grab the reins properly. He had opportunity to do little more than revive some of the better projects of his predecessors. Robert McNamara is generally regarded as the brightest, strongest, most effective leader the Pentagon has ever had—although not its most adept diplomat. Yet, even

McNamara has established reasonably tight control over only two elements: money and communications.

At its very best, the Defense Department can be a powerful, compassionate answer to an international plea for protection. At its worst, it is a sort of low-grade, gold-plated zoo. And always, to some of the people who work there, it is a frustration. Were it not for a deep dedication to cause and country, much of the most valued talent in the military wouldn't come near the place.

But for all the merit of dedication, the direction dedication takes is another matter. From his perch on top of the mountain, the Secretary can define the proper form with misleading simplicity, as McNamara did when he said, "Once you decide you intend to do what you think best for *total* national security, the rest is relatively easy." For a man anchored somewhere down the mountainside, there is a predictable tendency to define the total problem from his own vantage point. That difference in view has been, in the past twenty years, the launch pad for most of the Pentagon's internal squabbling.

Basically, there are several different caste systems in Defense. Any one individual can, and usually does, belong to several of them. The Secretary must understand and inspire them all. But they have problems of their own.

Two of these groups cut laterally across all Army, Navy, Air Force, and Marine Corps lines. They are: the career military (officers and enlisted men) and the career civil servants who fill approximately one out of every four top Defense assignments. It is difficult to tell which group outranks the other. Each thinks the other is better off.

They do the same types of work, mostly; put in the same long hours under the same working conditions; share responsibility equally; have jobs with essentially the same mission; represent just about every professional talent and service known. Yet, their pay is different; their eligibility for "fringe benefits"—and even the benefits themselves—are different. Their rules of proper behavior aren't the same, nor their criteria for promotion, nor even their job security. They are entrusted with wise and honest expenditure of 10 per cent of the nation's gross national product each year; yet, by law, they are considered susceptible—not as individuals but as groups, some more than others—to knavery and crookedness.

A civil servant can be outstanding on a weapon development

program for five years, and his career will probably be in wonderful shape. A colonel or a Navy captain can do the same job for the same length of time with the same success, and his career will face a major crisis. (Military people, for proper "career advancement," are supposed to change jobs every three years or so.)

Over these groups is a relatively small, powerful layer of temporary appointees, usually selected because of strong connections with the political party in power. These appointees, including the Secretary of Defense, sit at the top, not only in the Office of the Secretary of Defense, but in the military departments. As a rule, the appointees come and go more rapidly than Presidents are elected; in fact, they average less than two years on the job. Consequently, about the time many of them are just beginning to learn what's going on, they leave.

All these men at the top have told the Congress and the taxpayer, usually out of gratitude, that the 3.5 million or so career Defense personnel are, to quote one appointee, the "loyal, talented, unsung men and women who daily face the full brunt of Communist aggression." Secretary Robert McNamara has said of them, "In our society, no other group is paid less per unit of ability than our military leaders."

On his last day as Pentagon boss, Neil McElroy stated: "There are a couple of good things which I think I will be boasting about when I get into private enterprise. One of them is the quality of the people in the management of this Defense Department. I am talking both of people in uniform and people in civilian assignments.

"I was prepared to believe that there was a certain amount of dry rot in government, as I had been told there was. I am sure there is some in various levels of government around the country. I didn't find that among what I will call the management level of the civilians in Defense nor of the military people in Defense. I have tremendous respect for them, not only for their capabilities, but for their dedication. These people work in a way in which I don't see people work very much outside, and I plan to say that a few times, too."

Both the civilians and the military people are sorted out into job slots that read a lot like the organization chart of any company. Some are in the research and development office; some in what industry calls the marketing department (to the military, the "plans and requirements" divisions). Some are in the personnel office; some are in procurement, transportation, maintenance, training, the comptroller's office, and so on. Naturally, each of these functional specialists would like the Secretary to give "more" to research, or "more" to procurement, or to training, or to maintenance, depending on where that advocate of "more" works.

Finally, Pentagon personnel are members of another major set of fairly coequal castes. This membership, too, affects their personal attitudes toward doing what the Secretary wants done. There are five main castes: the Office of the Secretary of Defense, the Army, the Navy, the Air Force, and the Marine Corps. The situation is complicated in that the Army has its own air force and a small navy; the Navy has an air force and its own army—the Marine Corps. The Marine Corps, which also has an air force, does not, however, consider itself the Navy's army. For a long time, the Air Force had only an air force but, lately, it has managed to develop its own artillery, the intercontinental ballistic missile. When budget money is at stake, which means just about all the time, these groups don't get along very well.

Defense personnel also divide up and argue along other lines, closer to their combat members' hearts. The fighter pilots are certain they can do most of the necessary Defense job in the air better than the bomber boys—and vice versa. The young missile men, untested as a combat team, believe they can prove to the Secretary and the Congress that they can do the job better than any pilot.

Some military experts tell the Secretary that sea-launched missiles are better than land-launched. Other experts say not so. And they all have valid-looking estimates of probable kills to back them up, along with apparently cheaper price tags. Submariners know that they could accomplish a lot more for the same dollars than carrier admirals, who think submarines are, mostly, easy targets. Carriers are sitting ducks, too, insist many who fly aircraft or fire missiles or drive submarines. Paratroops know definitely that the regular Army is too big and slow to win any battles. The regular troops are sure that sky divers aren't going to win wars. And there are some chemical warfare people who will plot an "irrefutable" argument that the nation could retire all the rest of its military forces if *they* were put in charge.

Robert Lovett, the fourth Secretary of Defense, stated most succinctly the problem of meshing all these talents when he said, on leaving his job: "It is difficult for them to detach themselves from the hopes and ambitions of their own service. . . . The maintenance of an impartial, nonpartisan position becomes increasingly difficult in times of shortage of either men, money, or material. In fact, it is remarkable that the form of organization currently in being has worked so well and it is, I think, a tribute to the quality of the individual involved."

There are a lot of spurious reasons why these people don't agree. The major valid reason was summed up by one Navy admiral in 1959, in a bitter attack on that year's round of proposals to further "unify" the military organization: "Esprit de corps is an essential prerequisite to military success, and where it is absent, it is the first duty of responsible leaders to build it. It would be utter nonsense to attempt to convince a man that he should risk his life in a submarine, a jet aircraft, or as a member of a landing force, and to train for years to become proficient at his tasks, and at the same time to tell him that, after all, what he is doing is not really important; that others in other branches could accomplish the goals just as well; that there is no real necessity to perpetuate the skills.

"The dedicated submariner *must* believe in the importance of submarines—and a submarine service cannot be built without dedicated men who possess a deep conviction of the importance of their tasks and a loyalty to their organization. Thus, even within the Navy itself, there are competing loyalties. This is clearly recognized as a healthy situation, however, and the divisive effect is controlled, moderated, and kept within proper bounds by a loyalty to the Navy as a whole. The same is true of the other Services."

Even this argument, sound as it is, evades the basic question: Must the military today have a single command staff at the top level to properly pull all these combat threads together?

Thousands of people were killed during World War II, Harry Truman inferred in 1946, because we didn't have a truly unified Defense organization. A few thousand more men allegedly were lost during the Korean fighting for much the same reason. Billions of dollars were misspent on missilery in the late 1950's—an error caused, at least in part, by lack of the military cohesion the United States should have had.

For nearly a generation, this nation wasted fully 25 per cent of what it spent on national security. Some Pentagon professionals go so far as to insist that the figure should be fully 50 per cent. In any event, if James Forrestal and Louis Johnson had had, in 1949, the readiness that Tom Gates had in 1959, the chances are very good that there would have been no Korean conflict. If Robert Lovett and Charlie Wilson had had in 1953 what McNamara had in 1963, a "missile gap" wouldn't have materialized. A heavy price was paid to close that "gap," which, as close examination eventually revealed, did not really exist. (The charge that Russia had more missiles than the United States was widely publicized in the late 1950's. John F. Kennedy even made the supposed existence of the "gap" a Presidential campaign issue in 1960. Yet, in 1961, his Administration publicly agreed with McNamara's predecessor, Tom Gates, that there was no missile gap.)

During a stretch from late 1944 to mid-1947, the nation's military and political leaders, in one long, vitriolic argument, reviewed every review of earlier years; pondered all the imponderables of the past; exhumed all previously buried issues; and gave lip service to a conclusion that the country's military strength wasn't well enough managed, organized, or oriented to U.S. defense needs. The long and bitter analysis was prompted by rude disillusionment in high places with the military command machinery that had fought World War II. It was prodded into public view by the demands of Congress that the military eliminate "waste and duplication." The proposed solution to all the problems was the organization of a single Department of the Armed Forces, to be patterned after but made stronger than the somewhat informally coordinated Army, Navy, and Army Air Force combat commands, which, in the field, had planned and fought the latter half of the war. In effect, the objecters to inefficiency urged establishment of a sort of federal government for the military.

During the Capitol Hill debates, a wiry Wall Street investment broker turned brilliant government administrator, led the attack against this "autocratic" idea. He pounded and diffused it into a compromise more closely resembling a loose confederacy of autonomous military services. The design ended up being pretty much his—and President Harry Truman gave him the job of making it work.

II

Pioneer's Profile

PIPE-SMOKING, pensive James Vincent Forrestal, with his craggy features and broken nose, looked like a tough middleweight fighter. He gave most people who met him the impression that he was a man of great force, energy, and vigor. He was. Son of an immigrant father from County Cork, this lonely little 150-pound Irishman "loved the United States," said a close friend, "with an intensity only immigrants and the children of immigrants can wholly comprehend."

"His name," says a Pentagon veteran, "runs through the entire pattern of American foreign and military policies in the crucial years following World War II." But, if it hadn't been for chance, personal friendships, and politics, Forrestal might never have made it to Washington, nor have written his name so large—and, in the end, so tragically—in contemporary American history.

He was admired, respected, even loved for his seemingly tireless effort, dedicated devotion to duty, first as Under Secretary, then as Secretary of the Navy, then as first Secretary of Defense from September, 1947 to March, 1949. He was presented, on March 28, 1949, with the Distinguished Service Medal—highest honor the nation could bestow on a civilian—for his contributions to national security.

Less than a week later, he was rushed back from a Florida vacation to the National Naval Medical Center in Bethesda, Md., just outside Washington, D.C. Doctors announced that he was the victim of "an excessive occupational fatigue not unlike that suffered by servicemen in battle." After almost two months of treatment, toward the end of May, word circulated in a hopeful Washington that he might soon recover.

But, early on Sunday morning, May 22, a nurse on the Naval Medical Center's seventh floor heard something bang off a narrow ledge outside the fourth floor and thud into the hospital's third-floor abutment. Sometime between 1:45 and 2:00 A.M., James Vincent Forrestal, fifty-seven, had slipped out of his hospital room, crossed to a nearby diet kitchen, loosened a window screen held only by thumb latches, and plunged thirteen stories to his death. He was found with the sash of his dressing gown wrapped and knotted tightly around his throat.

His death shocked the nation, and leaders of governments around the world. Washington's reaction was a distressed, sometimes anguished, sometimes conscience-stricken "Why?"

Although the medical files on Forrestal were never made public, the virtually unanimous opinion of persons who had known him for a good part of his life was that, to quote one, "His safety valve was inoperable."

His freshman year at Dartmouth College in 1911 had been almost a total loss academically. Later, his grades at Princeton University were much better, and, in his senior year, his class voted him "the man most likely to succeed." His strong-willed mother wanted him to become a priest. He wanted to be a newspaper man. He became neither. Six weeks before graduation, he dropped out of school and took a job selling cigarettes. After that, he drifted through a series of jobs until he followed some Princeton classmates to Dillon, Read, and Company, a New York investment house.

He played a major role in building Dillon, Read into an aggressively successful sales outfit. That achievement started him on a meteoric rise that ended with his being named company president in 1938. By then, he was forty-six.

He had first caught official Washington's attention when he helped draw up the Securities Exchange Acts passed in 1933–34. His work impressed Washington lawyer Thomas G. Corcoran, drafter of the SEC legislation. "Tommy the Cork," as President Franklin D. Roosevelt called him, swung a lot of weight around the White House. In 1940, he suggested Forrestal's name when

Roosevelt needed another administrative assistant. At the time, Roosevelt was doing everything he could, short of war, to help besieged foreign nations hold off German, Italian, and Japanese aggression. Basically, that meant increasing U.S. industrial production of war materials. Roosevelt wanted someone to help him find the right men with "big names and organizing ability" to handle the build-up. Forrestal had been ferreting out management talent for Dillon, Read–backed firms for years, and already knew personally a lot of people who could get things done.

Corcoran described Democrat Forrestal to Roosevelt as "the acknowledged leader of your crowd on Wall Street." Moreover, Corcoran added, "He has enormous courage to do things that have never been done before, he understands the German situation thoroughly and bitterly, and he has followed you eagerly in your perceptions for the need to get the nation ready."

Forrestal heard about all this and asked his long-time friend Bernard Baruch (who was a sort of White House adviser without portfolio) what he thought of the scheme. Baruch advised him to accept the job, if asked. Even then, Forrestal was reluctant. In a note to Corcoran, he said:

> Dear Tom: I have some misgiving whether I can be effective in the role you outlined and I think there are better men available. Bob Lovett is one who comes to my mind. . . . the whole picture is too serious . . . for prima donna tactics. So I'm giving you my proxy—and I shall be happy either way it works out. I want neither publicity nor glory—the price of both is too high.

As matters worked out, Forrestal gave up a reported $190,000-a-year job and was sworn into office on June 23, 1940. He had barely gone to work when Navy Secretary Frank Knox saw him in action at a Pentagon meeting; shortly afterward, with Roosevelt's permission, Knox asked him to fill the newly created post of Navy Under Secretary. In August, just two months after moving to Washington, Forrestal took over the Navy's second highest civilian office.

Holding that responsibility meant, to Forrestal, total submersion in it. Spurred by an intellectual curiosity that ranged all over the map, he read voraciously, doggedly hunted after even the most minute details. He poured over several newspapers each day at breakfast and in his chauffeur-driven car going to and from the office. The breakfast, lunch, or dinner not spent on business was, to him, lost time. Washington cocktail parties were a chore, sometimes unavoidable because of his high position. When he had to, he hit them with a "Hello," one martini, and "Good-by."

Recreation he attacked—most often, at first, on the golf course, where his obvious, fidgety impatience to get started usually forced players ahead to let him go through. Later, he switched to less time-consuming tennis and squash. But always, as one partner said, a game "was medicine to keep his body in shape. The way he went at it I don't see how he could possibly have enjoyed it as a sport."

He covered his calendar pad with personal notes—reminders that ran from the very important "Obtain analytic study of British military procurement system" to the incidental "Regarding Kennedy midshipman appointment, you promised Lyndon Johnson to see Secretary Knox and let him know." He had an obvious dislike for idle conversation. By the end of the war, he had acquired a tough, humorless, no-nonsense reputation. People learned, too, that he never paid much attention to the clock. (The incident that became a classic Pentagon story didn't occur, however, until he was Secretary of Defense. Then, he once worked the staff through seven straight days, and soberly told them, as he left the office at 10:30 P.M. on Sunday, "Well, have a nice weekend.")

To Forrestal, one of the most important parts of his responsibility was Congressional relations, and he worked as hard at that as at anything he did. Early in the war, Knox asked several of his assistants, including Forrestal and Adlai Stevenson, to list the men they knew "fairly well" in Congress—the idea being to strengthen Navy relationships with Congressmen. While the rest of Knox's assistants could list only a dozen or so Congressional friends, Forrestal jotted down over seventy. By the time he became Defense Secretary, that list was considerably longer.

Strongest proof of what Congressmen themselves thought of him came from House Armed Services Committee Chairman Carl Vinson, a Georgia Democrat. Powerful Congressman Vinson, in his half-century-long Capitol Hill career, specialized in military matters and often shaped both House and Senate thinking on Defense. Twice, he called special meetings to honor Forrestal—once when Forrestal left as Secretary of the Navy to become

Secretary of Defense and again when he resigned as Secretary of Defense. At the first gathering, in a remark indicative not only of his own regard for Forrestal but also of the possessive Congressional attitude toward the military, Vinson announced, "Forrestal is the best Secretary of the Navy I have ever had."

When he came into the Navy, Forrestal had found plenty that needed doing. In 1940–41, Navy's industrial mobilization and procurement machinery was, as a result of long-standing disinterest among top Navy brass and splintered administration by top Navy civilians, an uncoordinated, inefficient mess. It got even worse under wartime need for a 70 per cent increase in Navy construction and buying. Tough businessman Forrestal set about clearing up the mess—and ran head on into tough military strategist Admiral Ernest J. King, Chief of Naval Operations, who wanted this business machinery under his own wing.

At the beginning of the war, Roosevelt had ordered King to streamline the way the Navy managed itself. King's idea of how to fill that order involved, among other things, pulling the logistics operation under his direct command. He may have had in mind, as justification, British Field Marshal Montgomery's advice that "Wars are won 25 per cent on strategy, and 75 per cent on logistics." Certainly, he had as precedent the fact that Secretary of War Henry Stimson had already placed the Army's procurement and supply operation, in effect, under Chief of Staff General George Marshall's control.

But every time King proposed his "streamlining ideas" to the White House, he got turned down. For one thing, Roosevelt could hardly have missed learning, as a one-time Navy assistant secretary, that admirals weren't inclined to tell their civilian superiors anything specific about operational planning. It wouldn't have taken much vision to project that general attitude past the end of the war, and to speculate that any centralization of Navy logistics under an admiral would quite likely freeze the civilian bosses out of Navy power altogether. Such a development would have been a clear violation of a long-standing American doctrine that military forces are to be under civilian control. But even more pertinent and practical, Roosevelt told King, was that the admiral's proposals amounted not to a streamlining but to a major reorganization. Roosevelt wanted to win the war first.

Still, King kept at his proposals, and, throughout the war,

Roosevelt was constantly standing him off with such comments as, "You plan the battles and leave the running of the business to Frank Knox." Knox, with plenty to do, delegated to Forrestal the authority to handle the key function of procurement.

Forrestal performed what came to be known as his special brand of management magic. Even though he lacked any clear-cut authority to change the business setup, he centralized control, anyway, and speeded up coordination. When Knox died of a sudden illness in 1944, Forrestal, primarily on the strength of past performance, was moved up to the job of Navy Secretary. Forrestal's confidential secretary, Katherine Foley, says that when she told him the Senate had confirmed his appointment, it was the only time in their nine years together that she saw a real ray of pleasure break over his usually inscrutable face. "He just sat there for several minutes smiling like a little boy."

At war's end, Forrestal, in spite of a frosty relationship with King, had become one of the first high-level civilians in a long time to get much more than the time of day from many Navy officers. Acceptance stemmed in part from admiration for his sheer, hard-working ability. His getting beer put in Navy ports for the enlisted men hadn't hurt his popularity any. Nor had his frequent wartime tours to the combat zones, as when he "hit the beaches" at Iwo Jima with the Marines. While he never interfered with the admirals' combat command, he felt he had to make these junkets to see for himself what the troops needed, in order to direct the logistics effort back home. (His transgressions of proper battle dress on these trips was typically civilian. Once, a sailor spotted him "out of uniform" and yelled, "Hey, buddy, where's your hat?" When the sailor learned he had just chewed out the Secretary of the Navy, he disappeared below decks and didn't reappear until Forrestal had left.)

By 1946, Forrestal had honed to a fine cutting edge those largely intangible but absolutely essential tools for successful government leadership: innate talent, appropriate experience, and key contacts in the right places. He was going to need them all, and more, for what lay ahead.

First, if the proposed unification of the military services were to be approved, Navy's traditional role as America's first line of defense could be lost to the atomic-bomb-carrying Army Air Force. Second, the White House and Congress were trying to slash military budgets, while fumbling with a foreign policy that kept committing the military to more supporting action than it was getting the money to provide.

Moreover, the nation had a new President, Harry Truman, and a new Secretary of State, a Truman crony and former Director of War Mobilization, James Byrnes. Both had had some exposure to military problems but knew little of foreign affairs. The nation also had a new Secretary of War (as the Army Secretary was then known), Robert Patterson. Only Patterson had had as much experience in the Government as Forrestal, having been Army Under Secretary for most of the war; Forrestal outranked him in seniority as a Service Secretary by less than a year. Prestige, experience, and seniority had made Forrestal a power to be reckoned with in Washington, but he was not one of "the close confidants of the White House." He never really had much chance to become one, because his vision kept leading him into one White House conflict after another.

Without authority, seniority and experience don't count for much. Even today, with all the publicity the Defense Secretary gets, there is a tendency to overlook the fact that it's not Congressional law that gives the Secretary his real power. It's the backing, or lack of it, that he receives from the White House. Secretary McNamara spelled out this fact in November, 1964, when he stated flatly, "I couldn't accomplish anything over here [in the Pentagon] without Presidential support. It is absolutely fundamental. I wouldn't and couldn't stay here one minute without it."

Unfortunately, in 1946, Forrestal kept pointing with alarm to problems his superiors either discounted or couldn't see at all. He had started his abrasive opinionating with a letter to a friend in 1944:

> I find that whenever any American suggests that we act in accordance with the needs of our own security, he is apt to be called a god-damned fascist or imperialist. While, if Uncle Joe [Stalin] suggests that he needs the Baltic provinces, half of Poland, all of Bessarabia, and access to the Mediterranean, all hands agree that he is a fine, frank, candid and generally delightful fellow who is very easy to deal with because he is so explicit in what he wants.

In 1944, Winston Churchill had begun warning of a "Communist threat," and had even directed a British fight to keep

Communism out of Greece. For that "unkind treatment" of Russia, Churchill was soundly and roundly criticized in a diatribe led by the U.S. Department of State. First, Roosevelt and, later, Truman clung to the delusion that the Russians, generally, and Stalin, specifically, could be "handled," although Averell Harriman, the Ambassador to Russia, was firing off warning dispatches that reached a peak in late 1945 with the admonition: "We must clearly realize that the Soviet program is the establishment of totalitarianism, ending personal liberty and democracy as we know and respect it."

The rest of the nation was beginning to anticipate peace, but Forrestal was warning, "The next eighteen months look to me to be the most critical this country has ever faced." Plans were being made to mothball armaments and discharge troops, but Forrestal was insisting, "Those who hate war must have the power to prevent it."

By 1946, Forrestal had delved deeply into a study of Communism in all its facets, to see what the Communist threat might mean to the United States and what the Government might need to deal with it. He was well aware that few, if any, of the military decisions he made, or was involved in, as Secretary of the Navy were decisions made on a purely military basis, and well aware that new phrases like "politico-military" and "military-economic-political matters" were suddenly cropping up in Washington conversation. Pushed by an early conviction that America had inherited Free World leadership whether she wanted it or not, Forrestal tried to quickly establish a stronger liaison between the military and the Department of State. But State Department officials, historically, and Secretary of State Byrnes, specifically, felt that they had privileged relations with the White House. They could not see much need to enlist support in the Pentagon for their foreign policy proposals and plans.

To a combat-victorious nation, Forrestal sounded like a temperance trouble-maker at a New Year's Eve party. Out of tune, he took to "crashing" meetings to make himself heard. Not invited to the Truman-Stalin Potsdam Conference in 1945, he went, anyway—by dreaming up another one of those "administrative expedients" that had made a success out of his efforts to improve Navy procurement during the war. He took off on an "inspection trip" of European naval operations. The trip just happened to include Potsdam, where Truman had gone to urge Stalin into the war with Japan, and to tell him that the United States was going to drop an atomic bomb on Japanese soil.* Armed with some just-intercepted messages from Tokyo to the Japanese Embassy in Moscow, Forrestal believed, and wanted to convince Truman, that the Japanese were anxiously looking for a face-saving way to surrender, that bringing Russia in would accomplish nothing except to extend Communist tentacles in the Far East, and that killing thousands of helpless civilians on the Japanese mainland was a brutal, and probably unnecessary, act. Much better, thought Forrestal, to drop the bomb on a solely military target or, at least, on a sparsely populated area and then issue a warning. That, he believed, might be all the face-saving excuse a desperate Japanese Government would need to surrender.

At least one other man, Allied European Commander Dwight Eisenhower, felt the same way. But Truman did not ask for Eisenhower's opinion, and Forrestal arrived at Potsdam too late. The deal, such as it was, had already been made. Within three weeks, 199,000 Japanese would die at Hiroshima and Nagasaki. Two days after the first bomb fell, Russia declared war on Japan. One day later, the second bomb fell, and, the next day, Japan gave up. In effect, the Communists gained control of large portions of Asia without having fired a shot. Similar U.S. miscalculations of a less dramatic nature in the next few years would prompt historians to dust off and reuse a standard old phrase about the "American talent for winning wars and losing the peace."

But, at war's end, winning the peace was not very high on the United States' list of priorities Economy-minded Congressmen were waving big, ominous-looking axes at the proposed military budget, cries for "unification of the armed services" had reached a crescendo, and there was almost no evidence that many of the nation's leaders were aware that a new enemy even existed. Lacking clear-cut authority, Forrestal took to looking for pretexts on which to position Navy forces in the right places to hold up Amer-

* Both these points were to be presented informally to Stalin. Since Russia was not then at war with Japan, the official agenda stuck to discussions about what to do with the defeated Axis powers in Europe. Truman himself says he "casually mentioned to Stalin that we had a new weapon of unusual destructive force. [He] showed no special interest." (Harry S. Truman, *Years of Decisions* [New York: Doubleday & Co., 1955].)

ica's new mantle of world leadership. In the spring of 1946, he found an excellent excuse, in the body of a man probably not one American in 10 million had paid any attention to at the time and probably not one American in 50 million remembers today.

His name was Munir Ertegun. He had been the Turkish Ambassador to the United States. When he died toward the end of the war, his remains had been interred temporarily in Arlington National Cemetery. After V-J Day, the United States offered to send his body home. A four-engine aircraft could have been used for the purpose. There would have been a few ruffles and flourishes, perhaps a nineteen-gun salute, and that would have been that.

But Navy Vice Admiral Forrest Sherman (later Admiral and Chief of Naval Operations) suggested sending the body home on a battleship. Forrestal seized on the idea, reasoning that it certainly couldn't hurt—and just might help—for the Eastern Mediterranean to see the American flag waved, with some naval guns beneath it. (Early in 1946, after swallowing up the East European satellites, Russia had attempted to force concessions from the Turkish Government, and had actually invaded nearby Iran. Greece had been feeling the threat of Soviet oppression since 1944.)

With assistance from Admirals Sherman and Chester Nimitz, Forrestal went to promote the idea at the White House. One sharp selling point: the Navy would use the battleship *Missouri*, named after Truman's home state. The request was not as routine-sounding as it now appears. In February, 1946, the clamor to "bring the boys home" was at its loudest, and the State Department still had high hopes of successfully negotiating with Russia the proper shape of the postwar world. Had it not been for the justification of having to take care of the late ambassador, any plans to send to that part of the world any naval vessel—let alone a battleship—might very well have been turned down. Truman endorsed the request. Secretary of State Byrnes, already under fire in the Senate and the press for treaty-table "softness toward the Russians," reluctantly agreed.

On March 23, the *Missouri*, on board which the Japanese surrender had been signed on September 2, 1945, sailed from New York. It was riding at anchor in Istanbul, Turkey, by April 5. Just seven months after V-J Day, the U.S. Navy was once again engaged in the historic Anglo-American policy of "showing the flag" in troubled parts of the world.

But Forrestal didn't get all he wanted. He had requested that a task force accompany the *Missouri*. He was turned down. On March 10, 1946, he mentioned the refusal to an old friend who was passing through Washington on his way back to England from Fulton, Missouri. The friend, Winston Churchill, had just made his celebrated "Iron Curtain" speech, calling for an Anglo-American alliance against the Soviet Union. "A gesture of power not fully implemented is almost less effective than no gesture at all," was Churchill's comment. Both Churchill and Forrestal felt that a solitary ship was not likely to "bar the Mediterranean door," as Churchill put it. A task force was needed. Forrestal came up with another of his improvisations.

Under the guise of making "courtesy calls," the *Missouri* went to the Athens port of Piraeus, and from there to Naples, Algiers, and Tangiers. More fascinating to those who watched closely in the next ten months, in addition to the *Missouri*, a total of two aircraft carriers, seven cruisers, eighteen destroyers, and four auxiliary vessels from the Atlantic fleet floated, a few at a time, into the Mediterranean to make, allegedly, similar courtesy calls on, by final count, over forty ports. The official alibi was that these visits were "in an area of traditional Navy interest." Interestingly, the Navy always made sure that its hosts, and anyone else watching, knew the ships had more-than-peacetime complements of Marines —and combat hardware—on board.

In May, 1946, at a foreign ministers' conference in Paris, came the first "firm but friendly" stiffening of State Department dealings with Moscow. In October, the New York *Herald Tribune* followed a Forrestal press release (explaining why all those ships were sailing around the Mediterranean) by observing that Forrestal "formally linked naval operations with American foreign policy for the first time."

In February, 1947, something happened to shake the by now rapidly growing number of visionaries who saw the Communist contest for what it was. The British announced that, because of their own war-devastated economy, they were withdrawing not only forces but also financial support from the Greek-Turkish area. As far as Forrestal was concerned, there was no question but that the United States had to move in.

In early March, Forrestal had lunch with Treasury Secretary John Snyder and "talked to him about my beliefs that if we are going to have a run for our side in the competition between the Soviet system and our own, we shall have to harness all the talents and brains in this country just as we had to do during the war." He discussed that thesis and its specifics with other top people in Washington, and got, apparently, at least a majority approval—but also got that standard government answer for a problem: "Let's have a committee study it." Forrestal was convinced that the United States didn't have that much time and decided to appeal directly to the White House.

He had his special assistant Marx Leva draw up a memorandum, checked it out with the President's special counsel, Clark Clifford, made some revisions, and then had Leva submit it—unsigned—to Clifford with a covering Leva-to-Clifford note. Fully aware of his move's possible onerous implications on White House leadership, Forrestal went through all these machinations so that Truman could take full credit for the memorandum's contents—if he used them. Never published, the memorandum may have been, think the experts who know about it, one of the most significant documents of recent history. Dated March 5, 1947, it said:

> For a long time now, it has been clear that there is a serious, immediate and extraordinarily grave threat to the continued existence of this country. These are the facts:
>
> 1. The present danger which this country faces is at least as great as the danger which we faced during the war with Germany and Japan. Briefly stated, it is the very real danger that this country, as we know it, may cease to exist.
>
> 2. From 1941 to 1945, we won a war by enlisting the wholehearted support of all our people and all our resources. Today we are losing a comparable struggle without ever having enlisted the strength of our people and our resources—and the consequences of our loss will be the same consequences that would have followed if we had lost the war of 1941–45.
>
> 3. Of the strategic battlegrounds of the present struggle, we have already lost Poland, Yugoslavia, Romania, Bulgaria, and a number of others; Greece is in imminent peril; after Greece, France and Italy may follow; and after France and Italy, Great Britain, South America and ourselves.
>
> 4. We lost strategic battlegrounds in the war of 1941–45 also—

but even while we were losing some battlegrounds, we were planning the offensive by which we were to win the ultimate victory. And we won the victory by pressing home our attacks—by landing our troops at Guadalcanal, North Africa, Guam, Iwo Jima, Normandy, the Philippines, and a host of other places.

5. This country cannot afford the deceptive luxury of waging defensive warfare. As in the war of 1941–45, our victory and our survival depend on how and where we attack.

6. By providing outstanding economic leadership, this country can wage its attack successfully—and can thereby build the foundations of a peaceful world. For the only way in which a durable peace can be created is by world-wide restoration of economic activity and international trade.

7. In order to be successful, our product—our economic leadership—will have to prove its superiority to the commodity which Russia has lately been so successful in peddling. Russia has a product which is skillfully tailored to appeal to people who are in despair—and thanks to German and Japanese aggression, Russia has had a wealth of customers who are sufficiently desperate to turn to anything. Moreover, the accomplishment of Russia's aim has been greatly simplified by the fact that we have heretofore offered the world no practical antidote for the Russian poison.

8. What we must do is create the conditions under which a Free World society can live. With that as our object, a group of our most competent citizens should be called together in order to enlist the full support of all elements of our economy in the accomplishment of this basic American task. For only by an all-out effort on a world-wide basis can we pass over from the defense to the attack. In making our all-out effort, we will be forwarding not only world stability but also our national interest—which includes, of course, business interest, labor interest and public interest.

9. . . . Financial support should be provided for local enterprises in those countries where a struggling economy needs a helping hand—but the furnishing of such support should, in every case, be handled by competent American personnel, in order to assure that the money goes into *productive* enterprises that are of direct use both to the country involved and to world trade. (Wherever possible, *private capital* in this country should render the necessary financial assistance . . . for this is essentially a business task, in which government's contribution is the creation of favorable conditions under which business can work.)

10. The group referred to above should be called together promptly. It should consist of our best brains—from manage-

ment, from labor, from both the executive and the legislative side of the government, from any source that has a contribution to make—for the issues to be faced are crucial, and we must attack if we are to survive.*

The memorandum was delivered March 6. Six days later, dramatically, before a joint session of Congress, President Truman announced a program of aid to Greece, Turkey, and any other foreign countries threatened by Communist imperialism. The Truman Doctrine, as it came to be known, marked a turning point in American foreign policy. To Forrestal's lasting credit, he led the launching, in 1946, with the help of Sherman, Nimitz, and a host of other individuals in uniform and out, in the Navy and elsewhere, of a decisive step that was followed in successive stages by the Truman Doctrine, the Marshall Plan, victory over Communism in the Italian elections of 1948, the Berlin Airlift, the Atlantic Pact, and the establishment of the North Atlantic Treaty Organization. Had it not been for that year-long 1946 maneuver, it might have been impossible, and certainly it would have been much more difficult, for the Truman Doctrine to say what it did in 1947. As Admiral Sherman noted to Leva, "There are a lot more things you can *say here* and *do there*, when your fleet is *there*, than there are that you can *say* or *do* when your fleet is *here*."

In March, 1947, Forrestal was just six months away from becoming the nation's first Secretary of Defense. The debates over "unification" of the Armed Forces were grinding toward decision. The whole Mediterranean episode and the improvisation required to get his memo to Truman convinced Forrestal that his proposal of a National Security Council, to formulate total government security policy, was of paramount importance in the impending reorganization.

* A copy of this memorandum was furnished to the author by Marx Leva, who includes it in his unpublished article "Secretary of Defense James V. Forrestal in Retrospect."

III

Creating the Cobweb

IN 1945, a study group appointed by Congress, and named after its chairman, retired Admiral James O. Richardson, finished interviewing some 800 top U.S. officers all over the world and sent its recommendations for Washington military reorganization to "the Hill." The Richardson committee report leveled some strong indictments. Among them:

> The Departments have no mission to perform nor any excuse for existence other than to direct and serve the fighting forces and to increase their efficiency.
>
> History forcibly indicates that as funds grow tighter and conflicting interests and personalities make themselves felt, agreements on major issues of policy, strategy and administration become difficult, if not impossible to reach. Teamwork disappears. Each Service withdraws into its own shell, as it has done in the past, and each concentrates on those things essential to its own profession without giving consideration to common problems.
>
> The fundamental reason unity of command on the battlefield has not accomplished necessary integration is that each component of the Army and Navy under a theater commander is actually part of a separate Department of the United States to which it owes its first allegiance. Components must owe allegiance and loyalty to the same organization. This is essential to attain singleness of purpose and to avoid jealousies and misunderstandings.

The Committee called for a "single military establishment" headed by a Secretary of the Armed Forces with the threefold job of (1) advising the President on the political, economic, and industrial aspects of military problems; (2) administering a "Department of the Armed Forces" backed by an Under Secretary for business activities and a military "Commander of the Armed Forces" for military activities; and (3) connecting these military and business functions in his communication with the President.

Almost no one argued with the Committee's accusations. Autonomous War and Navy departments no longer fit into the military environment. The war years had provided proof enough of the need for change.

Early in the war, the Services had pulled together a committee of the military Chiefs of Staff. The avowed purpose of this "combined Chiefs of Staff," was to produce unity in U.S. military thinking about how the war should be fought. The Committee was forced into existence by the need to develop a "single voice" in dealing with the British, who had had just such a "combined" organization since war's beginning and were finding it very difficult to mesh plans with a country whose "separate but equal" Services had their own individual, often uncoordinated plans.

President Truman leaned toward unification because of what he had witnessed as chairman of a military "watchdog" committee during his Senate career. Like many Congressmen since, he had spent uncounted days listening to anger-provoking accounts of what seemed to be waste and duplication, prejudiced treatment and favoritism among personnel, uncommon standards for common equipment, snarled supply lines, repetitious hardware development programs. As one military engineer put it, "A lot of us working for different Services spent the war inventing and reinventing each other's wheel." And, if sensible-sounding philosophy was not enough, the hard fact of the atom bomb, by itself, was sufficient to demand tighter, more cohesive control of the military at Washington's top level.

In December, 1945, borrowing the best from the Richardson report and from the opinions of military and civilian leaders, Truman sent a memo to Congress, saying, in part: "It is a necessity to make timely preparation for the nation's long-range security now while we are still mindful of what it has cost us in this war to have been unprepared." Urging adoption of legislation that would, in Washington, tie the War and Navy Departments into a single Department of Defense, he added, "One of the lessons learned which have most clearly come from the costly and dangerous experience of this war is that there must be unified direction of land, sea and air forces at home as well as in other parts of the world where our Armed Forces are serving. We did not have that kind of direction when we were attacking four years ago and we certainly paid a high price for not having it."

Some of that thesis Congress had heard just weeks before from visiting British Prime Minister Clement Atlee. Atlee had said, "There was a time which I remember when we in Britain enjoyed the same immunity. . . . Wars might devastate the Continent but we were safe behind our moat, the inviolable sea. Those days are past. Defensive frontiers, mountain barriers, the seas and even the oceans are no obstacle to attack. The old discontinuity of earth and sea has been replaced by continuity of the air."

Army Air Forces* General Henry "Hap" Arnold had told Congress, "In every war theater throughout the world, the pattern [of] an autonomous coequal Air Force under supreme command has emerged. It emerged under entirely different conditions, in widely separated parts of the world, impelled by entirely different influences and sets of circumstances."

General Douglas MacArthur had eloquently summed up the same ideas: "The great lesson for the future is that success in war depends upon a complete integration of the Services. In unity will lie military strength. We cannot win with only backs and ends. And no line, however strong, can go alone. Victory will rest with the team." With additional comments about the merits of strong central control in taking quick, correct advantage of research and development breakthroughs, and cutting waste in procurement and supply, all these themes had been echoed by the other high-powered advocates of a single military service.

Finally, Truman told Congress: "We cannot have the sea, land and air members of our defense team working at what may turn out to be cross-purposes, planning their programs on different assumptions as to the nature of the military establishment we need,

* To avoid confusion, the Army Air Forces will hereafter be referred to as the Army Air Corps or just the Air Corps up to the date, in 1947, when the U.S. Air Force was established as a separate military department. Former Air Force Chief of Staff General Curtis E. LeMay described the confusion over these terms in his book *Mission with LeMay: My Story* (New York: Doubleday & Co., 1965): "On 20 June, 1941, the Army Air Forces came into existence [and] the old Air Corps ceased to exist on that date, but the American public and press refused to be convinced. . . . All through World War II, it was, 'Our grandson is in the Air *Corps*.'"

and engaging in an open competition for funds. . . . The manner in which we make this transition in size, composition, and organization of the Armed Forces will determine the efficiency and cost of our national defenses for many years to come. . . . Unification is much more than a matter of organization. It will require new viewpoints, new doctrine and new habits of thinking throughout the Department structure."

While just about everyone endorsed the philosophy of a "single military establishment," precious few people agreed on precisely what a single military establishment should be. The argument had started during World War II and had grown bitterly personal by mid-1946. The residue of that argument grates the Defense organization even today.

Basically, there were, in 1946, (1) those (primarily in the Army and Army Air Corps) who wanted a strong centralized command under a powerful Secretary of the Armed Forces; and (2) those (primarily in the Navy) who pushed, instead, for a decentralized confederation of autonomous Services loosely tied together by a small number of key "coordinating" committees. The first opinion called, essentially, for a federal form of military government. The second contended that the Services were all right the way they were but just needed to agree to work together more.

A lot of different minor chords developed around these two main themes. The prime arguments, however, came down to (1) whether the President really needed a Deputy President for the Armed Forces or merely a glorified chairman, with little voting power, over a board "populated by members of the military Services"; and (2) whether the strategic bomber had made obsolescent the nation's "traditional first line of defense"—the Navy.

Behind all the viewpoints there were admirable motivations, but also there was an almost overpowering "what's-in-it-for-us" attitude. As the debate ground on through 1945 and 1946, the leaders of the separate Services took several in-house opinion polls and gradually got their "official" positions sorted out.

The Army—which had started the whole thing—called for a single Secretary of the Armed Forces, backed up by an Under Secretary and several assistant secretaries; a Chief of Staff of the Armed Forces, who would be responsible to and chief military adviser of the Secretary; and three major "coordinate and coequal" military forces (Army, Navy, and Air Force) with maximum autonomy "consistent with efficient and economic operation." In essence, the Army came out even stronger for centralized command than had the Richardson Committee.

General George C. Marshall had proposed such a single staff as early as 1943. It was really only an extension to higher levels of the General Staff system the Army had been organized under for over forty years; an extension, too, of the military-civilian chain of command that existed there, and in the Army Air Corps through an Assistant Secretary of War for Air. Naturally, the Chief of Staff of the Armed Forces would be an Army officer because "only he knew how to wage total war." His stature and authority would pull Army closer than it had ever been to something it had always felt a need for: short, effective, peacetime pipelines to the President and the Congress. Through these pipelines, Army leaders hoped, they could avoid the traditional budget disinheritance they had always suffered at the end of the war. They wanted the resources necessary to catch up with technology and to build and maintain an "adequately powerful" standing Army.

The Air Corps had been arguing that it should be a separate Service ever since Billy Mitchell started sinking "unsinkable" battleships in the 1920's by dropping bombs down their smokestacks. Since the Air Corps was already organized internally like the Army, it had a natural inclination to feel that "what is, is good." More to the point, in the early 1940's, the War Department had begun gradually to slacken its command reins to the point where the Air Corps was almost a separate Service, which—unlike the Navy air arm—even had its own representation on the *ad hoc* Joint Chiefs of Staff Committee.

Long before 1945, the Air Corps had concluded that probably the only way it would finally become a truly separate Service would be to back Army's long-standing drive for Service unity at the top Washington level. It knew the unification thesis fit the temper of the Congress, the President, and most of the people. (During its meteoric rise to prominence, the Air Corps had become very adept at ferreting out feelings.) Briefly, it knew the nation's leaders were disturbed enough about all the wasteful, scandalous confusion involved in having two autonomous Services. Any proposal to have three, *without* a strong coordinating control at the top, would be just too much to expect the country to swallow. In sum, to pick up Army support for making the Air

Force a separate Service, the Air Force was willing to pay the price of having a strong civilian leader at the top tying the monolith together.

The Navy was against the whole business. It felt it was going to be "not merged but submerged."

Most of the 800 officers the Richardson Committee had interviewed—including such blue-chip names as MacArthur, Eisenhower, Spaatz, Doolittle, Arnold, Nimitz, Halsey, and others from the Army and Navy alike—had endorsed a unified Washington organization. After all, in the field they were already, by 1944, operating under pretty much that kind of setup anyway, through common necessity if not by direct order and formal legislation. The Navy majority at sea also, reportedly, saw in the proposal what they thought was a chance to perpetuate the increased government stature gained, through wartime necessity, by their Chief of Naval Operations. This position of power in high Washington circles was one they had been after since 1915. "Traditional" Navy peacetime importance being what it had been, that proposed single Commander of the Armed Forces would, they believed, "no doubt" be a Navy man.

However, back in Washington after the war, the admirals suddenly realized why Admiral Richardson had ended up dissenting from his own Committee's report. If a muscular Secretary of Defense post was created, they now saw, it actually would not keep the Chief of Naval Operations as close to the White House throne as he had been during the war, but would push him one step further away. Moreover, while the Army proposed starting at once and working out the details later, it was precisely those details the Navy wanted to know about. What did the Army mean by "maximum autonomy for each Service"? Where would a legalized Joint Chiefs of Staff leave Navy admirals? The Navy, which had kept its air arm in a tight, subordinated position during the war, wanted to keep it that way. Whose airplanes would be a part of "Air Force"? How much had the atomic bomb affected military strategy? The heat of battle had proved that the Joint Chiefs Committee worked fine, said Navy officials, claiming that it was too soon after the war to start making drastic changes, since all the war's lessons were not yet understood. Navy men also believed that an organization that had worked well for 150 years would work at least a while longer.

What's more, argued the Navy in effect, the Germans had had at their top level a single Prussian General Staff, such as the Army wanted to install in the United States, and "look who lost the war" (neglecting to mention that the Allies had also beaten the Japanese, who had two departments, and the Italians, who had three).

At this juncture, James Forrestal told his own Navy that just being negative about the Army–Air Force proposal wasn't good enough. A change of some sort was in the wind, and to preserve any part of the Navy's position at all, he said, "We've got to come up with a positive alternative."

For Forrestal to fight unification by proposing an alternative was, in a way, to run against some of his own stated convictions. He was already on record as the leading Washington advocate (if not sometimes the only advocate) of better coordination among government departments (i.e., State, Army, Navy, Labor, Commerce, Treasury, *et al.*) in the formulation of foreign policy—a goal military unification could go a long way toward achieving. As an indication of its own majority opinion, Congress, he knew, had "unified" its own military committee structures in 1946, merging the Military Affairs and the Naval Affairs Committees, in both the Senate and the House, into one Armed Services Committee for each. But he also knew that, although the executive branch of the Government almost always decided what the military *did*, Congress jealously guarded its constitutional right to determine what the military was *to be*. Thus, he could speculate that any proposal was unlikely to pass Congress if it looked as though it would narrow the base of civilian checks and balances over the military by dropping so much power into the lap of, virtually, one man—particularly a nonelected executive who was not part of Congress. Certainly his close and powerful Capitol Hill friend, Georgia Democrat "Uncle Carl" Vinson (also nicknamed the "Admiral," for his long-standing support of the Navy) wouldn't sit still for any such deal.

What Forrestal proposed to counter the Army plan was a setup patterned, he later told Winston Churchill, after the British Committee of Imperial Defense. (From what he had seen in his wartime trips to Britain, he had been persuaded that the British cabinet form of government was far more efficient than the U.S. executive form.) His alternative also fit the Navy's desire to gain a stronger voice in foreign policy. Actually, Forrestal's counterattack on unification amounted to a reorganization not just of the military but of a large section of the whole executive branch.

The highlights of his "constructive alternative" were that there should be three separate Services (an admission that the Army Air Corps was by then virtually a separate Service, anyway) plus a series of boards and committees at the top level to interlock, theoretically, these autonomous Services. Forrestal's main point: he wanted some super-agencies set up outside the military—a National Security Council, a Central Intelligence Agency, and a National Security Resources Board—on which the military would have members.

What the Navy proposal accomplished, more than anything else, was to force the government's leaders to set their sights higher, and to emphasize that the whole hassle over the military organization should not have an increase in efficiency as its main objective. Indeed, Forrestal's group implied, there wasn't any need for efficiency, or, in fact, for a military force at all unless it was first and primarily an effective instrument for support of a carefully developed, cogent U.S. foreign policy.

Simple, sobering, and important as these differences of opinion among military leaders were, they weren't argued much, at least in public, in the tense years from 1945 to 1947. Instead, a lot of nervous irrelevancies forced their way to the forefront of the verbal combat. Listeners were subjected to many vague, inconclusive, unprovable fairy tales, which after a while began to sound like the real issues.

Of these nightmares stirred up by opposition to change, a key one could have been labeled the "multiheaded Prussian General Staff monster." As one observer sarcastically stated:

> Across the pages of American legislative history there flits a curious "man on horseback." He is a military man—usually a general and almost never an admiral, incidentally—who sits in the wings waiting to take over the government from civilians. He has, of course, never existed and yet he is quite as real as if he really had. Despite the fact that this "man on horseback" has always been a foreigner, and has grown up in other surroundings and circumstances, he plays and has played a very real role in the development of civil-military organization in the United States.*

* Dr. E. L. Katzenbach, in a lecture to the Navy War College, August 23, 1956.

The role is based mostly on superstition. After all, Congressional committees have staffs, and so do businesses. Most organizations operate on the principle that one man cannot know everything about everything and must have others to advise and assist him. Even the military has had staffs for centuries. But put an "all-powerful" Chief of an "all-powerful" General Staff in Washington, and there is immediate suspicion that a Genghis Khan will soon come charging down Pennsylvania Avenue.

Illogical as the fear of the "man on horseback" may be in the United States, talk about him did spice up what might otherwise have been a dull debate. And he had a lot to do with the form military reorganization finally took. As Forrestal said, in October, 1947, "A great many decisions, both in business and in government, have been reached more on emotional than on intellectual levels." In many respects, the National Security Act passed in 1947 was one of those decisions.

Rancor had run so high that, well into the fall of 1946, there were hardly any signs that anyone intended to budge from his particular position on unification. Even wives got involved. Army Secretary Patterson and Forrestal had grown quite close during World War II, as a result of having to sort out the Army-Navy competition for scarce war materials. At the height of the nerve-shattering unification arguments, Mrs. Patterson called Forrestal and asked him to support her husband. Her reason: "There is just too much bickering going on between friends."

In mid-summer, 1946, with the Navy still running behind on debate points, Forrestal had flatly ruled out "anything that would cost the Navy its status as a separate entity, cost its Secretary a seat in the Cabinet, and cost its officers access to the President." He hinted that, if the Navy had to pay such a price, he would resign. It was probably just as well that he only hinted. Among his opposition, the thought of his resignation had a lot of appeal. The Army and the Air Corps and even the White House wanted unification. Navy ringleader Forrestal's fight against it must have looked, on occasion, as if he were extremely close to subordinating his Commander in Chief's wishes to his own.

Finally, in late fall, 1946, the intramural war started turning toward a truce. Forrestal's friend and civilian aide Ferdinand Eberstadt believes that the first glimmer of sunshine showed on September 27. At that time, he, former Assistant Secretary of War

John McCloy, and about-to-resign Assistant Secretary of War for Air Robert Lovett met in New York. Out of that meeting came a victory for Forrestal: general agreement to have, not federation, but a confederation of three autonomous Services. The "Secretary of National Security" would exist mainly to coordinate various matters of common or conflicting interest among the three military departments. And if one or the other of them didn't like his decision, they could (and predictably would) appeal to the President.

Admiral Forrest Sherman gives credit for the decisive change in the intramural battle to Forrestal alone, and claims that a November 7 meeting Forrestal held at his Georgetown home in Washington, D.C., did the trick. It was there, says Sherman, that the contestants realized they would get a reorganization they could all live with only if they made important concessions to each other. Only five men were at the meeting, but they were key people. Besides Forrestal and Sherman, there were Rear Admiral Arthur Radford, who was Deputy Chief of Naval Operations for Air; Stuart Symington, White House "project manager" for unification, who had just replaced Lovett as Army Assistant Secretary for Air; and Air Corps Major General Lauris Norstad, head of the War Department's Plans and Operations Division. The participants, says one Forrestal fan, amounted to one more example of "Forrestal's amazing ability to pull together the right people, from among hundreds in complex Washington, to discuss problems." The question of who would control the airplanes had become the major chasm separating the Navy and the Air Force. All these men represented powerful authority in this area of decision. Moreover, as military professionals in the Pentagon knew, each of them was one of the smaller wheels whose influence made the bigger wheels move. All were up-and-coming men in their own right. Symington would become the first Secretary of the Air Force; Sherman was named Chief of Naval Operations in 1949; Radford became Chairman of the Joint Chiefs of Staff in 1953; and Norstad eventually filled the still unborn North Atlantic Treaty Organization's top military post as Commander, Supreme Headquarters Allied Powers Europe.

Out of their meeting came an agreement that actually endorsed the Forrestal-Eberstadt-McCloy-Lovett understanding: (1) three "separately administered" military departments; (2) a single Secretary of National Defense who, backed up by a very small staff, would coordinate the three military departments and direct policy; and (3) formal recognition of the Joint Chiefs of Staff Committee as it then existed, supported by a 100-man Joint Staff, but "better organized for getting things done."

Action came very rapidly. By January 16, 1947, a draft letter of the agreement, signed by Forrestal and Patterson, went to the White House. That same day, ex-Army, ex-National Guardsman Truman, who had strongly supported the Army attitude all along, softened his position and jotted a note to Forrestal and Patterson. Wrote the President, in part: "I am exceedingly pleased . . . that you have reached full and complete agreement on a plan for unification of the Armed Services. The agreement provides a thoroughly practical and workable plan of unification and I heartily approve of it." Sherman and Norstad were told to draw up a bill. Truman delivered it to the new Eightieth Congress on February 26, 1947.

Even while holding hearings throughout 1945, 1946, and early 1947, Congress actually seemed to be waiting on stage for a cue from the wings, reluctant to act on any reorganization of significance until it got an Army-Navy agreement on what it should legislate. Recognized in Congress by now as one of the most active men in the long, bitter inter-Service battle, Forrestal was called to testify first. In typical wound-healing fashion he told the Congressmen: "I should be less than candid if I did not admit that this bill is a compromise. But it is a fair compromise and, as the President stated, a sound and workable solution. It is a compromise which would not have been possible without the unselfish and cooperative attitude with which the negotiators of both Services attacked this problem."

To the knowledgeable politicians he was addressing, he then pointed out that the compromise was on such a touchy subject that "if any single item were withdrawn or modified to the advantage of any one Service" the whole thing would blow up. And he laid down a goal that has held ever since: "This bill provides an organization which will allow us to apply the full punitive power of the United States against any future enemy. It provides for the coordination of the three Armed Services, but what is even more important to me than that, it provides for the integration of foreign policy with national policy, of our civilian economy with military requirements; it provides for continuing review of our raw material needs and for continued advance in the field of research and applied science."

Forrestal also said something that a sudden twist in his own government career would make tragically prophetic: "Any step of this sweeping character . . . must rest fundamentally on the belief of all concerned that it is for the good of the country and that it will work. The good will of the working organization is necessary whether it is a business organization or a military one. . . . Conversely, the best organization chart in the world is unsound if the men who have to make it work do not believe in it."

At the time he was testifying, he didn't know that making the outfit work was going to be his responsibility. From bits and pieces of the Congressional Record can be culled other prophetic Forrestal admonitions such as "I do not believe you can, by law, direct the way organizations run," and "I think the success of this undertaking is going to depend upon the kind of men that man all these posts, not only the Secretary of National Defense, but also the Secretary of the Army, the Secretary of the Navy, and the Secretary of Air." Finally, in one exchange, he leaned on the point that "the man who takes . . . this top job would, I hope, have the right to select the men who work with him. If you hire men of good will, that is the important thing. I do not care what your right to fire is. You know as well as I do that once a man is in government for some length of time, it takes quite a lot of blasting to get him out."

By July 23, 1947, the National Security Act had cleared Congress. One public reaction was a flood of letters and telegrams that, added together, told Truman a number of men would be happy to run the new military establishment for him. On July 26, the President was aboard his private plane, the *Sacred Cow*, at Washington National Airport, about to fly to his dying mother's bedside in Missouri, when the bill was handed to him. He signed it into law before he took off. Earlier that same day, Truman had told Forrestal he was going to send his name up to the Senate as the proposed first Secretary of Defense. Forrestal was second choice. Army Secretary Patterson had been asked to take the post, but had turned it down because, it was reported, he was "so hard put to it for money that he felt he was unable to stay longer in government."

Congress was adjourning that day. The Senate rushed through the confirmation of Forrestal's appointment at the end of an all-evening session. The man who had done most to weaken the unification law was charged with making it function. He had been appointed to the highest government position he had ever held by a boss he neither liked nor admired. With one piece of legislation, Congress had performed a shotgun wedding uniting the Army and the Navy, had midwifed the twin births of the National Military Establishment and the Office of the Secretary of Defense, and had granted the Air Corps a divorce from the Army (which the new Air Force considered more of an emancipation).

About the best that could be said for the new Defense Establishment was what George Washington said when the Board of War and Ordnance was set up in 1776. Referring to what he called simply "the War Office," Washington predicted that "the Benefits derived from it . . . will be considerable though the plan upon which it is first formed may not be perfect. This like other great works in its first Edition may not be entirely free from Error. Time will discover its Defects and Experience suggest the Remedy . . . but it was right to give it a beginning."

The National Security Act's language was vague and confusing. It left plenty of room for autonomous military departments to move around in. Amid charges of "Service lobbying" and "military-officer insubordination," the Congressional hearings had side-stepped unification's main problem: what, specifically, should be the proper combat roles of the separate Services. In spite of high-flown talk about economy, efficiency, and operating simplicity, Congress had created an executive department that was not really a department at all. Unlike Commerce, or Interior, or Agriculture, or any department in which the Secretary was top man, the Secretary of Defense was merely the overseer of an "Establishment." He was responsible for about half the resources of the executive branch of government. Yet, his authority was questionable and his decision-making power doubtful.

IV

James Forrestal

[SEPTEMBER, 1947–MARCH, 1949]

ALMOST IMMEDIATELY, it became apparent that the new job in the new department wasn't going to work. For one thing, Forrestal didn't have enough people. Worried about a "plethora of assistant secretaries" sweeping into the Pentagon and unrolling large ribbons of bureaucratic red tape, Congress had authorized him only three key assistants. The three he picked were a lawyer, a budget expert, and a "troubleshooter."

Lawyer Marx Leva was hired by Forrestal early in the unification debate as Navy Secretary Forrestal's legal adviser and principal civilian special assistant. Besides being general counsel, Leva handled legislative problems, congressional contacts, public relations, and in addition, was Forrestal's closest staff confidant.

Budget expert Wilfred McNeil had been Navy fiscal director under Forrestal and had handled Pentagon budget details and certain related broad logistics problems. He was executive agent for the most significant authority Forrestal had gotten out of the National Security Act—coordination of money requests. That control would make McNeil, within ten years, one of the most powerful men in Defense.

The third man, Jack Ohly, handled "all the rest." A War Department lawyer in the years 1940–47, Ohly had been Secretary of War Patterson's top civilian special assistant. He gave a touch of tri-Service balance to a staff that, otherwise, amounted almost entirely to Forrestal's old Navy department team transplanted. Forrestal made Ohly secretary to the War Council, a committee set up by the National Security Act as, theoretically, a major connecting point, for the opinions of the military and of the civilians. Besides Forrestal, the Council consisted of the Secretaries and the Chiefs of Staff of each military department. Ohly also handled the needs of the Committee of Secretaries, which, manned by the three military department Secretaries, was, roughly, the civilian counterpart of the Joint Chiefs of Staff committee. Ohly was also Forrestal's monitor of the various Service-interlocking boards set up by the Act: the National Security Resources Board (to coordinate civilian, military, and industrial war mobilization planning among the various executive branches of Government, reporting not to the Defense Secretary but directly to the President); the Munitions Board (to coordinate industry war material production and mobilization planning for the Pentagon); and the Research and Development Board (to coordinate and integrate military research and development of weapons).

"Ohly," said one staffer, "was a real secret weapon. He could turn out more good work under pressure than any man I've ever seen." That kind of talent would be needed if Forrestal's concept of his proper mission in the military family were to be realized. Forrestal intended to coordinate tri-Service program direction and to develop, for common military tasks, single boundaries within which they would operate independently. He hoped to draw on the three staffs for the ditch-digging, detailed paperwork and wanted no part of directing their own internal management machinery in carrying out policy. In any case, he once said, "They're so clever at hiding their misdeeds, you'll never find out what they're doing, anyway."

Assuming the support and good will of the Services, "Eventually," Forrestal told McNeil, "this office, with forty people at the top, should be able to coordinate and set policy very nicely." (The modern version of McNeil's comptroller shop alone now employs nearly eight times that many.)

Blocking outright Service merger and diffusing authority were not the only concepts that had been written into the National Security Act the way Forrestal and the Navy wanted. He also got his National Security Council. Chaired by the President, it was to have as members the Vice President, the Secretaries of State and of Defense, the chairmen of the various Boards set up by the Act, the Secretaries and Under Secretaries of the Services and of other executive departments. Amounting to a kind of Cabinet-level subcommittee for military affairs, the Council's duties were to advise the President on (1) the "objectives, commitments, and risks of the United States in relation to our actual and potential military power; and (2) policies on matters of common interest to the departments and agencies of the Government concerned with national security."

Forrestal's idea was that any agreements reached at Council meetings would be binding on all executive branches of government. But Truman considered the National Security Council scheme an attempt to limit some of the prerogatives of the Presidency. During his term in office, he didn't use the Council much.

One other key feature of the Act: it edged warily toward the idea of a single military staff in Washington by giving legal stature to the Joint Chiefs of Staff Committee (but without a chairman) and by authorizing a 100-man Joint Staff for paperwork support of the Chiefs' joint deliberations. In practice, suspicious as they were of each other, the Chiefs relied mostly on their own people for such backup. As a result, the Joint Staff Director, Army Major General Alfred M. Gruenther, very soon became primarily simply a Forrestal military adviser.

Forrestal had stated repeatedly during the unification debates that "no single individual had the intellectual capacity to evaluate all the potential consequences" of a decision on which national survival depended. (A believer in unification, General Dwight Eisenhower countered at the time that, if that idea were right, one President of the United States wasn't enough, either.) As a result, Forrestal went in heavily for having committees grapple with issues. To control what one critic called "this dog's dinner of debating societies he set up," Forrestal planned to spend nine-tenths of his time eliminating human friction.

After the abrasive pulling and tugging involved in getting unification, there was plenty of human friction to eliminate. Unlike his smiling reaction when he was named Secretary of the Navy, "He had no illusions," said secretary Katharine Foley, "about what he was getting into this time." As he wrote playwright Robert Sherwood after his appointment, "This office will probably be the greatest cemetery for dead cats in history."

To survive, Forrestal counted on his experience in the Navy, the connections he had built up in the war years, and his well-publicized powers of persuasion. He hoped to convince, rather than order, the military Services to set aside parochial viewpoints and work together on the broad challenges to *total* national defense. At fifty-five, he thought he knew that job. Certainly, he worked hard at it, sixteen hours a day, six and seven days a week. He absorbed details like a sponge absorbs water, and he had a dozen different channels for getting information. None of these channels looked very logical on an organization chart. In fact, in the pragmatic sense, he had little appreciation of formal procedures and organization charts. He dealt with people, not with block diagrams on a piece of paper. His daily appointment calendar read like a biographical index. He demanded specifics and facts. The man who started off with "I think . . ." would be cut off with, "Don't think. Come back when you know."

Intense, totally consumed by his work, he had always expected and had gotten maximum effort out of the people around him. Looking back, one of them says, "I've never known a staff as dedicated as Forrestal's was. We knew he was there night and day, so we stayed with him. His problems were our problems." Apparently, however, Forrestal had little idea how his staff managed to get things done. His rapid-fire dictation, which sometimes started as he walked into the office, required a court stenographer's speed to keep up with. Literally the first to arrive in the morning and the last to leave at night, he had a phone set up in his office for late evening dictation. Alone one midnight, he dictated some messages into the machine, arrived at 7:30 the next morning, found no finished letters on his desk, and demanded to know why they hadn't been transcribed. Another time, a staff member fell behind on a report and struggled through a weekend in the office, while Forrestal was out of town, to catch up. At nine P.M. that Sunday, the staff member's Pentagon phone rang. Forrestal was on the line, calling in from his aircraft 200 miles out. "He said he wanted this and this and that documents to go over when he arrived in an hour or so. I'm sure it never occurred to him to even wonder what anybody was doing in the office at that hour."

Although he wasn't officially sworn into office until September 17, 1947, Forrestal started as early as July working day and night at being Navy Secretary and, at the same time, setting up the Defense Secretary's office. He was in his eighth continuous year of government service. (Yet, he still listed himself as an investment broker and his Washington address as temporary.) And he looked tired all the time. His main problem: few men in Washington authority saw the future as he did. He was like a pioneer trying to hack his way through a hostile jungle armed with nothing but courage and energy and a Boy Scout knife. With considerable justification, he felt that his nation suffered from the delusion, in the aftermath of World War II, that it could reorganize its way into permanent insurance against ever again making the mistakes it had made before and during that war. With the passage of the National Security Act, the national vision, which should have been looking to the horizon, seemed to him to turn inward.

Even so, Forrestal's theme of coordination rather than dictation in the new Department of Defense might have worked—had it not been that the military budget had dropped from $45 billion in fiscal year 1946 to $14.28 billion in fiscal 1947. The reduced figure still sounded like an awful lot of money to U.S. taxpayers worried about paying off a $270 billion war debt. Presumed economic experts were voicing fears that a high defense budget would generate further government spending deficits which, in turn, would force inflationary chaos. Even Forrestal said that he was apprehensive about the Pentagon helping to "eat the nation's economic head off."

President Harry Truman, talking more like a conservative Republican than a liberal Democrat, insisted on balanced budgets and "pay-as-you-go" and actually managed to take in more than he spent in fiscal 1947 and 1948. But the price being paid in combat readiness was shattering the nerves of military experts in the Pentagon and around the world. Economists worried about the dearness of the dollar but apparently gave little thought to the dearness of national security. No cohesive military-economic-political blueprint to challenge the spread of Communism had been drawn up, and warnings like Forrestal's anonymous memo to the White House had not been widely circulated.

Truman clamped down a $15 billion Defense budget ceiling. Although even that amount looked like a huge sum to U.S. citizens, the military was notably inept at explaining that about all the money was buying was the cost of maintaining occupation troops overseas. Precious little was left for developing and building new military hardware.

"It was," said Forrestal's old friend Stuart Symington, who had become Secretary of the Air Force, "like throwing a piece of meat into an arena and letting 300 hungry tigers go in after it." Particularly in Forrestal's own Navy, military leaders tended at that time—and even in the decade that followed—to give their loyalty on money matters first to their individual Chiefs of Staff and then, occasionally, to the Service Secretary, depending on how hard he fought with higher authorities for "an adequate slice" of the dollars. They hardly ever granted their loyalty to the Secretary of Defense and seldom even to the Commander in Chief.

As a result of the shortage of funds, the inter-Service rivalries that were supposed to be eliminated by the 1947 Act increased, if anything. While Communism was spreading in war-weakened democracies all over the world, the military spent their energies on a back-biting squabble over who should be king of the Pentagon mountain. They could not very well undercut their Commander in Chief. They could knock down the President's Deputy for Defense—and they did, mainly because they did not recognize him as the authority he was supposed to be. Nor, by the fall of 1948, did the White House appear to.

The Service team captains were a tough, experienced lot.

Former Under Secretary of War Kenneth Royall had moved up when Patterson resigned. Royall went through a swearing-in ceremony the day after Forrestal did, merely to note that his War Department had been renamed the Department of the Army. In the process, he grumbled about the new label, the National Military Establishment, and said that, if the Founding Fathers had named his department the War Department, that's what it should remain. Royall's Chief of Staff, General Dwight Eisenhower, resigned in February, 1948, after receiving a thinly veiled hint from the White House. (At the time, some young Democrats were in a public crusade to put the General on the 1948 Democratic Presidential ticket in place of Truman. Although Eisenhower's answer had been an adamant "No!" his presence in full public view created political problems.) By mid-February, Missouri-born General Omar Bradley, the "G.I. General," had been made Chief of Staff.

Secretary of the Navy John Sullivan had been Forrestal's Navy Under Secretary. By December, 1947, Admiral Louis Denfeld was Chief of Naval Operations, replacing retired Admiral Chester Nimitz.

Army Assistant Secretary of War for Air Symington had the new title of Secretary of the Air Force. His Chief of Staff, until April, 1948, was General Carl "Toohey" Spaatz. Then Spaatz retired to write for *Newsweek* magazine, blasting Navy views on air power, and General Hoyt Vandenberg became Air Force Chief of Staff, remaining until he retired in June, 1953.

Thus, although he had asked for "the right to hire, rather than the right to fire," Forrestal inherited many of the top Service officials in the organization. In his first few months in office, he inadvertently proved the truth of one of his fears about the pressures of being Secretary of Defense. It was, most assuredly, too big a job for one man—if that man stood alone.

On the day he was sworn in, Forrestal gave a buffet luncheon for most of the key people in the Pentagon. They were hardly in their seats, with Forrestal trying to generate a little of the spirit of cooperation, when they began sniping at each other. Right from the outset, says Ohly, "There was hardly a day or an hour when Forrestal's office didn't feel the pressures and constant battle for position."

There was conflict in virtually everything. Most of the headlines went to the issue of who was going to get to deliver the atomic bomb. The Army was out of that competition, largely, since the Air Corps had been granted its independence. But the new Air Force and the Navy battled continually over "roles and missions." In their ball park, the atomic bomb was home plate. Anything but a well-policed internal Pentagon debate, through press leaks and anonymous rumor-mongering, the quarrel had turned into one of the shoddiest spitting contests in U.S. military history. By mid-1948, it had become a public trial by newsprint on the major issues of survival.

And Forrestal was caught in the middle. In the summer of 1947, Truman had directed him to move his headquarters out of the main Navy building on Washington's Constitution Avenue and into the Pentagon. It didn't look right for the first Secretary of Defense to appear to be mainly the friend of just one Service. In spite of the move, Forrestal's understandable human tendency, when the pressure was on (which meant from the outset), was to turn to the men he had learned from experience he could count on to produce. Predictably, that meant looking to his Navy contacts for answers. In depending on the people at his former office address, he was sadly and, as it turned out, tragically disillusioned.

Within a year, incredible as it probably seemed to him, there had been enough unpleasant incidents to make him realize that a significant segment of his old outfit was telling him something less than the whole truth, even about little things. Typical was the note an admiral sent him charging a top Air Force public relations man with hanging around the National Press Club bar making slanderous remarks about the Defense Secretary. The man attacked didn't belong to the Press Club and had been there as a guest only once, eight months before the poison-pen note was written.

Such chipping away at Air Force integrity finally got so bad that, in the fall of 1948, Symington issued an "Eyes Only" order to his Air Force Chief of Staff. The reason: "I felt," said Symington, "based on conversations, that some of my messages had not been delivered to him." After a while, "I stopped giving information to him in writing, with his full agreement, because when the information went up there, it leaked out to the press and to aviation magazines, and when it leaked out it was invariably distorted."

Forrestal could, of course, challenge the top brass point-blank. But in the Pentagon, it soon became—and still is—virtually impossible to put a halt to anonymous indictments by missionaries tucked away at various staff levels. Uncontrolled (and sometimes encouraged) disciples of one or another point of view kept the running charges and countercharges by "informed spokesmen" going. Most of the time, Forrestal seemed at a loss on how to grab hold of and squelch the attacks and accusations. With substantive issues clearly needing attention, chasing such frustrating ghosts around the building was a dismaying distraction. "It aggravated Forrestal," says a close friend, "irritated him, and tired him very much—but he couldn't come to grips with it."

The Navy was not the only villain. "All the Secretaries tended to be uncooperative," said one Forrestal staffer. "Even the Army was in it on the issues themselves, although they stayed away from the personal attacks." The Air Force, said another Forrestal aide, "was just pouring it out," riding as it was on a crest of public popularity. Speech-making Air Force generals were telling a nation that believed science had made war cheaper what it wanted to hear. Why listen to all the arguments for maintaining a strong

Navy, when one relatively inexpensive Air Force bomber, or maybe one of the projected new missiles, armed with one atomic bomb, possessed more firepower than the United States had shot off during all of World War II?

Symington was faced with almost as demanding a challenge in his own camp as was Forrestal. After splitting off from the Army, the Air Force was the great "have-not" Service, with clear title to little more than its airplanes. It was looking for its own place in the sun. The Army Air Forces had ballooned from 26,000 men in 1939 to 2.4 million in 1944. Many of its air bases, research and test stations, recreation facilities, and much of its on-base housing, were still, in 1947, on loan from the Army, which wanted everything back except the short-term, jerry-built structures thrown together to last only through the war. Moreover, soured by what it considered the poor logistics support the Army Technical Services had given it during the war, the Air Force planned to build a supply structure of its own as much unlike the Army Technical Service operation as it could logically be. In essence, the Air Force had to assemble a multibillion dollar business overnight from scratch.

Still, for all the problems the Secretary of the Air Force faced, Forrestal's staff considered much of Symington's behavior inexcusable. "He would call six, eight, even ten times a day to bitch about the most minute things," claimed a Forrestal aide. "If the telephone didn't get results, he'd page Forrestal on the squawk box [a raspy, direct-line intercom hookup connecting all the most important offices] sometimes with as many as four or five calls an hour."

Symington certainly wasn't the only one harassing Forrestal. Talk that he was helped to convince the Air Force that Forrestal's own staff still "thought Navy." That belief showed up most clearly the morning an ex-Navy Forrestal assistant arrived in Symington's office and handed him a budget dissertation, saying, "Here's the testimony you're to give Congress this week." The Secretary of the Air Force skimmed through a document on what he was supposed to think about air power and snorted, as he threw it back, "Young man, if you ever get that blue water wrung out of your pants, you'll be a lot more useful around here."

Such in-fighting erupted over questions that ranged from the important down to the ridiculous. At one stage, Forrestal nursed the idea of adopting a common uniform for all three Services. The Army went along. The Air Force said it would agree, provided all the Services did. The Navy said that it would have to study the proposal, and later announced that any such move would wreck Navy morale. The Air Force then countered, with tongue in cheek, that it had reason to believe a great many Navy enlisted men would welcome any uniform other than the one they were wearing (bell-bottom trousers with a thirteen-button flap in front). The proposal quickly degenerated into a name-calling hassle, and Forrestal gave it up. At that point, the Air Force announced that, if a distinctive uniform was so important to morale, it wanted one, too. In due course, a highly classified meeting was attended by what was later described as a "short, strange-looking man." No one thought to ask who he was. As the meeting closed, an Air Force representative introduced him, saying, "Like you to meet our tailor. And outside are two boys wearing the new Air Force uniform."

Next, the Air Force demanded, in addition, its own dress uniform, and hammered away at the subject every week for months—at Joint Chiefs' meetings, meetings of the Service Secretaries, with Forrestal, with individual Chiefs, with anybody who looked as if he might have some authority. Mountains of Joint Chiefs' "position papers" were written on the matter. By the time approval finally came, this and similar distracting games had stacked the case load of unresolved Joint Chiefs' issues virtually ceiling high.

Forrestal began attending meetings of the Joint Chiefs. He either had to get decisions out of them or find other ways to handle problems they couldn't, or wouldn't, tackle.

And the Pentagon did have other problems. All around the world in the spring of 1948, events were particularly threatening. In Czechoslovakia, the Communists had just pulled off a sudden and successful *coup d'état*. The Chinese Communists were pushing Generalissimo Chiang Kai-shek's Nationalist army toward the sea. France had acquired what one diplomat called "the Communist infection," and the French Government was as unstable as a bottle of nitroglycerin. South Korean Communists had begun a wave of sabotage in and around Seoul and Pusan. The Italian national elections were due in another month, and Communists were heavy favorites to win government control. (In addition to his Defense duties, Forrestal was privately hard at work raising money to finance Italian anti-Communist electioneering.) Turkey and Greece were under Communist pressure and the Yugoslavian Communist Government was threatening to take over the free port of Trieste. Although no public announcement had been made that the second series of U.S. atomic tests was about to begin on Eniwetok, a non-U.S. snorkel submarine had been sighted in the Pacific near the atoll.

The United Nations was debating the proposal to partition Palestine into two nations: one for the Arabs and one for the Jews. U.S. sentiment was running strongly in favor of creating the new Jewish state of Israel. The whole Middle East was a tinderbox. What concerned Forrestal, among others, was Russia's probable attempt to move in "to restore peace" once the predictable fighting broke out. If successful, the Russians could choke off strategic Middle East oil pipelines. Most important, Forrestal knew that, if the United States were asked to send troops to preserve order, a dollar-starved Army would be able to scare up only about 15,000 men, and even to get that many would require going back on a temporary war footing. Moreover, such a token force would be far more than just embarrassing. It would be an open confession of military weakness. The British had about 57,000 troops in Palestine carrying out a protectorate responsibility dating back to the League of Nations. They would pull out if the United Nations voted partition. To maintain even an uneasy peace, the Pentagon's Joint Staff estimated, could require anywhere from 80,000 to 160,000 troops, depending on how hot the likely Arab-Jewish civil war burned.

Forrestal advised postponing partition until the United States could build up its forces. That suggestion earned him a tumult of vicious "anti-Zionist" charges from those favoring the establishment of Israel. He was attacked in many unfair ways. His one-time shares in a Canadian stock-holding company were dredged up, with the implication that he was at least a tax dodger, if not a crook. A story was fabricated about his behavior—alleged to have been cowardly—during a nearly forgotten robbery at his home. The partition decree approved by the United Nations in May did not, fortunately, result in quite the disaster the Pentagon had anticipated—mainly because Israel was strong enough militarily to defend itself. But hard as he tried, with fact sheets to the press,

Forrestal never quite shed himself of the "anti-Zionist" smear. It was not dropped until after his death.

On the fifth of March in that tense spring, the U.S. Army Berlin garrison commander, General Lucius Clay, fired off an "eyes only" wire to Army intelligence in Washington. Its contents had about the same emotional impact as would a time bomb set off in the White House:

> FOR MANY MONTHS, BASED ON LOGICAL ANALYSIS, I HAVE FELT AND HELD THAT WAR WAS UNLIKELY FOR AT LEAST 10 YEARS. WITHIN THE LAST FEW WEEKS, I HAVE FELT A SUBTLE CHANGE IN SOVIET ATTITUDE WHICH I CANNOT DEFINE BUT WHICH NOW GIVES ME A FEELING THAT IT MAY COME WITH DRAMATIC SUDDENNESS. I CANNOT SUPPORT THIS CHANGE IN MY OWN THINKING WITH ANY DATA OR OUTWARD EVIDENCE IN RELATIONSHIPS OTHER THAN TO DESCRIBE IT AS A FEELING OF A NEW TENSENESS IN EVERY SOVIET INDIVIDUAL WITH WHOM WE HAVE OFFICIAL RELATIONS. I AM UNABLE TO SUBMIT ANY OFFICIAL REPORT IN THE ABSENCE OF SUPPORTING DATA BUT MY FEELING IS REAL. YOU MAY ADVISE THE CHIEF OF STAFF OF THIS FOR WHATEVER IT MAY BE WORTH IF YOU FEEL IT ADVISABLE.*

The nerve-racking rush of international crises forced the United States to send some A-bomb–armed B-29 bombers to air bases in England. Nuclear devastation of the Russian motherland was about all the United States could threaten to counter the massive Russian ground forces. Apparently, the threat was enough.

The Russians did not launch all-out war. (Most U.S. military leaders assumed, at the time, that all these brushfire wars were merely a prelude to direct Russian attack on the United States. They could have made a much better argument for an increased Defense budget if they had heeded, as they did ten years later, the argument of some experts on Communist methodology. That minority argued that so-called tactical Communist victories actually were ends in themselves, part of a long-range plan to avoid provoking atomic retaliation while, at the same time, gradually dismantling capitalism.)

In March, 1948, Forrestal charged the military departments to work out some plans for sharing their shortages, and, at the same time, went after Truman to loosen the chain on his budget anchor.

* Quoted in Walter Millis (ed.), *The Forrestal Diaries* (New York: Viking Press, 1951).

But Harry Truman was a marked underdog in the national elections that were just seven months away. He had antagonized many Southern voters in his own party by endorsing civil-rights legislation. He had irritated a good many people by vilifying, at every opportunity, the Republican 80th Congress, which had just cut taxes. Senator Robert Taft, was calling, despite the tax cuts he favored, for Defense expenditures in the neighborhood of $25 billion to handle increasing world pressures. Truman's vote-hunting point: cutting taxes and raising the Defense budget didn't go together.

Ordering the Chiefs not to complain (which, through "informed observers," they promptly yelled was "gag rule"), Truman requested, in his January message to Congress, an $11 billion Defense budget for fiscal 1949. Military experts, the White House press releases implied, had agreed it was enough. One year earlier, the President had spelled out the Truman Doctrine, in which he had said, in part, "I believe . . . it must be the policy of the United States to support free peoples who are resisting attempted subjugation by armed minorities or by outside pressures." Fortunately for White House political ambitions, nobody had yet put a realistic price tag on that promise.

The budget ceiling was based, instead, on a kind of "guts" judgment on what Congress and the public were willing to pay. Military needs, based on contingency war plans, based in turn on threat estimates, were then cut to fit the dollars—which was like cutting the man to fit the suit. The worst of it was that the U.S. military didn't just demobilize after World War II. It nearly disintegrated.

The Army, in the spring of 1948, had shrunk to 127,000 men below its Congress-authorized 669,000-man strength. Not only were there not enough dollars appropriated to support the full count, but enlistments were running way behind discharges. The Navy was 200,000 men short, including the 29,000-man gap between actual and authorized strength in the Marines. It hoped to ease its troubles somewhat by mothballing 107 ships. Air Force manpower shortages were almost as critical, but the Air Force was more worried about a different threat to its future. The Navy's budget request asked for money for a new supersized aircraft carrier capable of launching and landing B-29 bombers.

To the Air Force, which already had had to mothball more than

50,000 of its World War II aircraft, the request was a clear-cut Navy attempt to steal its strategic bombing mission. The Air Force launched a hard-sell campaign for a 70-group aircraft fleet. Then authorized 55 groups, it actually had resources to fill only about 49. If the Air Force got what it wanted, there would be nothing much left under the budget ceiling for anyone else. As a hedge against failure to consummate that effort, Air Force officials proposed some fascinating deals. An Air Force official's quiet suggestion to a top Navy aviation expert that they "get all this flying stuff in one department" is supposed to have been buttressed by the promise that "If you agree, Admiral, we'll let you be Chief of Staff of the new Service." The admiral said he'd have to think about it. Later, the Air Force's top strategic bombing general was asked to bring his bombers over and join the Navy. According to one report of the conversation, the general was told: "We've got a completely integrated fighting outfit including our own transportation, communications, fighters, even the beginning of an Army. Join us and we'll put the War Department out of business." The Army, in its turn, proposed that the Marines be assigned to them.

Without getting into the military science of it, Forrestal accepted the premise that each Service contributed something of value to total security. "You cannot separate in modern war," he said, "any one segment from the other two. They march together." Thus, in spite of the wave of popular support for putting most security eggs in the Air Force atomic-bomb basket, Forrestal favored a concept of "balanced forces." The idea was the embryonic stage of what came to be known fourteen years later as the "strategy of flexible response."

In budget terms in 1948, it meant that, for every $2 the Air Force got, the Navy got $2, and the Army got $1.95, or thereabouts. Poor third in a three-horse race, and aware of its position, the Army bought the concept, naturally. The Navy, a close second, did, too. The Air Force disagreed, not having heard any analysis of what enemy forces the balanced forces were supposed to be balanced against.

Forrestal really had no Pentagon machinery strong enough to force the Joint Chiefs to agree on dividing up the roles and missions implicit in the budget battle. He decided to haul all of them, along with their aides, "away from the telephone" to the seclusion of the Key West, Florida, Naval Base. At a press conference on March 10, just before the four-day meeting began, Forrestal announced that the session would decide "who will do what with what." And he added that if the Joint Chiefs failed to come to terms, "I shall have to make my own decisions."

The theme at Key West was to be teamwork. The military department bosses were to develop plans for combating the dollar shortage by switching forces around to back up sister Services. The Navy and the Air Force were particularly instructed to "give much more thought and help to the third Department, the Ground Forces, who are the catchall for the unwanted and unglamorous jobs."

During the Key West meeting, a note arrived from General George Marshall, who had replaced James Byrnes as Secretary of State the year before, outlining a proposal by British Foreign Minister Ernest Bevin that had features startlingly like the debate on "cooperative effort" going on at Key West. Bevin asked that a joint security pact be put together for the North Atlantic nations. It was the seed for what would eventually become the North Atlantic Treaty Organization. The Joint Chiefs, preoccupied with their own headaches, noted it and filed it away.

By the last day of the meeting, the Chiefs had managed to agree to the *status quo*. The Marines would hold at four-division size, and would not try to create another land army. The Navy would not develop a separate strategic air force. The Air Force would let the Navy use aircraft to hit inland targets that might attack the fleet and "permit" the Navy to participate in an "all-out air campaign."

With that much out of the way, a half-hour before lunch, Joint Staff Director Gruenther told the Chiefs that their joint war plan required larger forces than they had. In essence, relying on voluntary enlistments to fill the ranks was a failure. Universal military training, which Truman had been promoting since he became President, wouldn't provide men fast enough—even if the UMT bill passed Congress. And passage of such a bill was doubtful. The Chiefs voted to ask Congress for revival of the Selective Service draft.

Plenty of mental wounds were inflicted at that meeting. In an attempt to restore order, which cost him support from the rest of the Navy, Chief of Naval Operations Louis Denfeld suggested:

"The words of our understanding are clear. Interpreted properly, they will instill the spirit of 'all for one and one for all.' Any agreement will work only if the personnel of each Service work together with sympathy and really desire to make it work." (Five months later, the Chiefs had to meet again, this time at Newport, Rhode Island, in another attempt to achieve harmony. Like the Key West meeting, the Newport get-together was just another unrewarding vacation away from the Pentagon.)

On March 17, President Truman addressed a joint session of Congress and issued an emotion-stirring call to rearm. From the ringing tone of his speech, Congress fully expected to be asked for, and was ready to give, more armaments, more men, and a great deal more money. Instead, Truman requested only prompt enactment of the European Recovery Program, commonly called the Marshall Plan (basically, a financial transfusion for war-wrecked Allied economies); enactment of UMT, and "temporary" reenactment of the Selective Service legislation.

Forrestal hurried to the White House, armed with a Joint Chiefs' request for some $9 billion in add-ons to the Truman budget request of January—which Congress had not approved yet. In light of the tense world situation, Truman indicated, he might go for about $1.5 billion more. Forrestal did not even consider taking that bad news back to the Pentagon. Instead, he argued until Truman agreed to let him present his own add-on budget request to Congress, the additional request to be "in the neighborhood" of $3 billion.

Because of the time spent in argument, more than a week passed after Truman's ringing speech before Forrestal got to the House Armed Services Committee to spell out in dollars what the President had meant. Even then, while he had Truman's permission to talk, he did not have endorsement of the substance of what he was going to say. In the meantime, the only specific hardware rearmament proposal the nation had heard from anyone was an Air Force plea for an increase in size to seventy groups. The result was a general assumption that, if rearmament started, it would start with building up the Air Force.

On the contrary, what Forrestal asked for was a balanced boost in air, sea, and ground forces. He proposed spending the bulk of the budget add-on to strengthen the Army by 240,000 men, the Marines by 11,000. The rest of the $3 billion would be used, he said, to fill out the existing, but undermanned, 55-group Air Force. The Key West accord he thought he had supporting him as he went to Capitol Hill started coming unstuck almost before he finished speaking there. Symington called, saying he and his generals were "not in agreement with a press release to the effect that agreement had been reached in all major areas at Key West." (At the same time, the serious undertone to all this discord was struck by the Central Intelligence Agency, recently set up by the National Security Act. Reported the CIA, with probably unintended irony, "War isn't likely for at least the next sixty days.")

In House testimony following Forrestal's presentation, the Air Force clearly implied that it thought it had been betrayed, and added that the full 70-group Air Force would cost only another $800 million on top of the Truman budget proposed in January. Someone, thought Congress, was giving it a run-around.

Back came Forrestal. If one Service got all it wanted, the other Services should, too, he said. Therefore, the price tag for additional bombers would, in the final analysis, amount not to $800 million, or even the $3 billion he was asking, but $15 billion. He requested that the $800 million be voted for UMT instead. In so doing, he assumed, of course, general support of his balanced-forces concept. The Committee was immediately confused because it wasn't assuming any such thing.

Out of the wrangling that followed came an embittered Air Force and a frustrated Forrestal. Congress voted $822 million to go to the Air Force, primarily for new intercontinental B-36 bombers, but the bill was undercut with "stretch-out" clauses that meant the President could freeze the money. Truman made plain his attitude: "I'm in favor of a 70-group Air Force—when the Nation can afford it." The Air Force failed to get what it wanted. So did Truman, since Congress killed UMT.

Meanwhile, on March 31, Russia put up her first, if temporary, roadblocks on the supply routes into Berlin. Next day, in a move that was a prelude to the later, famous Berlin Airlift, some food was actually flown into the city. After three months of on-and-off harassment, Russia clamped down hard on her blockade in the same week the Republicans were holding their Presidential nominating convention in Philadelphia. Britain, France, and the United States answered Russia with more supplies of food and fuel flown into Berlin. "Operation Vittles," as it was officially named, hit its peak on September 17, hauling, on that day alone, 7,000 tons of supplies. The airlift effectively broke Communism's drive to push the Free World Allies out of the city. It was a magnificent accomplishment—and it was well that it worked. In the face of massed Russian armies on the East German border, Europe's democracies could muster only piddling military strength. Apart from the B-29 atomic bombers, which had been swiftly deployed to England, U.S. forces in Europe were not much stronger.

Still, the White House refused to lift its budget ceiling. The Joint Chiefs had finally "compromised" on Forrestal's general request for a fiscal 1949 budget add-on by asking specifically for some $3.481 billion. That amount was to give the Army 790,000 men and the Air Force sixty-six groups, mainly by reactivating B-29's rather than building B-36's. The Budget Bureau chopped the Pentagon's request to $3.17 billion, and forwarded it to the President. Then Truman told the Chiefs, in effect, that he would send their proposal to Congress only if they would agree not to spend the money. One nonplussed military officer was quoted in the press at the time retelling the story of comedian Eddie Cantor talking to his sidekick Jimmy Wallington about how Cantor's wife, Ida, was always needling him for more money.

"That does sound pretty bad," sympathized Wallington. "What does she do with all that money, anyway?"

"I don't know," said Cantor. "I never give her any."

In the fall of 1948, Forrestal tried once more. The fiscal 1950 budget (covering the period from July, 1949, to June, 1950) would be the first jointly developed by the Army, Navy, and Air Force working, however reluctantly, together. (The budget for July, 1947, to June, 1948, had been prepared, of course, before there was a National Military Establishment. And, since the request for July, 1948, to June, 1949, was presented to Congress in January, 1948, just four months after Forrestal became Secretary of Defense, it too, in preparation, had been virtually one budget for the Navy and another for the Army, with the Air Force promised an agreed-upon share of the Army request.)

Forrestal came up with a scheme for fiscal 1950 to outflank, he thought, the budget ceiling. He asked the Chiefs for a coordinated budget request in two sections. First, he wanted the run-down on what each Service would buy with its share of the $14.4 billion the White House would make available. (The projected $15 billion for Defense included $600 million earmarked for stockpiling scarce raw materials.) The foregone conclusion was that there would be only enough bought to launch a strategic A-bomb strike against Russia, with the bombers stationed in England, if war broke out. Very little else could be provided for. But Forrestal also wanted from the Chiefs an alternative "in, say, the $18.5 billion range," based on the balanced-forces concept. These budget figures, he said, were to represent their best considered professional judgment of the absolute minimum necessary to (a) support U.S. foreign policy commitments implied in promises like the Truman Doctrine, and (b) provide the skeletal strength on which to build quickly if total war broke out.

The Chiefs refused Forrestal's request. They merely dumped back in his lap three separate, uncorrelated budgets, totaling slightly more than $30 billion, and calling for a 70-group Air Force, an Army of 700,000 men, and a start by the Navy on construction of its super aircraft carrier. One cynic observed, "I doubt if the Joint Chiefs will reach an amicable solution under a $15 billion ceiling."

Admittedly, it was difficult for the military departments to be much concerned about coordinated budgets at that time. The Services really had no clear guidelines on what foreign policy they should support. Also, they were preoccupied with their donnybrook over who should have the important hardware. Their own strategic war plans were no more tightly coordinated than their budgets. What's more, they were convinced the United States would soon be involved in another shooting war. Where and on how big a scale they weren't sure, but certainly they believed that when it did happen, all this budget business would be forgotten. In view of the world situation, the Services had a good deal of confidence that the $15 billion was a show figure to be flourished until the election returns were in. Even Forrestal implied that he would be able to renegotiate that ceiling after the votes were counted—whether with Truman or (said the odds-makers) with a new President from the Republican Party.

However, Forrestal still insisted on working within the stated limit. "The division (of $15 billion) will be disposed of before supplemental appropriation discussions are taken up." He threatened to replace the Joint Chiefs if they could not agree and announced he would set up a tri-Service board to work out compromises. That shook the Chiefs enough so they beat him to it, setting up a board themselves. It sliced the $30 billion they had first asked to $23.6 billion—just about what the electioneering Republicans had indicated they would be willing to support. Before the Defense Secretary could figure out a new way to coerce the military closer to his $18.5 billion goal, Truman won his smashing upset election victory. Completely hamstrung now, Forrestal mulled over calling back to active service some recently retired senior officers. He hoped that these old military friends could pull the Chiefs together.

His staff didn't think much of the idea, claiming that there's nothing more out of date than a Pentagon war horse who's been away for a year. They told the Secretary that any officer recalled to duty would listen to the briefings and repeat what the Services wanted. And that, they said, "We already know."

Forrestal fussed, "We've got to do something. We can't get these people to agree, and we can't get a higher budget out of Truman."

He decided to ask in national military hero Dwight Eisenhower, who had just become president of Columbia University. Forrestal told an aide to call the General.

In a moment, the aide reported back, "He's gone fishing, sir, and can't be reached."

Forrestal bounced off the roof. "He's alive, isn't he?"

"Yes, sir."

"Well, get him on the telephone."

Eisenhower's main contribution was a "red bricks and purple bricks" concept. The red bricks were those absolutely essential building materials that hold up the roof of the house. The purple bricks, although useful, too, had a primarily decorative function and could be left out of the budget for a while. The only fault with this concept was that to the Air Force its seventy groups all seemed to be red bricks, while most of the Navy's fleet looked to the Air Force like purple bricks. And, of course, to the Navy, carriers were red bricks, while most strategic bombers were purple bricks.

But, despite disagreements, faced with the facts of political life, the Chiefs cut and chopped their way through an exercise that surprised even them. They scaled down their requests to $16.9 billion and took this compromise to the White House, where they made a flip-chart presentation of it. Truman listened and watched politely, thanked them very much, and left the budget ceiling at $15 billion.

Domestic issues had been the keynote of the election campaign. Worry about world conflict had seemed relatively muted. Truman's economy-in-government crusade had just been vindicated at the polls. Who was to say he was wrong?

By now, an almost overwhelming mass of evidence indicated that Forrestal had lost, if indeed he personally had ever had, the one absolutely essential weapon a Secretary needs for effective Pentagon control—unwavering White House support. He was trying to boost the Defense budget at the same time Truman and the Bureau of the Budget were trimming it, as part of an announced intention to cut the public debt to $200 billion by 1952. Ground into this conflict over money was a distinct White House feeling that "the Navy," Forrestal's heritage, "was the worst offender in spending."

Although the White House was endorsing the United Nations, "warmonger" Forrestal had the audacity to contend that the United States should not rely on the Security Council, because Russia had a veto power there. Forrestal wanted military control over atomic weapons. Truman insisted that control must remain in a civilian agency, the Atomic Energy Commission, reporting directly to the President. Forrestal wanted the National Security Council to be an executive committee with authority. Truman considered that idea a "Forrestal grab" for Presidential power.

Forrestal's "member-of-the-team" image had suffered in mid-1948 when he was frequently suggested as a possible Presidential candidate in place of Truman. Although he contributed large sums privately to the Democratic campaign fund, he had refused to let the Pentagon be drawn publicly into politics. With Truman needing all the help he could get, that closed Defense door had antagonized a great many professional Democrats. Finally, just prior to the November balloting, Forrestal had briefed Republican candidate Thomas Dewey on the state of U.S. national security. Although such briefings became a fairly standard (and certainly wise) procedure a few years later, at the time Forrestal's action was viewed as an attempt to curry favor with, and indirectly endorse, the favored Republican candidate for the Presidency.

Forrestal's balanced-forces budget had angered the Air Force and its many friends in Congress. He had antagonized influential Jews who either didn't understand his attitude on Palestine partition or refused to give weight to his reasons for advocating delay. He had soured organized labor and some so-called liberal groups by favoring the Taft-Hartley law, which Congress had passed over a Truman veto. The unions did not share his concern over the threat to effective industrial war mobilization of some 4,500 unregulated strikes a year—and cared not at all for his philosophical observations that, historically, when governments were "overzealous" in their favors to labor, Communists moved in and took over first the unions and then the nations.

With so many arrayed against him, Forrestal, in addition, had almost incontestable proof that many of his old Navy friends could no longer be trusted. Gone were many contacts he had carefully cultivated on Capitol Hill. Gone was Secretary of State George Marshall, whom he admired and with whom he could reason, replaced by Dean Acheson—who clearly had Truman's backing. Gone, too, was his long-time friend and close working companion Under Secretary of State Robert Lovett, replaced by James E. Webb, former foe in the Bureau of the Budget.

The Secretary had been breaking new ground in Defense. There were no benchmarks against which to measure his claims that significant economies had been achieved in the first seventeen months of his reign. Promoted by press leaks and public military rivalries, a general impression of Pentagon waste, duplication, and extravagance persisted.

Truman's election victory in November, 1948, started rumors rippling through Washington that Forrestal was on his way out. Many staff members, whose devotion bordered on love, insist that they saw nothing unusual in Forrestal's behavior after November. But other aides noticed that he appeared to become gradually more and more preoccupied. He started repeating things over and over, acted worried about making big decisions, seemed afraid that he couldn't trust people. His concentration was not as good as it had been. What he said and did wasn't up to his past talent for substituting brilliant improvisation when clear administrative authority was lacking. Dwight Eisenhower, who by then was operating as Forrestal's key military adviser, noticed the change in the Secretary's behavior, but discounted it as nothing more than an understandable caution in dealing with a problem as grave as national survival.

On at least one occasion, however, Forrestal alluded to his shaky position in Washington. "This job," he said, "not only has to be well done but the public has to be convinced it is being well done."

Then, in December, Truman asked Forrestal "to consider Louis Johnson," 1948 Democratic campaign fund-raising chairman, as a possible successor. Forrestal briefed Johnson at least twice in January, 1949, on the Defense operation, what made it tick, where Forrestal's proposals intended it to head, what its headaches were. But, by February, Forrestal began to sound as though the predicted request for his resignation would not come soon.

There were, after all, little pieces of progress he could point to. "A great deal of what was easiest to do," says Ohly, "was done." Most of it was in areas where there was some basis for Service compromise. All sorts of study committees had been set up, some temporary, some that soon began to have a status comparable to the statutory boards created by the Security Act itself.

Probably the biggest step forward had been the setting up of the Military Air Transport Service (MATS), merging the old Air Force Air Transport Command and the Naval Air Transport Service into one. Run by the Air Force, MATS was called the "executive agent" for all military air transportation. In format, it was the forerunner for many such "single-manager" organizations, which, in the future, would handle several different kinds of common tasks for all the military departments. (The Navy, in near mutiny over this move, had been calmed by being promised command of the same sort of office controlling ocean transportation, the Military Sea Transport Service.) A uniform code of military justice for all three Services had been developed. Numerous joint officer advanced training courses and maneuvers had been set up—to start the long, arduous process of developing tri-Service teamwork through understanding of the other man's perspective.

Unfortunately, most of what Forrestal started was the kind of study work that wouldn't make headlines—except for somebody else, later. Across-the-board studies were done on (1) military pay levels and compensation inadequacies; (2) consolidation of the separate Service medical departments; (3) the problems of the poorly trained, badly equipped, and weakly organized Reserve and

National Guard forces; (4) proposals for what would eventually become the single-manager agencies for Defense Supply, Defense Communications, and Defense Intelligence.

Forrestal had set up the Weapon Systems Evaluation Group, a collection of "independent military experts" whose task was to give the Secretary nonparochial military opinion on the relative merits of separate Service weapons. He had gotten the Joint Chiefs to take the first steps toward setting up "unified commands" in overseas areas where the United States had committed major forces. Granted that, among the Joint Chiefs, the idea of unified commands was a horse-trading proposition ("the Air Force can have the Alaskan theater if the Navy gets the Pacific if the Army will accept the Caribbean"), still, the guidelines would lead, in about a decade, to a standard policy of assigning to one theater commander forces from all three Services.

Forrestal could also point to the first attempts at tying down individual Army, Navy, and Air Force roles and missions, tenuous and sensitive though those definitions were. He could take credit for the formulation of the first joint long-range and short-range strategic plans (even though there weren't enough resources to back them up) and for the writing of the first integrated military budget (controversial and unrealistic though it was).

All these embryonic programs certainly would need a firm, knowledgeable man to help them to fruition. Forrestal began indicating that he felt Johnson might come to the Pentagon in a secondary position and move up gradually as he gained experience. But suddenly, at 12:30 P.M. on March 1, 1949, Forrestal was called to the White House and asked to resign. He was shattered. Late into the evening, he worked, drafting and redrafting his resignation. He made two calls to New York to consult old friends about it. He told an aide he had been given until June 1 to get out, but, the aide recalls "He said he wanted out earlier." When he named March 31 for his departure, the date was accepted.

That last day, he was invited to the White House. There he was surprised, and left speechless, by being awarded the Distinguished Service Medal, highest accolade the Government can bestow on a civilian employee. Later, he went to Capitol Hill, where he heard "Uncle Carl" Vinson and other leading House and Senate Armed Services legislators heap high praise on him.

Yet, to Forrestal, 1948 had been an unacceptable year of failure.

Said one Pentagon veteran, nearly two decades later, "Only a few of his very close friends and advisers really felt the depth of his thinking and his vision."

That evening of March 31, he cracked. Friends flew him to Robert Lovett's winter home in Florida, hoping that, with a little rest, he would recover. Instead, he got worse. He kept insisting that the beach was covered with hidden microphones, and that "they" were out to get him. He was flown back to Bethesda, Maryland, to the Naval Medical Center, on April 2.

More than anything, the illness seemed to be the price of his tireless efforts. Forrestal was admired and respected for his dedicated devotion to national duty: first as Under Secretary, then as Secretary of the Navy, and, finally, as the first Secretary of Defense. Those who had attacked him so bitterly in the parochial, intramural Washington wars must have felt a twinge of conscience. Looking for scapegoats, some whispered that Louis Johnson had precipitated his breakdown by "driving him out of office." In fact, Johnson made almost daily checks on how he felt and what more could be done for him.

Symington, too, as spokesman for the "antagonistic Air Force," was given part of the blame, despite a friendship dating back to the 1930's when Dillon, Read's Forrestal had pulled Symington out of an early retirement to revitalize an electronics company in which Dillon, Read had an interest. At that time, Forrestal's clinching argument had been: "All you are doing is loafing around learning how to play golf so well I can't beat you. I need you back at work." Symington now checked on his old friend constantly.

At 1:30 A.M., on Sunday morning, May 22, a medical corpsman, stationed outside Room 1618 in the hospital's white granite tower, looked in on the Secretary and, later, reported him asleep. Under orders to check every fifteen minutes, the corpsman, at 1:45, looked again and found him awake. He asked him if he wanted his usual sleeping pill and was told "No." The corpsman went to report on the patient to a psychiatrist stationed next door, returned in five minutes, and found Room 1618 empty.

On the bedside table was a copy of Mark Van Doren's *Anthology of World Poetry* opened to an English translation of Sophocles' dark and solemn "Chorus of Ajax." Some lines had been copied onto hospital memo paper: "Worn by the waste of time—comfortless, nameless, hopeless save in the dark prospect of the yawning grave."

The snake pit in which Forrestal had worked was rough enough for any man. He had made it worse by locking his emotions inside himself, sharing few, if any, of his problems with his wife, his two sons, or his small list of close friends.

For himself, as for others, he set impossibly high standards of performance. Even his achievements resulted in little self-satisfaction, but instead caused him to set his sights even higher. "He chose to kill himself," said one friend, "at least in part because of his own profound conviction that he had been an utter failure as Secretary of Defense."

In the biography of Forrestal, the man, no specific clinical blame for his death ever was fixed, nor is it probable that it ever will be. A student searching the impersonal archives of the Office of Secretary of Defense may read the tragedy of his death in many different ways. But one conclusion is inescapable. His suicide wrecked any slim chance Louis Johnson had of making an unqualified success out of replacing him.

V

Louis Johnson

[MARCH, 1949–SEPTEMBER, 1950]

THERE WAS NOT much neutral ground around fifty-eight-year-old Louis Arthur Johnson by the time he was sworn into office March 28, 1949, on the Pentagon quadrangle. The big (250-pound), tough, ambitious Virginia-born lawyer had begun muscling his way into politics and the military early. A 1912 graduate of the University of Virginia, he had started, in Clarksburg, West Virginia, what eventually was built into a highly successful law partnership, Steptoe and Johnson, with offices in Clarksburg, Charleston, West Virginia, and Washington, D.C.

Elected to the West Virginia House of Representatives in 1917, young Democrat Johnson had hardly begun his term (majority floor leader, judiciary committee chairman) when he was called into World War I. Infantry officer Johnson later helped to organize the American Legion and became its national commander in 1932. National Chairman of the Democratic Advisory Committee from 1936 to 1940, he was named an Assistant Secretary of War in 1937.

By 1939, Johnson was arguing openly with Secretary of War Harry Woodring over U.S. neutrality and mobilization. He stomped across the country demanding rearmament, "obviously," said one observer, "with the consent, if not the active support, of President Roosevelt." Johnson pushed universal military training ("UMT" the press called it for short) and urged industry production of 24,000 military aircraft a year. Although that construction rate would be beaten four years later, at the time of election year 1940, industrialists hooted at such nonsense. So did a good many others, blistering Johnson with a counterattack of pacifist speeches and student "keep-us-out-of-war" rallies.

Although Johnson's orders came directly from the White House, President Roosevelt, then candidate for an unprecedented third term, wanted to stop the front-page battle between his top War Department civilians. He ousted Woodring, intending to name a Republican to the top Army slot, in order to have a bipartisan cabinet behind him if he had to declare war. Johnson, who wanted the post himself, said "If you do that, I'll have to resign." Harry Stimson was picked, and Johnson quit.

However, less than two years later Louis Johnson was back in White House favor, and he had grown into a Washington political power by war's end. Named chairman of the Democratic Party's finance committee in 1948, with characteristic drive he raised the bulk of Truman's campaign funds—much of it after the upset election from favor-seekers calling to offer congratulations and, often, to plead something like, "By the way, I'm ashamed to confess this, Louis, but I just discovered my secretary forgot to mail that donation you asked for. It'll be over today by messenger." Being named Defense Secretary was Johnson's reward for backing the long-shot winner.

Initially, a new Secretary and his organization always enjoy a pleasant honeymoon, filled with lip-service promises of support and jockeying for position. Johnson's was the shortest-lived honeymoon on Pentagon record.

Without benefit of notes and as fast as he could talk, two days before he left, Forrestal had dictated a rundown on every going Pentagon program. Other than that memorandum, the largely inexperienced Johnson had little more than a superficial, seat-of-the-pants opinion about what the military needed. The handful of American Legion cronies he gathered around him—"gauleiters," the Pentagon called them—weren't much help. The new Secretary's strongest asset was Forrestal's veteran staff, still headed by Leva, McNeil, and Ohly. "Please stay," Forrestal had asked them. "He's going to need so much help."

"Colonel" Johnson (respectful buddies used the nickname liberally, with galling effect on military generals) held a press conference the day after his swearing in, and another two weeks later. Both times, it was apparent that he hadn't had proper briefing. A typical exchange from the record of that second meeting with the press:

"Will you comment on the scope of the arms aid program to Europe?"

"No, sir. That really isn't, at the moment, my responsibility."

"Will guided missiles be divided between the Services?"

"The one thing that I, until I was sworn in, did not get into was guided missiles and atomic energy."

"Would you include biological warfare in that, too?"

"Yes, sir."

"What is your position on the race integration between the branches of the Armed Services as now proposed by the Air Force?"

"You'll not have much argument with what we decide there, I'm quite sure."

"Are you in favor of your predecessor's recommendation to federalize the Air National Guard and the Army Guard?"

"We'll not duck it when we are informed on it. It is in the process . . ."

"Last week, the House Appropriations Committee voted to give the Air Force $800 million more, that old UMT $800 million, and to take some away from the Army and the Navy. What do you think about it?"

"I am supporting the President's program."

"Does that mean you won't let the Air Force spend the money?"

"I am supporting the President's program. I am not quarreling with Congress."

"Explain your position on that."

"The language will speak for itself."

"How can you support the President's program and not fight with Congress?"

"The language will speak for itself. Next subject."

"Would you comment on Atlantic Pact countries asking for more troops to be sent to Europe?"

"I've been looking into it."

"There's been some talk of abandoning the huge carrier for the Navy. The keel is to be laid next week. Will it or will it not be built?"

"I'll play fair with this group. We won't pull something behind your backs on this."

Johnson did not hold another press conference until the following year. He took the squawk boxes out of the Secretary's office to stop the nuisance interruptions that had plagued Forrestal. Like Forrestal, he arrived in the office about 7:30 A.M., worked until 9 or 10 at night, and took a briefcase full of reading home with him. Describing initial impressions, one Pentagon employee said, "He was very approachable, gregarious. He made a point of meeting everyone his first day here, circulated around the offices periodically to see what we were doing. He had an 'open door' policy for his own office."

The friendliness didn't last long. Very quickly Johnson demonstrated, in one of those small ways that can become significant in retrospect, that he was not going to run operations the way Forrestal had. The first Defense Secretary had been so concerned about starting off with the smallest possible emotional tremor among Pentagon employees that he had moved into a vacant office overlooking the Pentagon's mall entrance rather than into Room 3E880, which was reserved on the floor plan for the Secretary of Defense but happened to be already occupied by the Army. Soon after he took office, Johnson ordered the Army out—"to show who was boss," he said later.

The staff soon discovered, too, that he could be personally brutal to people who disagreed with him. The briefing officer who stood before him reading from flip charts would be cut short with, "Say what you have to say. I can already read." In one nasty exchange, an officer outlining some projected cost figures for the Pentagon's top brass was chopped down in front of the others at the meeting by Johnson, who snapped, "General, you're a liar. Come back tomorrow and apologize. You only missed it by $300 million." After a few exchanges like that, the staff pushed him off at arm's length and kept him there.

With his staff meetings every morning, his quick trips around Pentagon corridors, his long hours, Johnson, according to his gauleiters, "had his finger on everything the Department was doing." Pentagon regulars didn't believe it. He also was described as "really very human. This stern exterior is just a front to command respect for his office." Not many people believed that either. Chastized employees were soon mumbling that he intended to use the Pentagon as a springboard to succeed Truman in the White House. Some even felt, as one said in private, that he was "the closest thing to a man on horseback trying to take over the Government since John Wilkes Booth."

Forrestal's people had been closely knit—in many ways, more like a family than a staff. Even fifteen years later, one of them would write, "A great deal of me lies buried in Arlington National Cemetery beneath a simple headstone marked 'James Forrestal—Lieutenant, U.S.N.R.F., World War I. Born 1892. Died 1949.'" None of the Forrestal holdovers felt that way about Louis Johnson.

After Forrestal had killed himself, slanders flitted through Washington that Johnson had helped the disaster along by blunderbussing Forrestal out of office. "Johnson," whispered the witch-hunters, "wanted this job badly to restore the prestige he lost when he was fired in 1940."

Johnson countered, "The President drafted me." He added, "Actually, the first suggestion that I take this job came from Forrestal in a White House meeting." Forrestal was alleged to have implored, "I'm not well. I need a rest, and you have the guts to do the job." Truman had supported the idea, so the story went, and Forrestal had come to Johnson's house one January midnight and had talked until 2:30 A.M. "trying to convince me to accept." Purportedly, even Generals Marshall and Eisenhower endorsed the idea. Just to show what a reluctant bridegroom Johnson was, the press "learned" that he had been having a 7:30 breakfast in Washington's Mayflower Hotel the day after his announced appointment, when Truman had called, wanting to know "why I hadn't been over to thank him for giving me the job."

Forrestal enthusiasts couldn't quite believe this story. They found it incredible, in those tense times, that Forrestal, who knew well many able, experienced Pentagon leaders, would be so strong on a neophyte he had hardly met. They believed, rather, that he was bitterly opposed to Johnson. Johnson could no more have changed that notion than he could have rewritten his political biography to prove he was not a politician.

"Forrestal could be spoken to frankly," said one of the faithful. "For all his impressive intellect, he would hold a problem up to the light, turn it around, analyze it, mull it over, scrutinize it some more before he made a decision. Johnson never has any doubts."

"He tries to operate by fiat," grumbled one succinct Pentagon veteran, "more than he really can by fiat."

Forrestal had pleaded for voluntary Service help in late 1948 when he said: "I should like to re-emphasize that true unification of the armed might of the United States cannot spring from legislation alone. The spark generated by the Unification Act must be fanned into flame by the thoughts and actions of generals and admirals, ensigns and lieutenants, soldiers, sailors, airmen, and civilians. We must all learn that we are working together for a common cause—the security of our country—and that the good of all transcends that of the few."

Louis Johnson didn't bother with such diplomacy. Instead, he merely summoned Pentagon leaders to his office and announced that anyone who couldn't actively and enthusiastically back unification had better get out before he got thrown out.

Forrestal had created scores of committees, trying vainly to push the military into reaching decisions through majority agreement. Johnson snorted, "There are too damn many committees for efficiency's sake," abolished 68 of them before he had been in office two months, wiped out another 141 by the end of the year.

Even Forrestal had admitted, a few weeks before he left, that he had made a mistake about the dangers of placing all Pentagon authority in a single man. To Senate Armed Services Committee Chairman Millard Tydings, he wrote, "I am convinced that a failure to endow this [Secretary of Defense] with sufficient authority to control effectively the conduct of our military affairs will force upon us far greater security risks than will be the case if singleness of control and responsibility are achieved."

In leaving office, Forrestal asked for, and Congress enacted in August, 1949, changes in the 1947 National Security Act. Most of the changes looked like simple alterations of language, but they effectually chopped off the semantic pegs on which the separate Services had been hanging justification for their "rights" to autonomy.

The National Military Establishment was renamed the Department of Defense. In the subtleties of government vernacular, that change meant that the Secretary of Defense was *the* principal military adviser to the White House. His three special assistants were boosted to the rank of Assistant Secretary. He became sole Defense member of the National Security Council. He acquired an alter ego in a Deputy Secretary of Defense. A Chairman for the Joint Chiefs of Staff was approved, in a move that recognized the role Dwight Eisenhower had been filling off and on for several months.

The most significant 1949 addition to the Act was a Title IV section. It required Defense to set up uniform budget and fiscal procedures. In practice, that requirement meant that Congress-appropriated funds would be distributed by the Secretary of Defense, not by the individual Services. Among the unwritten rules of government control is one that says: "Power flows where the money goes." Put another way, the Secretary's real command resided in his comptroller's shop. And sharp, tight-fisted Comptroller Wilfred McNeil already had a reputation "for knowing where every dime was in Defense."

But Louis Johnson didn't wait until the August legislation passed to grab hold of the Pentagon. "The President put me over there to take charge," he said later, "and I did." To prove it, less than a month after taking office he canceled construction of a huge (65,000-ton) flush-deck aircraft carrier, the U.S.S. *United States*. Planned to be capable of launching and landing B-29 bombers, it was the Navy's bid to gain a piece of the Air Force's strategic bombing mission. The Navy had just completed well-publicized keel-laying ceremonies a week earlier at the Newport News, Virginia, shipyards. When Johnson halted the project, Navy Secretary John L. Sullivan exploded and sent a bitter "farewell message" to "a Navy no *foreign* foe has ever defeated." In his letter of resignation, he snarled at Johnson:

> My Dear Mr. Secretary:
> On Saturday, April 23, without discussion with the Chief of Naval Operations, without consultation with the Secretary of the Navy, you directed the discontinuance of construction of the [flush deck carrier] U.S.S. *United States*, the construction of which had twice been approved by the President.
>
> This carrier has been the subject of intensive study in the Navy Department since it was first proposed early in 1945 by the late Marc A. Mitscher whose combat experience had convinced him of its necessity. In a hearing with the Director of the Budget on December 16, 1947, with the approval of the Chief of Naval Operations and the Chief of the Bureau of Ships, I volunteered to surrender $307 million which was the cost to complete the approved construction of other vessels, to insure that funds would be available for the U.S.S. *United States*. Its construction was ex-

plicitly approved by the reports of the Armed Service Committees of the Senate and House on June 2, 1948, and June 9, 1948, respectively. In the Naval Appropriations Act for the fiscal year 1949 the appropriation for the first year of construction of the U.S.S. *United States* was approved by the Congress. Again on December 17, 1948, in a conference with the Secretary of Defense and the Director of the Bureau of the Budget, with the approval of the Chief of Naval Operations and the Chief of the Bureau of Ships, I abandoned construction of other vessels in the amount of $57 million to insure the continuance of the carrier and (its supporting) vessels. Additional funds for the continuing construction of this vessel in the fiscal year 1950 were included in the budget message which the President sent to the Congress on January 3, 1949, and were included in the National Military Establishment appropriation bill passed by the House on April 13, 1949.

Professional naval men, charged with the task of planning for a Navy adequate to the defense of America believe that the construction of the U.S.S. *United States* is so indispensable to the continuing development of American sea power that they have twice sacrificed other substantial construction because of the carrier's highest naval priority.

On Monday, April 18, while discussing a variety of subjects with you, the question of the continuance of work on the U.S.S. *United States* was raised, and my opinion was asked. I started to give my opinion, but before I had talked more than a minute you advised me that you had another appointment and would discuss this matter with me at a later date. The following day I sent you a very brief memorandum touching on only one phase of the justification of this carrier. In this memorandum I referred to my desire to resume the discussion that had been interrupted the previous day. I heard nothing about this again until Saturday, April 23, when in Corpus Christi, Texas, I was advised by long-distance telephone that you had sent me a memorandum directing the discontinuance of construction.

I am, of course, very deeply disturbed by your action which so far as I know represents the first attempt ever made in this country to prevent the development of a power weapon. The conviction that this will result in a renewed effort to abolish the Marine Corps and to transfer all naval and marine aviation elsewhere adds to my anxiety.

However, even of greater significance is the unprecedented action on the part of a Secretary of Defense in so drastically and arbitrarily changing and restricting the operational plans of an armed service without consultation with that service. The consequences of such a procedure are far-reaching and can be tragic.

In view of the foregoing I am sure you will agree with me that no useful purpose can now be served by my remaining as Secretary of the Navy. I have accordingly submitted my resignation to the President.

I deeply regret the circumstances that lead to my departure from the National Military Establishment at such an interesting and crucial period of its development.

Sincerely yours,

John L. Sullivan

Sullivan was promptly replaced by Omaha lawyer Francis Matthews, who made it clear that he thought Louis Johnson was the finest thing that had ever happened to the United States.

Although comprehensive, Sullivan's letter told only part of a longer story. Forrestal had implied, when he had agreed to the supercarrier idea, that it was mainly insurance against possible Air Force failure to perform effective strategic bombing. As he was leaving the Pentagon, he questioned the wisdom of his own decision. That doubt was all the opening economy-minded Johnson needed. Both the Army and Air Force Chiefs of Staff had accepted the carrier program at the Key West meeting. Now, Johnson asked them for a new opinion, and they scooted into his corner on a technicality. The March, 1948, endorsement had merely accepted, they claimed, a decision already given by "Navy man" Forrestal and the President. Preferring at the time to negotiate rather than fight, primarily because Navy Secretary Matthews was not so much a Navy crusader as he was a "Johnson man," Chief of Naval Operations (CNO) Louis Denfeld did little to contest the other Service Chiefs' sudden change of heart. That decision cost Denfeld considerable Navy prestige.

Predictably, the new vote showed the Navy for, the Army and the Air Force against the carrier. On April 22, Johnson showed Truman the majority rejection, and got permission to kill the program. Johnson also collected, he says, approvals from Vinson and Tydings, and polled Eisenhower (who was at Key West recuperating from an ileitis attack). Next morning, as Denfeld—senior Joint Chiefs' member in Eisenhower's absence—formally handed the opinions of the separate Chiefs to Johnson, the reporters one floor below him in the Pentagon got word that the

U.S.S. *United States* had been scuttled. Denfeld learned about the quick action forty minutes later when an aide showed him the press release.

The Navy's aviators immediately launched what came to be tagged the "Revolt of the Admirals." It soon degenerated from an excusable, legitimate military debate over strategy into a summer-long near mutiny, filled with press leaks and character assassinations. The focal point of the Navy's attack was a ten-engine, propeller-driven monstrosity known as the B-36, designed and being built for the Air Force by the Consolidated Vultee Aircraft (Convair) Company.

This plane had been a long time developing. Seven months prior to the Japanese attack on Pearl Harbor, while carrier admirals were wrestling with the battleship admirals for shipbuilding money, Roosevelt had concluded that Hitler was likely to overrun all of Europe. Air-power advocates convinced him that the United States must build a bomber capable of hitting the Nazi dictator from U.S. air bases. Specifically, the aircraft they had in mind must be able to fly 10,000 miles nonstop and cruise 240–300 miles per hour at an altitude of 40,000 feet—high enough to escape air-gulping, 1940-vintage, piston-engine interceptors. When the United States decided, in the middle of the war, that it would not need a B-36 to win, the program was cut back. But by 1947, Russia had become the enemy whose massive, mobile armies could conquer war-flattened Europe overnight. Limping B-36 development speeded up. Now, on Capitol Hill, it became the keystone in an Air Force campaign for funds to build a 70-group air arm. Although far short of the nearly 70,000 planes that fought World War II, that goal was still a good deal better than the 48 groups then flying. The 70-group Air Force called for 6,869 aircraft, including 436 medium and light bombers, some 1,800 trainers, 936 transports, 2,188 fighters, and a variety of miscellaneous planes. But the headline item was a request for 988 heavy bombers. The glamour girl in that category was to be the B-36.

High-powered Air Force speech-makers helped to convince U.S. citizens, anxious to return to peacetime pursuits, concerned about high federal budgets forcing runaway inflation, enamored with simple solutions to complex problems, and awed (to say the least) by the atomic bomb, that the B-36 was the answer. After all, even Dwight Eisenhower had stated, in 1948, "What we are able to do in the first sixty days of another war will be decisive in its determination of our ability to carry the war to a successful conclusion."

That same year, a Truman-appointed Air Policy Commission had analyzed reports on U.S. World War II strategic bombing and had concluded that the United States could "no longer rely entirely on the Navy as our force in being in peacetime. Defense of the United States must be based on air power." A Congress-appointed study group, covering the same subject, had announced that (a) air-power capability was most likely to discourage an aggressor's attack, (b) air power would be the most effective method of thwarting an attack once it started, and (c) of all military weapons, air-power–delivered atomic bombs were best able to deal out retaliatory damage that would discourage future attack. Both reports included Navy aviation in their endorsement but, to a thoroughly brainwashed American public, air power meant the Air Force.

House military expert Carl Vinson "deserted to the Air Force," according to an irate Navy. He declared that the $800 million Truman wanted for universal military training "would be spent instead" for a 70-group Air Force. Ten days before Johnson killed the carrier, House Appropriations Committee Chairman Clarence Cannon (a Missouri Democrat), revealed, "The Air Force is now considered the first line of American defense and will get the lion's share of military air-power funds."

To Johnson, this contest of aircraft carrier versus B-36 was "the issue that gave me a chance to run the department. The secretary didn't have control before. This was the thing that gave me control."

The Navy deployed for battle, setting up in the Pentagon a scholarly-sounding Organizational Research and Policy Section. Known informally as Op 23 (Navy lingo for "Chief of Naval Operations, office number 23"), its main function was to lead the Navy's fight against the Air Force. The Navy's goal: to sell their conviction that naval power was still, and should remain, the nation's traditional peacetime defense.

As early as mid-December, 1947, an outspoken aviator, Rear Admiral Dan Gallery, had warned his Pentagon Navy leaders that strategic atomic bombing would probably be the key mission in deciding the next war. "It is time right now," he urged, "for the

Navy to start an aggressive campaign aimed at proving the Navy can deliver the atom bomb more effectively than the Air Force can."

In 1948, the Navy could have made a strong case. Even Air Force fighter pilots were criticizing the B-36. After more than 200 flights, the airplane still hadn't lived up to performance demands spelled out as long ago as 1941. Its "go-stop-go" development had had a history of mismanagement, of wasted and weak engineering effort. And a revolution in military hardware technology was about to engulf the B-36. Forrestal had pinpointed the implications of this revolution in 1948—to an admiral, of all people—when he questioned whether the Air Force "had really faced up to the urgent strategic and tactical problem of whether or not the bomber could survive against modern radar defenses and the new jet fighters armed with rockets."

Top Air Force officers felt the same concern and split almost fifty-fifty in mid-1948 on canceling or going ahead with the B-36. If they had had anything better, they would have scrapped the B-36 then. But jet bombers were still too many years away, they believed, and intercontinental missiles were no more than a drawing board dream. Air Force Secretary Stuart Symington cast the deciding vote to push on with the best of a bad deal.

Some Navy aviators were appalled, and set out to thoroughly discredit the bomber. They wanted ownership of some atomic bombs, themselves, believing that, without this title, the Navy would become a taxicab service, hauling other people's combat hardware around. Combat, not transportation, troops have most of the promotion opportunities. Careers were at stake, they felt. So were shares in Defense budgets and national influence. If the main issue had not been military needs for national survival, the superficial sideshow might have been very entertaining comedy.

Two Navy humorists wrote B-36 lyrics that were sung in bars around Washington to the tune of Gershwin's "It Ain't Necessarily So": "Oh, the Bomber goes 10,000 miles. Oh, the Bomber goes 10,000 miles. But a bomb the size of a cherry is all it can carry—when the Bomber goes 10,000 miles." Air Force songsters countered with a ditty about the "80,000 tons that disappeared," claiming that an atom bomb dropped from one B-36 would obliterate the 65,000-ton carrier, plus its full load of aircraft, fuel, and munitions.

An admiral got national publicity with a speech challenging the Air Force's bombing concepts. Symington retaliated in the *Saturday Evening Post*. In *The New York Times*, a pro-Navy columnist wrote a series of biased, anti-Air Force articles for which, it is alleged, he nearly got fired. The Air Force, in turn, backed a series for the *Reader's Digest* cutting up Navy aviation.

Army Chief of Staff Omar Bradley became so worried about the possibility that all this ballyhoo would obscure the importance of the Army in modern war that he went on a nationwide speaking tour.* Nobody paid much attention. Things were too interesting back in Washington.

In the spring of 1949, the family squabble grew especially wild—probably because that is the time of year when Congress first looks at budget requests.

On March 1, Secretary Symington ran into CNO Denfeld in the lobby of a Boston hotel and offered to fly him back to Washington in an Air Force plane. Denfeld declined, saying that he already had tickets for a commercial flight. Symington pressed him, in words to the effect: "I'm not stopping, but I'll be happy to let you off." Not until the next day did Denfeld learn that Symington was on his way to Fort Worth, Texas, to greet, along with planeloads of Washington reporters, the arrival of the *Lucky Lady*, a beefed-up B-29 that had just completed a historic round-the-world, nonstop, aerial-refueled flight. Trumpeted Air Force General Curtis LeMay, "We could drop an A-bomb any place in the world."

Hurriedly, a Navy P2V patrol bomber took off from a Caribbean-based carrier's flight deck, flew nonstop with an atomic-bomb-weight cargo to Alaska, circled a mythical target a few times, and returned to an air base in Florida. Total flying distance: some 8,000 miles. Air Force spokesmen snorted publicly, "Yes, but it couldn't land back on the carrier"; privately, it is alleged, they offered the pilot an Air Force brigadier general's commission.

In a few days, the Air Force sent a B-36 winging 9,600 nonstop miles, 5,000 of them with an 84,000-pound bomb load. Word leaked to the press that seventy strategic targets within that range

* General Omar Bradley was Army Chief of Staff from February, 1948, to August, 1949, when all this debate occurred. What his being caught in the middle of the argument cost the other Services, in terms of his personal attitude and support, became clear when he moved up to serve as Chairman of the Joint Chiefs of Staff from August, 1949, to August, 1953.

had been earmarked for complete destruction "if total war comes." It took reporters about two minutes to learn from an atlas that in Russia there were precisely seventy cities with populations of 100,000 or more. The Air Force gloated that, until the advent of long-range missiles, the B-36 would be outmoded only by a better airplane, and added that Russia "has no adequate defense" against the bomber. Maybe the Russians didn't, but the Navy did. Notice was slipped to newspapermen that a Banshee jet fighter could climb to 40,000 feet in seven minutes. The Air Force sneered at such nonsense. So Navy wags hung an aerial photograph of Washington on the wall of the National Press Club bar, told journalists the picture had been taken by a Banshee from 50,000 feet ten minutes after takeoff. Navy aviators challenged Air Force pilots to a duel between the B-36 and a Banshee.

The Joint Chiefs, including Denfeld, promptly shot that thought down, saying it wouldn't prove a thing, no matter what the results. "Just like Billy Mitchell didn't prove anything twenty-five years ago," complained a Navy aviator, "when he challenged the battleship admirals to a duel." Symington fired a note to Johnson, "Are we back in the same old rut with two Services doing what they are told and the third what they think best?"

All this battling was just a bit too much for Carl Vinson. On April 5, his House Armed Services Committee, in words startlingly similar to a Forrestal plea to the military the previous winter, warned that he wanted it "clearly understood if persons in the Armed Services or in their employ continue to pass statements to the press which are calculated to deprecate the activities of a sister Service and which, at the same time, jeopardize the national security, the Committee will step in with a full-scale investigation."

Clearly ahead on publicity points, anyway, the Air Force decided "our proper court of appeal is the Congress." And, simply because Air Force leadership as far back as 1947 had demanded that generals clear in advance, with a single Air Force press relations man in Washington, any public statements they wanted to issue, the Air Force was able to make the order stick. Not so the Navy. Its admirals had always assumed a good deal more independence and were much more inclined to state their minds without bothering to get approval from any civilian boss. One of them even told Navy Secretary Matthews when he opposed arguing with the Air Force, "If you issue that order, we'll resist it."

Then, the Navy committed a fatal error. With the help of a manufacturer who was losing Air Force contracts to B-36 builder Convair, Navy zealots pulled together a list of fifty-five specific allegations, circulated it to the press and on Capitol Hill. Generally referred to as an "anonymous document," it disparaged the B-36 and "exposed" Louis Johnson as having been a member of the Convair board of directors before he became Secretary of Defense. The scandal sheet charged further that in 1948 Johnson had persuaded Missouri Democrat Stuart Symington to bring pressure on Convair's president for a $6 million campaign contribution, on threat of losing the B-36 contract, and said that Symington reportedly had "advised" "Northrop and/or Curtiss-Wright" aircraft builders to merge with Convair or "business would be bad for them." Symington, according to this "Document," intended to launch a new "General Motors of the Air" by handing it the B-36 contract, resign from the Air Force to become its boss, and kick back to Johnson to keep the program well-funded after he left. A Congressman up for promotion in the Naval Reserve laid these "charges" before the nation in a House speech; Congressional immunity protected him from legal action.

Carl Vinson ran out of patience and ordered an Armed Services Committee investigation, which, it turned out, lasted well into the autumn. His probing questions exposed the list of allegations as mere rumors, which Navy extremists had tried hard to prove, found they couldn't, and issued, anyway. For instance, Johnson testified that he had asked Forrestal to make all B-36 decisions before leaving office and had actually taken an $85,000 loss through dumping stocks—his Convair holdings among them—on the market to avoid any possible charge of a conflict of interest.

A high-level Navy special assistant, Cedric Worth, who had no clearance for but did have access to top secret documents, finally "confessed" he had written and distributed the "Anonymous Document." Still, the Navy didn't fire him until a year later when Vinson publicly said it should. Observers of the whole shabby scene came away convinced that Worth "took a dive" to protect a good many more important Navy officers and civilians "up above and around him." In the Navy's own court of inquiry, convened shortly after the Vinson hearings started, one exasperated investigator characterized the contradictory, cover-up testimony both the Navy court and the House committee were hearing. Renouncing the last in a long line of witnesses, he snapped, "I suppose you understand that some of the stories you have told us are incredible beyond belief."

From time to time, the hearings got close to the real need, the devising of correct military strategy. But most of the testimony amounted to nothing but hand-wringing recitations of Navy unhappiness. A Navy captain publicly maligned his superiors and justified his insubordination as "a patriotic obligation" to tell the nation that its Navy's offensive power was being "nibbled to death." A vice admiral moaned, "Morale of the Navy is lower today than at any time since I entered the commissioned ranks in 1916," and described what he called "genuine fear in the Navy for the security of our country [as a result] of policies followed in the Department of Defense since the National Security Act became law." The commander of the Pacific Fleet said a majority of his officers agreed with the admiral.

These self-appointed critics not only renewed the Navy's attack on the B-36, calling it, "the billion-dollar blunder"—but also, with witnesses often seeming to contradict each other, went on to challenge the destructive power of the very weapon the Navy was trying to get hold of—the atomic bomb.

One admiral discredited the bomb's power at almost the same time some of his own staff experts related engineering advances that had made possible new warheads even more awesome than the one used at Hiroshima. Another admiral argued that the whole idea of strategic bombing was a myth. "It actually failed in World War II," he said, "because [enemy] factory production had actually increased in spite of it." He didn't think it possible, he added, to "buy a cheap, quick, easy victory based on a bombing blitz." A third Navy man insisted that the weapon should be outlawed on moral grounds and compared "blowing up helpless civilians in cities" to the use of poison gas in World War I. Then, as the climax to stumbling through several weeks of such talk, Navy spokesmen finally went one sentence too far. A commander told Vinson's committee, "You could stand in the open at one end of the north-south runway at the Washington National Airport, with no more protection than the clothes you now have on, and have an atom bomb explode at the other end of the runway without serious injury to you."

Southern Democrat "Uncle Carl" Vinson pulled his rimless glasses down onto the end of his nose, stared over them at the young commander, and drawled, "Well, if it is going to drop that close, I want to be down in Georgia."

What the commander had wanted to emphasize was that pinpoint bombing was still necessary even with the atomic bomb and "wasn't possible from a B-36 at 40,000 feet." The Air Force countered this, and all the other attacks, by noting that it had never said it could win an entire war alone (although a lot of taxpayers thought it had said as much). Backing away from its previous adamant insistence on the magic 70-group goal, it now allowed, sensibly, that all decisions should be made on the basis of the size and changing nature of the threat to national security.

Louis Johnson, who had managed to avoid being caught up in most of the bickering, now stepped forward and accused the Navy of waging a "campaign of terror" against unification. Secretary of Navy Matthews decried the uncontrollable, insubordinate "officers, with an obligation to support the Constitution and the Laws of the United States, who have deliberately engaged in the indefensible procedure of surreptitiously disclosing information to persons unentitled to it."

On October 13, 1949, Denfeld's staff persuaded him to drop all attempts to mediate between his Navy and the rest of the Pentagon. He finally, but far too late, became the Navy's spokesman. Among his charges in Congressional testimony: pouring funds into the untested B-36 was starving both the Army and Navy of essential resources; a twenty-five-year lead in carrier and amphibious warfare know-how squandered on "false doctrines" of war; the Army wanted to abolish the Marines, and the Air Force wanted to abolish carriers; the Navy had not been granted full partnership in Defense. He warned: "Improper operation of unification is more injurious than no unification at all."

For the press, one Navy subordinate elaborated: "A political appointee and a bunch of dog-face soldiers are cutting Navy out of the military family. [Clearly, he was referring to a meeting the previous July, at White Sulphur Springs, West Virginia, at which Johnson had ordered, with Omar Bradley's agreement, a 50 per cent reduction in the Navy air arm and about the same thing in fleet size.] A West Virginia lawyer and an infantry officer. What the hell do they know about ships?"

Openly attacked by his own outfit, Johnson's disciple and handpicked Secretary of Navy, Francis Matthews, stormed red-faced out of the hearing room.

By this time, Omar Bradley had become the first official chairman of the Joint Chiefs. He took the witness stand, and in 15,000 wrap-up words, castigated what he called the "fancy Dans" in the Navy who had always opposed unification. ". . . I believe," he said in part "that this is a most serious matter—one which must be resolved if this organization is to be allowed to proceed effectively. While the whole world relies upon the leadership of the United States as they face a common enemy, Americans at home are offered a spectacle of dissension within our own Department of Defense."

Three million words of testimony and almost all of 1949 had been spent on what amounted to not much more than (1) public confession that military morale was shaky and (2) disclosure of some heretofore classified information. Rapped Bradley, "Careless detractions of the power of this [atomic] weapon have done national security no good and may have done our collective security, in these precarious times, untold harm."

The week following the end of the hearing, Denfeld learned—from his limousine driver, who had heard it on the radio—that he had been fired by Matthews, with Johnson's support. Next day, he went to the Navy–Notre Dame football game and received a standing ovation from the assembled brigade of Naval Academy midshipmen. Admiral Forrest Sherman was flown in from the Mediterranean, to become, on November 1, the first naval aviator appointed Chief of Naval Operations in peacetime. Navy fliers had lost the year-long debate, but "one of their own" was now in the top Navy officer post.

The Navy later managed a last, hollow laugh when Johnson, Symington, Bradley, and two congressmen traveled to sea to ride in a P2V during a carrier takeoff and landing. The same pilot who had made the run to Alaska when the Navy was fighting for press attention the year before was at the controls.

Turning to Johnson, he pointed toward the control tower superstructure and announced, just before he rammed his throttles forward to the cockpit firewall and kicked in the JATO (for Jet Assisted Takeoff) bottles, "Mr. Secretary, if I get off line at all, you're going to have a flush-deck carrier whether you want it or not." Seconds later, the plane's right wing zipped past the tower by a slim three feet.

At hearing's end, the Navy had succeeded only in receiving a sharp reprimand for, said the Vinson committee, trying to undercut Johnson's Pentagon authority, trying to take over strategic bombing missions, and forcing disclosure of secret information.

Less than three years later, the object of all the bitterness, the B-36, which had never fired a shot nor dropped a bomb, was replaced by the jet-powered B-47's and 600-mile-per-hour B-52's. Meanwhile, the Air Force had mended some fences by promising a worried Army "to do something" about its long-neglected tactical and transport aviation responsibilities.

In late 1949, a poll showed some 74 per cent of the American people believed that the Air Force would be decisive in winning any future war. At about the same time, former President Herbert Hoover, then heading a bipartisan commission to improve federal government operating efficiency, testified in praise of Johnson for "his courageous attempts to economize" in Defense. And Carl Vinson said publicly that Johnson "deserves the full support of the [House Armed Services] Committee and the country in his difficult task."

Johnson needed some applause. His heavy-handed drive to take charge was beginning to backfire all over the Pentagon. His unwise naming of a public relations man, Steve Early, as the first Deputy Secretary of Defense had earned him smears of being more concerned with his national image than with improving Defense, and ordering the Services to clear all B-36 versus Carrier testimony with his new alter ego got him charged with dictatorial gagging of military free speech.

Vinson's applause gratified the Secretary, but it did nothing to raise his rating in the Navy. The admirals were convinced Johnson was "out to get" them because of their stand against unification. Their "proofs": his turning down the supercarrier had been followed by Congress' approving a Johnson-endorsed, Air Force-oriented budget. In addition, they said, Johnson was "listening sympathetically" to an Army proposal that the Marine Corps be merged into the Army. (He was, but the proposal was not carried out.) Any one of the so-called proofs was enough to permanently alienate Navy support.

And Johnson's stature in the other two Services had been plummeting rapidly for other reasons. Army and Air Force anger centered primarily on his tight-fisted reluctance, as they saw it, to let them spend any money at all.

In early 1949, at a White House meeting, Truman had informed top Pentagon officials he was scrapping the "high Defense budget" Forrestal had talked him into. The new ceiling for fiscal year July, 1950 to June, 1951, was to be $14.6 billion. After deducting some $1.6 billion earmarked to stockpile scarce raw materials, to pay for a military salary increase Congress had passed, and to build a new guided missile test site at Cape Canaveral, Florida, the Services had about $13 billion left to spend. And the following year, Truman said, that amount would shrink to $11 billion.

"Can we argue?" asked Johnson.

Truman said no.

The military Chiefs of Staff, who had once freely beaten Forrestal about the ears with their vitriolic demands for far higher "absolute minimums," didn't say a word. Back in the Pentagon, each Service ran through a series of fiscal gyrations, and each concluded it might just be able to squeeze by on $9 billion, while the other two should be able to operate very nicely on about $2 billion each.

Unlike Forrestal, Johnson didn't bother much with what the Services' individual military motivations might be. If the three couldn't get together voluntarily, that was their problem. He was after economy. "He became a great one for across-the-board percentage cuts," said one fiscal expert.

Defense, Johnson told Truman, was "still suffering from the costly war-born spending habits." It was, he said, "like a fat man . . . in poor condition to run a race until the fat could be transformed into muscle."

He had promised Congress early in 1949 that, if it passed certain proposed National Security Act changes to give him more authority, he would be able to cut Defense spending $1 billion the first year, $1.5 billion the next. Technically, Truman's $13 billion ceiling was, in July, 1949, a year away from going into effect, but Johnson saw no point in waiting. He ordered the Services to "bleed down" to the projected 1951 spending pace in their fiscal 1950 programs—for which Congress had not yet even appropriated funds. His message was clear: the military would spend more efficiently what money it already had before it was given any more.

He showed publicly what he meant one afternoon in 1949 by sending a telegram to every member of Congress, asking them to be in the Pentagon auditorium the next day. At 8 A.M., startled employees were greeted by the sight of almost the entire Legislative branch of the Government rushing up the Pentagon steps. They learned later that Johnson had coldly announced the closing of seventy-seven "nonessential" bases, including six hospitals with 25 per cent or less occupancy. Pork-barrel–minded Congressmen, who thought he understood their political needs, were stunned. They wanted economy—but not that much.

To help the Services along toward cost-cutting, he began reprimanding them for their wasteful ways. Buying by one Service of what another already had too much of particularly roused his ire; he claimed, later, that his forced coordination of procurement had saved $49 million in one electronics area alone during just his first year in office. He complained about military family housing costing $35,000 a unit, demanded standardization of housing specifications, and bragged of a resultant price cut to $17,000 a unit. Suppressing "excessive" buying of spare aircraft engines by the Navy and Air Force saved another $56 million, he said.

He cut Air Force officers with desk jobs off the flying payrolls, costing them the extra-risk, weekend flying income that had supplemented their low regular pay. That move got the ranks mad at him. Higher levels lost their tempers when he impounded most of the $822 million Congress had voted for a 70-group Air Force and told the Air Force it would have only $4.1 billion to spend in fiscal 1951. That action meant that the Air Force could sustain just 47 groups into 1951, only 39 by 1952, and, with inflation pushing the price per item up, only 34 by 1956 (the year in which it was estimated the Soviet Union would reach its strategic airpower peak).

By the spring of 1950, Symington had had enough. He went quietly to the White House and loyally warned Truman, "I can't accept that man. I don't want to make a mess . . . but I want out." Now that Johnson had put the Navy in its place, Symington's staff speculated that their Missouri Democrat boss, loaded with key Congressional contacts, head of the most popular Service, was likely to be Johnson's next target. Truman shifted Symington to head the National Security Resources Board. From a prestige standpoint, the job was on par with Johnson's. As chairman, Symington was co-equal with Johnson on the National Security Council. The rest of the Air Force squirmed over losing their Service leader by default.

The Army suffered in silence, nearly one-third under its authorized manpower strength by then but without any single expensive piece of glamorous hardware to attract attention—and never very adept at public relations, anyway.

Johnson sailed energetically on, wielding his economy bludgeon. In January, 1950, he had revealed that $20 billion in fiscal 1951 money asked by the Services had been trimmed to $13.5 billion, which, he said, was "adequate to defend the nation against any situation that may arise in the next two years." If Joe Stalin, he bragged later, "starts something at 4 A.M., the fighting power of the U.S., spearheaded by the Air Force, will be on the job at 5 A.M."

In March, he said, "We're farther ahead than ever in peacetime history removing waste and eliminating the fancy trimmings." The military, cowed into letting him make the speeches, was convinced privately that it wasn't efficiency but a reduction in strength that had lowered Defense spending. In the face of military agitation that war was imminent and more funds had to be spent to prepare for it, Johnson said, "I don't think it is necessary for this country to do everything to be in a readiness for full, all-out war on a moment's notice. It will bankrupt us."

One perceptive Congressman commented, "The real question is just how much is enough? If there is peace, a $13 billion budget is entirely too much, and if there is war, this is entirely too little."

But low budgets indicate low intentions. With all the public wailing about American military weakness, Russia had good reason to believe that, if she picked her target carefully, the United States could not retaliate. At 4 A.M. on June 25, 1950, 3 Communist North Korean army columns, spearheaded by about 100 Soviet T-34 and T-70 tanks, jumped across the 38th parallel into South Korea.

"Louis said we could lick the Russians," snapped one bitter admiral. "He didn't say anything about the North Koreans."

Immediately under fire, Johnson tossed the nation a bunch of statistics. It is noteworthy that, in March, 1948, only 28 per cent of total Army strength was in combat units. At the time of the Korean invasion, 43 per cent of Army's military personnel were in combat units, with the number of combat personnel increased by over 67 per cent.

"There are lies," answered one general privately, "there are damn lies, and there are statistics."

Of the $90 billion spent on Defense from 1946 to 1950, $42 billion went just to liquidate the costs of World War II. Maintaining peace overseas had kept nearly half the Army occupied in Europe and Asia, substantial portions of the Navy in the Mediterranean, and a large part of the Air Force budget committed to the Berlin airlift. Operating and maintaining aircraft, ships, tanks, and military installations—the bulk of U.S. military strength—drained $3 billion, or 26 per cent, out of the annual budget. To pay, feed, clothe, and house the military soaked up another $5 billion annually. Johnson's proudest argument was that he had raised the percentage left to spend on new hardware from a low of 6 per cent in 1947 to a high of 19.5 per cent by fiscal 1950. His military and public critics claimed they could find little hardware in the inventory to support that boast.

Asked if he was going to fire Johnson, Truman said, "He'll be Secretary of Defense as long as I'm President."

The answer bantered around Pentagon lunch counters was, "That means for about another thirty days."

But Presidents don't resign. Nor, particularly in war, do they admit mistakes. Scapegoats are found. By September, the United States was just a short breath away from being driven off the Korean peninsula. One Sunday morning in September, a "White House spokesman" disclosed that Johnson was out. On a West Coast speaking tour at the time, Johnson immediately hurried back to Washington and roared into Truman's office to insist on a public denial.

Pentagon obedience, he explained, was tough enough to come by when military men knew he had unquestioned White House backing. If they once got the idea he was through, making them carry out orders would be well-nigh impossible. Answered Truman, "Well, Louis, if you feel that way about it, in your resignation, mention George Marshall as your successor."

Grim, white-faced, with tears in his eyes, Johnson returned to the Pentagon, picked up a pencil, and did as instructed. Aides, recalling Forrestal's similar reaction to the same order a year and a half earlier, stayed close to him until he met his wife that evening. He had been told to resign just as Far East Commanding General Douglas MacArthur was launching a successful amphibious flank attack at Inchon, Korea, which temporarily turned the tide of war. Four days later, Johnson's departure was announced.

Much later, Johnson told a Senate committee:

> I caught more hell when I resigned as Secretary of Defense, but time showed the record then was all right; and I have every confidence that the work we did for unification . . . getting the military establishment ready to receive these additional [Korean build-up] appropriations will be some day, even by the severest critics, recognized as not a disservice; but, to the extent they want to admit it, as a service to the thing I dedicate my life to—the security of America.

Asked why, in that case, he had been fired, he answered, "Truthfully, under oath, I don't know. I don't know to this day."

In all fairness to Johnson, it should be said that, if he had one glaring fault, it was his loyal soldier's unbridled enthusiasm in carrying out the Truman Administration's orders. Well aware of this side of his record, most of Washington fully expected him to lash back at the White House. His biting answer to one friend, "I don't tell stories like that!"

The economy drive it had once demanded of him, a rattled nation now considered his "arbitrary, unreasoned exercise of power." He returned to practicing law, and said nothing more about his stormy Defense career. Even his enemies grudgingly granted, as one of them said, "He took his spanking very well."

To restore Pentagon morale, Harry Truman picked a man he had once called "the greatest living American."

VI

George C. Marshall

[SEPTEMBER, 1950–SEPTEMBER, 1951]

George Catlett Marshall was only three months away from his seventieth birthday when he became Secretary of Defense on September 21, 1950. He had been an international military hero even before the Pentagon was built—and had been trying to retire for about six years. Tall, white-haired, ruggedly handsome, he had in the twilight of his career an unsettling reputation for being able to command attention without seeking it.

"In an ordinary gray business suit," said one top Washington official, "he could walk into a cocktail party full of high-level U.S. and foreign dignitaries dressed to the collars in gold braid, and the minute he entered, their chattering din turned to whispers."

The "Old Man," as long-time associates privately and affectionately called him, was, they said, "a pretty fearsome type, until you got to know him."

He was treated with a "veneration due your elders" by veteran Pentagon civil servants. "He was awesome," said one, "a man of history sitting behind that desk. The only thing like it was the White House." His decades-old habit of calling even important people by their last names ("Get me Vandenberg of the Air Corps!") merely emphasized to the awe-struck the new boss's stature.

The Services were, of course, generally delighted. The man who had commanded many of them personally when they were mere majors and colonels in the 1930's, had led them during World War II, had been a key backer of unification and at the same time of independent air power, had helped set up the North Atlantic Treaty Organization, had created and launched the famed Marshall Plan to put Europe back on its postwar economic feet, who knew the military ways of doing business—and for that matter had created many of them—was once again leading.

"The 'Old Man' was the one who kept people steady on course. The Chiefs knew his language, knew how he expected problems to be handled, knew how he operated. It was an understood but unwritten thing. It played a tremendous part in bettering Pentagon activity," one of his staff recalls.

In marked contrast to Johnson, Marshall had a reputation of "such evident integrity and honesty. He never did an expedient thing. What's good for the whole country was all he was after."

One colonel said, "He rated in my book just about even with the Holy Ghost."

"No," topped a brigadier general, "It's George Marshall and *then* the Holy Ghost."

"There is no limit to the good one can do," Marshall once said, "if he doesn't care who gets the credit." By the time he replaced Louis Johnson, he had built on that creed a prodigious success story.

Son of a Uniontown, Pennsylvania, coal merchant, he graduated from the Virginia Military Institute in 1901, and began his military career by shuttling back and forth between posts in the Philippines and the United States. He was on the first U.S. troop ship to France in 1917. His World War I battlefield command and operations planning earned him selection as General John J. Pershing's personal aide-de-camp; he served in that role from 1919 until Pershing retired in 1924.

Marshall's wife, Elizabeth—"Lily" he called her—died of heart failure in 1927, while he was an instructor at the Army War College. Wrote Marshall to close friend Pershing: "Twenty-six years of most intimate companionship, something I have known since I was a mere boy, leaves me lost in my best effort to adjust to future prospects in life. . . . However, I will find a way."

The way was dedicated hard work. The Army praised him for working "a magical change" at its Fort Benning, Georgia, infantry training center, strengthening the curriculum and revamping instruction techniques. He married again in 1930. In 1933, he was publicly praised again—for his work setting up Civilian Conservation Corps camps in Georgia and South Carolina. Asked at the outset how many officers he could spare for the chore from his 8th Infantry command, he replied, "Leave my post surgeon, my commissary officer, my post exchange officer and my adjutant and I will run this command with first sergeants." As he sent officers out to organize the fifteen camps assigned him, he warned, "I'll be out to see you soon and if I find you doing something I will help you; but if I find you doing nothing, only God will help you."

With spirit like that, the Army took about as long to set up 275,000 men in 1,330 companies and camps across the nation as it had taken to mobilize 180,000 men for war in 1917. The performance effectively squelched Congressional agitation to slash Army's officer strength by half. Young Army Chief of Staff Douglas MacArthur applauded the job and said of Marshall, specifically, "He has no superior among infantry colonels."

The military, however, do not necessarily, nor even very often, promote on talent. Time in rank is the basic measure, and, after that, variety and importance of assignments. For all his rare, consistently demonstrated combination of talents—effective combat leader and able staff administrator—Marshall's promotion in rank had gone strictly according to the system. A captain in 1916, a lieutenant colonel by 1923, promoted to colonel ten years later, he finally got his first star in 1936 with a promotion board comment, "Too bad he's not already a brigadier general because he deserves to be promoted to major general."

That comment didn't help Marshall's peace of mind much. He had spent nearly a decade watching men with less impressive records, but more time in service, pick up the best duty tours and earlier promotions. He was fifty-seven, discouraged, thinking of retirement, when his career caught fire. Summoned to Washington to head the Army war plans division, he was soon being touted as the next probable Chief of Staff. Of the thirty-three men ahead of him on the official promotion list, he actually had to beat out only four. (The others were disqualified by a rule that a Chief of Staff must be able to serve the full four-year term before becoming sixty-four.) In 1939, on the day Hitler attacked Poland, Marshall was jumped in rank from brigadier to full general, and appointed to the Army's top post.

He was on the threshold of world military leadership. By March, 1942, he was responsible directly to Roosevelt for military strategy, tactics, and operations. He led the Army's build-up from a scattered combat force in the United States of some 174,000 troops and 1,000 planes to a total, by May, 1945, of 8,250,000 men and 69,000 aircraft.

He was U.S. leader of the Allied Combined Chiefs of Staff; attended every Roosevelt-Churchill-British-Chiefs-of-Staff meeting; went with Roosevelt to every Allied Powers conference, including the ones at Casablanca, Quebec, Cairo-Teheran, and Yalta; was with Truman at the Churchill-Atlee-Stalin Potsdam Conference.

When, in 1944, he asked to command personally the Allied invasion of Normandy, Roosevelt turned him down, saying, "I feel I could not sleep at night with you out of the country." Eisenhower was assigned the burden, instead. A year later, Marshall, having reached retirement age and living as always by the rulebook, asked to be relieved, and Eisenhower succeeded him. President Truman awarded the retiring Chief of Staff an oak leaf cluster for his Distinguished Service medal, and said of him, in part:

> In a war unparalleled in magnitude and in horror, millions of Americans gave their country outstanding service. General of the Army George C. Marshall gave it victory.
>
> His was the vision that brought into being the greatest military force in history. Because he was able to make the Allies understand the true potentiality of American greatness in personnel and matériel, he was able to exercise greater influence than any other man on the strategy of victory. . . . To him, as much as to any individual, the United States owes its future. He takes his place at the head of the great commanders of history.

Marshall's British military colleagues wished him farewell with more of the same kind of praise.

Months before retirement, he had begun shipping personal belongings piecemeal from his quarters near the Pentagon to his home in Leesburg, Virginia, forty miles away. The day he retired, he and Mrs. Marshall had only to toss a couple of suitcases in the car, and they were gone.

After a historic, whirlwind decade of pressure-packed decisions, he looked forward to puttering around the yard idly for the rest of his life. While his wife unpacked upstairs, he went to make her a highball. The telephone rang. It was President Truman: "I want you to go to China. I think it'll take a year."

Marshall was dismayed. Between the graft-ridden Nationalist Government and the warring Communists, China was a thankless problem. Besides, he had already served more than forty-five years. He hesitated two or three minutes, but finally agreed to take the assignment. "Cornball as it sounds," said one aide, "only the strongest sense of duty made him go. Nothing else did."

Knowing how it would upset his wife, he put off telling her. Later, coming downstairs from a nap, he heard the radio blaring "Marshall to go to China!" His wife glared at him. "I didn't think they would announce it that fast," he apologized.

He arrived in China as personal ambassador from the President, a few days before Christmas, 1945. He had to try to solve what, in his own words, was "an impossible situation." Chiang Kai-shek's Nationalist Army and the Communists had some 4.5 million men fighting in the field. "My job was first to create an armistice so there would be no active fighting during political meetings [of the two parties], and later act as an adviser in the [hoped for] integration and demobilization of the military forces, Communist and Government."

Both from London (where Churchill was temporarily out of power) and from Washington, Marshall was constantly harassed and second-guessed by lobbyists and intriguers. He handled the Washington end of it as best he could by sending his messages from China through War Department communications channels to be sure they reached the White House untampered with. State Department lines, which he properly should have used, meant a proliferation of message copies to various desks, and in turn, a security risk. "Any time two people in Washington know something," he said, "it is no longer a secret."

He had also to contend with a very poor supply system. Whether by design or accident, armaments for Nationalist forces would arrive with something missing—trucks with no engine magnetos, cannon with no breech blocks.

But the incurable headache of the job was politics, an area Marshall was, theoretically, supposed to stay out of. The U.S. objective in China was to create a coalition government of the Nationalists and the Communists. But each uneasy truce he arranged on the battlefield kept falling apart through what he called "inability to produce any agreements between the two political groups which did not involve such extreme suspicions on both sides that a coalition cabinet to my mind was just out of the question."

In January, 1947, Marshall was called back to the United States to replace James Byrnes as Secretary of State.

At State, Marshall's orderly sense of military routine was shocked by his discovery that nineteen independent individuals reported directly to the Secretary. Working-level coordination was, at best, haphazard, and often studiously avoided. He set up an executive secretariat, a sort of telephone central peopled by bright young men who stopped every request coming in for a Marshall decision. They saw that each bureau concerned was given a chance to comment before Marshall saw a paper. This system meant, in essence, that the Secretary nearly always received well-rounded, thoroughly cross-referenced background on a problem and rarely had to make decisions on the same subject more than once. "The 'Old Man' was a great one for orderly conduct of business and for those people who had responsibility getting their day in court before a decision was reached," said one assistant.

Reorganization of the State Department through the executive secretariat was not Marshall's only contribution to foreign policy. With the help of Deputy Secretary Robert Lovett, he developed a European Recovery Program. Quickly named the Marshall Plan, it was unprecedented in its size, scope, and humanitarian objectives. As it ran its course, the multibillion-dollar project enabled war-devastated Europe to climb back on her economic feet and, under the U.S. atomic umbrella, build some measure of her own military protection against aggression. That Marshall got the program off the ground at all in those tight budget times was a tribute not only to his administrative ability, but to the high regard lavished on him by Congress and, particularly, by Truman. (Forrestal tried to exploit that rapport in 1948 by asking Marshall to back his $18 billion defense budget. Wrapped up in launching his aid program, Marshall replied too late; Truman had already decided on $13 billion, and, as the Pentagon had learned long ago, when Truman made a decision, further discussion was pointless.)

In whatever he did, Marshall never neglected people, no matter how small their role. "Morale is a state of mind," he had once said. "It is steadfastness and courage and hope. It is confidence and zeal and loyalty. It is *élan, esprit de corps* and determination. It is staying power, the spirit which endures to the end—the will to win. With it, all things are possible. Without it, everything else, planning, preparation, production count for naught."

An example of how he acted on this belief occurred at a meeting of the Organization of American States in Bogota, Colombia, in April, 1948. The Secretary of State and the rest of a sizable American mission were apparently trapped in a well-organized Communist riot. As Red violence intensified, Lovett called Bogota to find out if Marshall needed rescue. A Marshall aide answered the telephone. Asked how the General was, he answered, "The 'Old Man' is fine. To tell you the truth, I think he is having more fun than he has had since the Philippine insurrection. A little while ago he was out in the garage telling a young Colombian Army lieutenant how to position his men," the aide went on. "He pulled most of them in out of the rain to be warm and get some coffee and left on duty only the minimum necessary to sound an alert, so the others, warm and rested, could come out fighting mad to repel any attacks."

Before Marshall had left for Bogota, he had ordered Lovett to see a doctor and "be over that nasty chest cold by the time I get back next week." Now, when he came on the line, his first question was, "Lovett, how's that cold?"

"My gaskets blew," said Lovett later. At the time, with appropriate Anglo-Saxon adjectives, he asked, "General, never mind about me. How are you and the delegation?"

"Everything is fine at the moment. We've had a little excitement down here."

"Do you need any supplies?" Lovett asked, implying that he meant small arms and ammunition.

Marshall's answer: "A gross of candles, some evaporated milk, some Karo syrup and several thousand ponchos."

"I remember," said Lovett later, "hanging on to the desk while I digested this weird list, wondering who was going to hold a taffy pull at night in a rainstorm."

"Curiosity almost killed me on the ponchos," he recalled, "until

I learned the Colombian troops had come up from jungle heat to the high, 50-degree Bogota altitude wearing only thin cotton uniforms."

Realizing that having to stand around in the drizzle and cold would make the troops miserable and that they would thus not be as reliable in facing a mob as they would be if they were dry and warm, Marshall had decided to take direct action. The ponchos were issued, the troops were enthusiastic about them, and the delegations, instead of canceling the meeting, got on with business. (Marshall had also asked that troop transports stand by on call at the Panama Canal Zone, so he could assure the other delegations they, too, would be airlifted out if the riot became uncontrollable.)

Lovett later observed, "Calm, steadfastness, instinct about a soldier's needs and concern for them, in addition to ability to inspire confidence turned something that might have been a shameful disaster into a minor irritating event." Two years later, rumor had it that the bill for the military supplies Marshall had ordered during his Bogota trip was still bouncing back and forth between State and Defense, caught in an argument over who was going to pay it.

In late 1948, Marshall had a major kidney operation, which slowed him up perceptibly. He even needed the support of a cane for a while. To get him away from middle-of-the-night pressures but still keep him close, Truman angled him into the directorship of the American National Red Cross. But the comparative rest he was supposed to receive turned into a grueling series of trips around the country, checking various Red Cross offices and relief projects.

Still not entirely recovered from his operation in July, 1950, he was vacationing in northern Michigan's Huron mountains, with the closest telephone at a country store thirty minutes from camp, when Truman called him. There was urgency in Truman's voice, but he asked only that Marshall consider becoming Secretary of Defense, and that they discuss it when he returned to Washington.

In August, Marshall agreed. For military morale, his decision came none too soon. Although battle lines around Pusan, Korea, had stabilized by then, United Nations (mainly U.S.) forces knew they would long since have been driven off the peninsula if the North Koreans had been better organized and led.

Louis Johnson's impressive-sounding percentages about improved combat readiness had glossed over hard facts: military strength 150,000 shy of an authorized 1,617,000 men; Army units fleshed out with poorly trained draftees; Navy machinists building Pershing tank parts at a destroyer base in California because the Marine Corps couldn't obtain funds to buy them; all Services using antiquated equipment because no money was available to modernize.

On July 4, when Johnson learned that bazooka shells wouldn't penetrate the new Russian-built North Korean tanks, he called the Research and Development Board together. Showing its members a piece of the finest steel made, he asked, "Do you have a shell that will penetrate this and explode?"

They said they did "but only on the drawing board."

"By August 4, I want a ship in San Francisco loaded and on the way to Korea with those shells."

"But, that'll mean working twenty-four hours a day, seven days a week!" somebody protested.

"That's right!"

The carrier *Boxer* left San Francisco on August 3, "so loaded the flight deck was almost awash," claims one Johnson disciple.

But this achievement was not much of a bright spot in the storm. To the military, Korea was proof their fears had been well founded. Decrying the penny-pinching days, they said that matters had been made worse by lack of any solid coordination between military plans and foreign policy. Hindsight identified all manner of mistakes.

As early as 1946, and again in July, 1947, career foreign-service officer and Russian expert George Kennan, in Moscow, had urged a "firm containment" policy against Communism. A short time later, the State Department had asked the Pentagon to back up such a policy by developing a balanced variety of forces to fight "limited war" as well as nuclear holocaust. Specifically, the State Department urged creation of two highly mechanized and mobile "fire-fighting" divisions. Such talk was lost on the Joint Chiefs, whose strategic debates were preoccupied with bickering over control of the atomic bomb, wrestling against the rush of unification, and complaining of small budgets that wouldn't finance what they considered only marginally important projects.

The best Pentagon politico-economic-military analysis of Communist intent had been done by Forrestal. But, as early as the month after national elections in November, 1948, Forrestal had become walking proof of a Washington axiom—"There is nothing more frustrating in this town than to be right and be out of power." On May 29, 1949, a week after Forrestal's death, *The New York Times* ran on its inside pages a story headlined "U.S. to Quit Korea in July."

The previous January, Symington had warned the White House not to count indefinitely on an exclusive monopoly of the atomic bomb. That fall, at the height of the B-36 controversy, Truman disclosed that the Russians had exploded a nuclear device. Forced by the meager budget to build little more than a nuclear holocaust capability, the Chiefs downgraded any notion that the Communists might try some other tactic. In October, 1949, for example, Bradley had argued, "Large-scale amphibious operations will never occur again. The first prize of any aggressor is Europe." And, in late 1949, he observed of Forrestal's year-old proposal to dole out total defense dollars among the Services in roughly equal amounts, "The budget balance may not hold as we continue to evaluate the capabilities of the only aggressor in sight."

When the Navy's supercarrier was chopped down, Air Force Chief of Staff Hoyt Vandenberg had said, "I see no necessity for a ship with those capabilities in any strategic plan against the one possible enemy." To this, Bradley had added, "The carrier's fundamental purpose is included within the primary function of Air Force; the U.S.S.R. is not a sea power nor is it dependent upon the sea for obtaining raw materials; the United States and Britain have a vast preponderance of naval power already; the use of carrier task force planes against land targets should be limited."

On January 12, 1950, Dean Acheson, Marshall's replacement as Secretary of State, had told a National Press Club audience, among other things, that Korea was outside the U.S. defense perimeter. Low in Department of State priority, it was low on the Joint Chiefs' list, too. In January and again in April, the Air Force had concentrated even more funds on the B-36.

In mid-June, Johnson had gone to Japan to see Supreme Allied Far East Commander Douglas MacArthur. While there, he was handed a Central Intelligence Agency report which stated that the North Korean Army was ready to move on an hour's notice. But, said Johnson, " 'Wolf!' had been cried so often we didn't believe it." The Communists attacked just after he returned to the Pentagon.

When MacArthur proposed his amphibious landing halfway up Korea's west coast to outflank the Communists and regain the offensive, the Joint Chiefs opposed it. Hazardous terrain and dangerous tides made the plan look potentially disastrous to generals unfamiliar with Marine Corps operations. Besides, the Chiefs did not want to risk further reduction of the forces they expected Europe would soon need. Korea, Bradley complained, "is the wrong war in the wrong place at the wrong time with the wrong enemy."

MacArthur thundered, "Victories are not won through timidity in some office thousands of miles away!" Only "Colonel" Louis Johnson backed him.

Although Americans were warring and dying in Korea, the fighting there was technically a United Nations "police action." That legal status allowed Truman to avoid asking Capitol Hill for a declaration of war he probably could not have gotten, anyway. It also left him the lonely, unsupported Commander in Chief in what most U.S. citizens considered a deadly charade.

"The United States doesn't fight wars," said one military oldtimer. "It fights crusades." Because of some new, arbitrarily established, "turn-the-other-cheek" ground rules, Korea didn't look much like a crusade. Bitter rumors spread across the country that, with 1950 national Congressional elections coming up, Army units in the least politically sensitive states were being sent overseas first—"from Oklahoma," went the indictment, "which has to vote Democratic, anyway, and California, to show those Democrats who jump the party fence to vote Republican."

Venom at home was matched by blunders in combat. Green Army combat units in the war's early stages frequently broke and ran under pressure, or were captured. (Almost two-thirds of all U.S. troops seized during the three-year war were taken prisoner in the first six months of fighting.) Close air support, which the Air Force had promised "to do something about" months before, was often so bad it was tragic. Air Force jet fighters, operating from bases in Japan, could carry fuel for only a niggardly fifteen or twenty minutes in the target area. Worse, they could—and some did—ignore ground command instructions on how to attack, succeeding, as a result, in shooting up a few forward Army and Marine units. B-29's from Okinawa hit the United Nations brigade trying to lead a counterattack north from Pusan. One Marine general even ordered an Air Force plane shot down because it refused to obey his strafing instructions and was about to fire on his own troops.

"It took those pilots awhile," muttered one Army general, "to figure out that the guys on the ground standing up and waving might not be Communists at all but Americans."

Navy fighters, carrier based just off shore, were able to stay over the battlefield five times longer than Air Force squadrons. Below them, Marine divisions, better trained than Army, and possessing their own integrated, ground-controlled close air support, became the bulwark of defense. (In September, the lead elements in MacArthur's counter offensive were the same Marines that Pentagon Army experts a year earlier had called obsolete.)

The Navy's 7th Fleet, which Washington experts said in 1949 need worry only about fighting other navies in the future, was rushed to police duty in the strait between Formosa and the Chinese mainland. Its mission was (a) to show the Chinese Communists that Formosa would be defended, too, if they had any rash idea about trying to take it while U.N. forces were distracted with battling in Korea, and (b) to halt Nationalist "military adventurism from Formosa."

Late in August, 1950, Washington received the first inkling that MacArthur didn't agree entirely with its ideas on how the Far East clash should be handled. In a speech written for delivery at a Veterans of Foreign Wars convention in the United States, MacArthur urged more aggressive action not only in Korea but "elsewhere in Asia." Translation: he wanted the Chinese Nationalists on Formosa to start shooting more at the mainland.

U.S. allies in the United Nations were appalled at the idea, angry at what they considered MacArthur's brazen intention to say such a thing publicly without first asking their approval. Truman ordered the proposal stricken from MacArthur's speech, but word of it had already reached the press. The State Department pressed the White House for MacArthur's dismissal. Louis Johnson's answer to that was an adamant "No!"

Into this tense and tangled situation walked Marshall. When he relieved Johnson in late September, the Inchon landing, 150 miles behind North Korean forward lines, was already a week old. Communists were fleeing back toward the 38th parallel to avoid being trapped. After three bitter months of fighting to hold onto a little piece of the peninsula, U.N. forces cleaned their enemy out of South Korea in just fifteen days. On October 1, Marshall cabled MacArthur, "We desire that you proceed with your operations without any further explanation or announcement and let action determine the matter."

That done, Marshall turned to the Pentagon's intramural snags. Congress didn't seem at all worried that a General was running Defense. For generations, it had frowned at the thought of military force without civilian control, had even written a provision in the National Security Act that no man who had been a commissioned officer within the previous ten years could be Secretary of Defense. A law exempting Marshall from that limitation was rushed through the Senate one September morning and cleared the House in the afternoon.

When he heard he had been confirmed, Marshall left his Red Cross headquarters, climbed into an old Studebaker, and rode over to the Pentagon to take charge. Once in the office, he muttered, "Guess we have to go through the oath business." Steve Early, who would soon be replaced as Deputy Secretary by Lovett, said it should be recorded. A photographer dashed up from the second floor. The Deputy General Counsel was called in to officiate.

"You could count on two hands the people who knew what was in process," said one Marshall aide. "When this ten-minute affair ended, the Joint Chiefs were called in and we were in business."

That rush to work was jarred in its first moments by unintended interruptions. On the side of Marshall's desk, level with the blunt end of his big leather chair's arm, were three buttons. One buzzer summoned the Deputy Secretary, one Marshall's top military aide, and one his secretary. Until they figured out what was happening, all three kept rushing into his office simultaneously about every fifteen minutes from different directions when he accidentally shoved his chair arm into all those buttons at once.

As he had insisted on being met during his World War II travels by a post commander only, without ceremony, in order not to draw people away from important jobs, so he was well aware, in 1950, of the effect his presence created. He spared Pentagon office staffs as much distraction as possible by mostly staying behind his closed office door and letting others stand in the limelight.

He gradually eased out Johnson's gauleiters, and brought in experienced men who shared a mutual confidence developed from years of working together. The same splintered, uncoordinated, direct-to-the-Secretary reporting existed in Defense, he found, that he had tried to correct at State. To cope with it, he set up the same kind of executive secretariat he had utilized so successfully before.

He also re-established diplomatic relations with the State Department at the unsung lower staff levels, among the "pick-and-shovel men" as he called them. Johnson had cut off such liaison, at least partly because he was convinced that State's Averill Harriman was after his job, that Harriman's "biased input" was warping Secretary of State Acheson's opinion of Johnson, and that State wanted to run Defense. Johnson's order had amounted, at the working level, to separating specialized experts in military planning from those in foreign policy. As Marshall well knew, the two could not—or at least should not—be separated. He also began inviting the Secretary or Under Secretary of State and the head of the Central Intelligence Agency to Joint Chiefs' meetings. "When he does something like that," said his aide, "it points up to the military the political implication of what they do."

In contrast to Johnson, Marshall never tongue-lashed ineffective people. "He just quietly shipped them off without a lot of 'foofooraw,'" said one assistant, "usually by volunteering some question like 'Hasn't so-and-so indicated a desire to serve in North Africa for awhile?'" Marshall's reluctance to criticize people was so strong that, after World War II, he turned down offers of more than $1 million for his memoirs. Even Truman begged him to write them. "It was the only thing he ever refused the President," said a friend.

"He remembered that General Pershing had written a book." That book had won a Pulitzer prize but had "created a lot of ill will. Marshall would have insisted on his book being just as factually accurate and just as frank. That would have meant being unkind to people he assumed had been trying to do their best." Besides, as he once told a reporter, his government had paid him a salary for his work and that, he believed, was ample compensation.

While his memory was "a fantastic storehouse of information that counted," it was fantastically bad about remembering people's names. Office staffers in World War II had helped him over the hurdle and kept guests at ease, by seeing that the name of a visitor he should know was worked into the conversation early. The day he became Defense Secretary, he warned a sergeant who was assigned the name business, "And I'm a little hard of hearing [30 per cent loss in one ear] so when you come in here, speak up!"

He operated almost completely without front, had fewer aides than many subordinate officers, wrote all his own speeches in longhand on a yellow, legal-sized note pad. Historians got after him almost immediately to keep a diary as Forrestal had. "I'm not ready to start looking back yet," he snapped.

At seventy, he could still come up with the Marshall brand of swift, sure decisions, still not flinch in the face of tough ones. Unlike Forrestal (at least after the first Defense Secretary's crippling mental illness set in) Marshall "never had brooded—and still didn't—over a decision after he made it," said an aide. "He believed, if he did brood, it would not improve the decision any, but it would improve his chances of blowing the next one."

In sum, Marshall was to the United States a symbol of stability in a volatile hour, the incarnation of past military victory, and, with his Marshall Plan, of political sympathy with U.N. allies.

The Pentagon needed such stability by the fall of 1950. In mid-October, Truman had traveled to Wake Island with a fourth oak-leaf cluster for MacArthur's Distinguished Service medal, and a five-pound box of candied plums for Mrs. MacArthur. He told MacArthur that the United States was to pursue a "benign Asia" policy. Before Inchon, that had meant just driving the aggressors out of South Korea. After Inchon, since much of the routed North Korean Army had escaped MacArthur's mousetrap, the policy was "reinterpreted" to mean driving farther north to destroy North Korean forces on their home ground so they could not wage war again.

Through neutral envoys, Peking threatened to send Chinese troops into Korea if U.N. forces crossed the 38th parallel. MacArthur assured Truman that Peking wouldn't. Attacking U.N. forces were split into two widely separated columns charging up each side of the peninsula. MacArthur asked approval to cross the Yalu into Chinese Communist Manchuria if he were still in hot pursuit of North Koreans when he reached the river. Thirteen U.N. allies sent Washington a unanimous "No" to that request. Washington added orders that he was to send only South Korean troops to the border.

MacArthur ignored that instruction as he stretched his supply lines and communications razor thin trying for quick victory over his disintegrating enemy. Then, on November 7, he reported that the Chinese Communists had done exactly what he had told Truman they would not do. They had jumped south across the Yalu and "there is a new war going on now with the Chinese Communists." Before MacArthur's announcement, Washington and the U.N. had fussed for nearly a month over whether organized Red Chinese combat units fighting in Korea in October were "volunteers." By the time diplomats fearing World War III decided they were being lied to, Communist forces were well into their counterattack back toward the 38th parallel. MacArthur asked authority to hit the new enemy in its U.N.-granted sanctuary north of the Yalu. He was turned down.

On November 24, he announced a new "Home by Christmas" offensive, complaining bitterly and publicly about the lack of support for his efforts in Washington and the U.N. Within two days, the United States learned that its military might was vastly outnumbered, its troops freezing in the winter cold and short of ammunition. A massive Red assault right after Thanksgiving crumpled MacArthur's right flank, tore a hole in his western defenses, and forced Allied withdrawal all along the front. Washington was in a panic. On December 16, Truman declared a national emergency.

Ten days earlier, Washington had issued two directives addressed to all top military leaders but really written for MacArthur. One said that statements concerning foreign or military policy should be cleared with State or Defense. The other added that officials overseas should "exercise extreme caution in public statements," clear all but the routine, and "refrain from direct communications on military or foreign policy with media."

But MacArthur was no ordinary field general. When, on his seventieth birthday the previous July 8, he had been named the first U.N. commander in history, he was already at least as large a legend as Marshall. Youngest Army Chief of Staff ever, hero in two world wars, conqueror of the Japanese, he was, in 1950,

Supreme Commander of the Allied Powers in Japan; Commander in Chief, Far East; and Commander of the Far East Army. He had virtually set up the Japanese democratic government, was running the Japanese nation of 83 million people as though he were president, even receiving and dealing with foreign ambassadors.

He had strong ideas of his own about what ought to be done in Korea. By the end of December, the Chinese Reds had driven back south of the 38th parallel, and were threatening Seoul, the South Korean capital. MacArthur asked the Joint Chiefs for permission to: blockade the Chinese coast; bomb Red industry, communications, supply depots, and troop assembly points in China; reinforce his combat units with Chinese Nationalists; let Chiang Kai-shek hit the mainland. All this, he said, plus a counterattack in Korea, would not only insure victory there but "save Asia from the engulfment otherwise facing it."

Again, Washington turned him down. Still more than half certain that the Communist moves were a diversionary tactic prior to Russian assault on Europe, the Pentagon sent four divisions across the Atlantic and named Eisenhower NATO commander. Reminded of the way his Far Eastern theater had had to take a back seat in World War II until Europe was won, MacArthur now argued that Europe's first line of defense was not in Germany. Korea, he said, was the real test of NATO. "The issue is a global one and failure to comprehend this fact carries the germ of freedom's ultimate destruction."

Although cold war strategists might have agreed with him in theory, the practical fact was that the United States didn't believe it was equipped to engage in a world struggle. In January, the Joint Chiefs debated pulling out of Korea altogether, decided finally to stay. The high-flown diplomatic explanation given was that the United States could not permit Red China to shoot its way into the U.N., either in Korea or Formosa. Idealism was helped considerably, however, by the fact that, as early as January 10, retreating U.N. forces had dug in and held along a line running across the peninsula from a point twenty-five miles south of Seoul. While MacArthur blasted away at restrictions "without precedence in history," his troops began to fight their way back north. By March 15, they had retaken Seoul.

In Britain, the ruling Labour Party argued that Red China

should be admitted to the United Nations. To many U.S. observers, this point of view smacked of coddling Communism. A majority of the small member nations in a shaken United Nations were willing to accept peace at almost any price. Truman said that if the United Nations were strong in Korea there would not be any new aggression later. Churchill, still out of power in England, mused, "I cannot help feeling that it would have been well if all these matters had been talked over at the right moment and in good time in Washington by the highest authorities in both countries." They were not.

With his troops still moving north, MacArthur wired Truman on March 20 that he would shortly announce a willingness to discuss with the Communist field commander suitable terms to end the bloodshed. The Joint Chiefs fired back a dispatch telling MacArthur, "State planning a Presidential announcement shortly that, with clearing of bulk of South Korea of aggressors, the United Nations now preparing to discuss the conditions of settlement in Korea." They ordered him to halt his advance, fight a holding action, and leave politics to the diplomats.

Instead, on March 24, he broadcast:

> Even under inhibitions which now restrict activity of the United Nations and the corresponding military advantages which accrue to Red China, it has been shown its complete inability to accomplish by force of arms the conquest of Korea.
>
> The enemy therefore must by now be painfully aware that a decision of the United Nations to depart from its tolerant effort to contain the war to the area of Korea through expansion of our military operations to his coastal areas and interior bases would doom Red China to the risk of imminent military collapse.
>
> These basic facts being established, there should be no insuperable difficulty arriving at decisions on the Korean problem if the issues are resolved on their own merits without being burdened by extraneous matters not directly related to Korea, such as Formosa and China's seat in the United Nations.

Not only had he not cleared that declaration with Washington (in violation of the December 6 directive), in three paragraphs, he had managed to set for diplomats the terms on which he would talk truce; to flush down the drain virtually completed U.N. plans to have Truman call for armistice talks; and to gum up delicate State Department behind-the-scenes stage-setting efforts with Britain, India, and Russia for the actual start of peace negotiations.

The Communists apparently thought MacArthur might be right. They called him a warmonger. Most Europeans and some Americans thought he might be wrong. They labeled him dangerous and irresponsible. MacArthur insisted, two months later to a Senate committee, that he spoke when he should have stayed quiet because, "I was operating in what I call a vacuum. I could hardly have been said to be in opposition to policies which I was not aware of even. I don't know what the policy is now."

He added that "to go on indecisively fighting, with no mission for the troops except to resist and fight in this accordion fashion, up and down, means that your cumulative losses are going to be staggering. It isn't just dust that is settling in Korea, Senator; it is American blood."

For all the ignorance he pleaded about U.S. foreign policy objectives, MacArthur could hardly not have known what they were. He simply would not accept being prevented from using his clearly superior naval strength and air power to hit Asian Communism's stronghold on the Chinese mainland. He said, "The greatest political mistake we made in a hundred years in the Pacific was in allowing the Communists to grow in power in China. I think, at one stroke, we undid everything starting from John Hay, through Taft, Leonard Wood, Woodrow Wilson, Henry Stimson and all those great architects of our Pacific policy. I believe it was fundamental, and I believe we will pay for it for a century."

He privately scorned the fears, as he called them, of "the Truman-Acheson-Marshall-Bradley-general staff group" that Russia would commit its armies "to a war in China's behalf at the end of an endless one-track railroad to a peninsular battleground that led only to the sea. Russia could not have fought us."

Was he right as he had been at Inchon, or was he wrong as he had been about the Chinese Communists poised above the Yalu?

Arguments that a Korean standoff would buy the United States time to build its military strength were, to MacArthur, specious. In the first place, he insisted, the United Nations could win with what it already had. Secondly, "You make the assumption that we increase our strength compared with the enemy's. That is too speculative. If we add fifty divisions to our forces, he might add sixty. He can do it just as quickly as we can."

The point, however, was not whether or not he was right, but that his field commander's public statements were usurping Washington authority to direct military and diplomatic strategy. The State Department demanded his removal. Marshall was hesitant. He was, after all, well aware of MacArthur's penchant for ignoring proper channels in expressing opinions and handing out orders. He had been warning MacArthur about the dangers of this habit as far back as 1942.

But, on April 5, a MacArthur ploy that even Marshall couldn't discount came to light. House Republican leader Joe Martin released a letter written to him by MacArthur two weeks earlier. The opening paragraph complained:

> It seems strangely difficult for some to realize that here in Asia the Communist conspirators have elected to make their play for global conquest, and that we have joined the issue thus raised on the battlefield; that here we fight Europe's war with arms which the diplomats there still fight with words; that if we lose the war to Communism in Asia the fall of Europe is inevitable, win it and Europe most probably would avoid war and yet preserve freedom. As you pointed out, we must win. There is no substitute for victory.

MacArthur had not cleared that letter with Washington, either. Summoning Harriman, Acheson, Marshall, and Chairman of the Joint Chiefs Bradley to a White House meeting the next day, Truman demanded to know why he shouldn't fire MacArthur. Marshall cooled him down, suggesting that he first take a look at "all the facts and data." Truman ordered a complete review for his attention by the next morning, Saturday, April 7. "At that meeting," said Marshall, "the President directed we think the matter over that weekend. Meanwhile, I was to obtain the views of the Chiefs of Staff on the purely military aspects. Those were obtained Sunday afternoon, and we met on Monday morning."

The upshot was that Truman indicted MacArthur for not clearing in advance his public statements, for opposing U.N. policy to confine the war, and for challenging Truman's right to be the U.S. foreign policy spokesman. The President said, "If I had allowed him to defy the civilian authorities in this manner, I myself would be violating my oath to uphold and defend the

Constitution. MacArthur left me no choice. I could no longer tolerate his insubordination."

The next afternoon, April 10, notice was sent to Army Secretary Frank Pace, coincidentally already in Japan, to tell MacArthur he was fired from all his jobs. U.S. 8th Army General Matthew Ridgway in Korea was instructed to take over.

Later that day, Washington learned that news of the firing might have leaked to the press. Believing that Pace had already delivered the dismissal order to MacArthur, Truman hurriedly called a press conference for 1 P.M. on April 11, and announced what he had done. Unfortunately, through a breakdown in communications, Pace had not received his message. Thus, MacArthur first heard the news from Mrs. MacArthur, who heard it from their chauffeur, who heard it on the radio. (Youngish, inexperienced Frank Pace later denied the suggestion of a waggish friend that he had feared venerable warhorse MacArthur's reaction so much he had slipped the official order under the General's office door, knocked, and sneaked off.)

America was first shocked, then incensed. Washington mail ran ten to one against the decision. Questions of "possible impeachment" of the President were raised. Truman was booed that week when he went to a baseball game and burned in effigy on several college campuses. His victim was eulogized at home and halfway around the world. The Japanese monarch paid MacArthur the highest possible honor by making a farewell visit to him. As MacArthur's limousine drove to the Tokyo airport, 230,000 persons lined the streets to wave good-by. As he climbed into his plane, he listened to a 19-gun salute, while 18 jet fighters and 4 Superfortress bombers roared overhead. Along a 20-mile parade route in Hawaii, 100,000 persons greeted his arrival. Another 500,000 did the same when he reached San Francisco. An estimated 3 million more watched the homecoming on television.

Not completely confident about who would end up winning the Truman-MacArthur argument, some cautious Pentagon employees fixed up an expensive executive suite in the building for MacArthur to use if he chose. (He chose not to.) When he reached Washington he received another thunderous ovation. Called to address a joint session of Congress on April 19, he concluded a highly emotional speech with, "Old soldiers never die; they just fade away." But he didn't fade very fast. On to New York, he was met by a horde of people—one estimate put the number at over 7 million—who shrilled themselves numb for more than six hours, hailing the national hero.

In the midst of this uproar, the Senate convened hearings to find out why MacArthur had been fired. As he had been for most of the previous decade, Marshall was again the stabilizing element in a potentially explosive drama that could have torn to shreds the fabric of Free World leadership. Through nearly a week of continuous grilling, he calmly answered and re-answered probing interrogators with the same consistent, unbending theme:

> The Joint Chiefs of Staff, the Secretary of Defense, and the President, who are responsible for the total security of the United States . . . must weigh our interest and objectives in one part of the globe with those in other areas of the world so as to attain the best overall balance. . . .
>
> We have brought to bear whatever has been necessary, in money and also in manpower, to curb the aggressor; and we have sought in every possible way to avoid a third world war. . . .
>
> It is completely understandable and, in fact, at times commendable that a theater commander should become so wholly wrapped up in his own aims and responsibilities that some of the directives received by him from higher authority are not those that he would have written for himself. There is nothing new about this sort of thing in our military history. What is new, and what has brought about the necessity for General MacArthur's removal, is the wholly unprecedented situation of a local theater commander publicly expressing his displeasure at and his disagreement with the foreign and military policy of the United States. . . .
>
> General MacArthur had grown so far out of sympathy with the established policies of the United States that there was grave doubt whether he could any longer be permitted to exercise the authority in making decisions [which] normal command functions would assign to a theater commander. In this situation, there was no other recourse but to relieve him.

The Administration's case was helped by the simple fact of Marshall's presence. "Not the least of his talents was that he was just dynamite on Capitol Hill," said one reporter. He was invariably introduced by Congressional investigators tossing effusive bouquets at his "nationally renowned integrity and devotion to duty." His performance in committee could be, and usually was, electrifying, charged with a casual, unintentional dropping of great names from contemporary world history.

Although he went to painful, patient length to give politicians meticulously accurate answers, he usually left the distinct impression that he hoped they did not have too many questions because he had work to do back at the office. He was an enigma to the status-seekers who showed up for these solemn sideshows because he obviously had no interest in playing to the galleries or seeing his name in print. He had long since disarmed the nation's newspapermen simply by being completely candid with them. They had never enjoyed such treatment before. Editorial criticism of Marshall had been as rare as snowfall in May—until the MacArthur firing.

The Senate kept its balance during the tense inquiry. The military stuck by Truman and Defense policy. But MacArthur disciples in the press wanted "satisfaction." When they didn't get it in the Senate, in spite of their backing of what polls said was the more popular cause, they began a newsprint attack that included Marshall as a primary target. Typically, as always in such hate campaigns, the insinuations were silly and superficial.

One charge was that he knifed MacArthur because he had always been jealous of MacArthur's earlier success in the Army. (To be sure, because they were two different kinds of men—Marshall didn't consider himself a "man of destiny"—their relationship had never been cordial. But it had always been what one mutual acquaintance called "coolly correct.")

"He's a bad Secretary, too old for the job," said angry gossips. "A couple of drinks before lunch and he's no good for the rest of the day." And, "He's developed the old man's forgetful habit of telling and retelling the same stories."

One fact served to support the smear campaign: Marshall did work much shorter hours than had either Forrestal or Johnson. In the office by 7:30 A.M., he always tried to leave by about 4:30. But the reason was not old age. He was only backing up, by performance, his advice to Pentagon workers to protect their health. Twice in his much younger years he had suffered breakdowns from precisely the kind of overwork that had precipitated Forrestal's illness. For that reason, he didn't take, and didn't want other people to take a lot of paperwork home at night, either. "There is only so much productive work in a man," he said. "There comes a time in the day when your efforts no longer have any meaning. Your energy is gone. When you pass that point, you are operating on reflexes. The loss then is that of whatever faculties make you better than run-of-the-mill. So, when you go home, relax."

To MacArthur lovers, that was senility. The charges hit Marshall hard, but he never tried to rebuke them. "He felt," said a friend, "if he did, it would detract inexcusably from the time he should spend building toward constructive ends."

Marshall was more of a civilian in his performance as Secretary of Defense than Johnson had been. He firmly backed the generations-old American doctrine that military forces must be controlled by civilians. Even during World War II, when he had a virtual blank check to do anything he wanted, he took pains to see that War Secretary Stimson was counseled and kept informed.

The military was servant to the public, he felt, not partner. In 1952, when Eisenhower and Adlai Stevenson were running against each other for President, Marshall was asked which one he favored. They were both his boys, he said, one from his Army career, the other from his tour at the State Department. Besides, he added, "I've never voted in my life and don't intend to start now."

His Assistant Secretary for Manpower collared him, complaining that he was setting a bad example for voters in the military ranks. "You aren't exercising the first right of citizenship." Marshall countered that he didn't vote because he didn't think a military man should choose up sides. Anyway, he said, the question was academic because the "American people will never pick a military man for President."

When Marshall accepted the post of Defense Secretary, primarily to restore respect for it in the eyes of the military and the nation, he told Truman he should be able to get that trend started in about six months. He added that then he would leave at some appropriate time during a lull in demands on the Secretary's office. One year almost to the day from the date of his swearing-in, he submitted his resignation, telling Truman that the rush of Pentagon problems never lets up and "There just is no 'best' time."

In February, 1952, five months after he finally retired, he was invited to England for the coronation of Queen Elizabeth II. He was assigned the first seat in the first row of the first pew—the position of highest honor for visitors. He hadn't changed any in seventy-one years. He was still unshakably modest and unassuming. As he entered Westminster Abbey and started to walk up the long corridor to his seat, trumpets blared and applause rang through the cathedral. Winston Churchill and Field Marshal Montgomery broke ranks—and tradition—to come over and shake his hand. Busy glancing over his shoulder to see who was being honored, Marshall almost ran them down.

A year later, while pressure groups were wading through the Truman administration looking for villains and trying to smear Marshall with some of their "soft-on-Communism" charges, the rest of the world was a good deal kinder to him. In December, 1953, in Oslo, Norway, he was awarded the Nobel Peace Prize. As he accepted it, he said, "For the moment, the maintenance of peace in the present hazardous world situation does depend in very large measure on military power, together with Allied cohesion . . . but (for the long term) we must, I repeat, we must find another solution."

When Marshall died in October, 1959, friends announced that his last wish had been that his funeral be kept simple and unostentatious. Those he had asked for as pallbearers included mostly enlisted military men who had worked for him. The list, made up the year before he died, also included the man to whom he had turned over Pentagon command eight years earlier.

VII

Robert Lovett

[SEPTEMBER, 1951–JANUARY, 1953]

IN MIDSUMMER, 1943, Assistant Secretary of War for Air Robert Abercrombie Lovett was in Marrakech on his way back to the United States from an inspection tour of Air Corps operations in England and North Africa. He was flying in a battered old B-17 bomber that had been converted to the semi-retirement of hauling VIP's around the European combat theater. Lovett was soaking wet when he took off in the 110-degree North African heat, and shivering a few seconds later when the aircraft reached cruising altitude.

He walked forward to the crew compartment to change into a dry shirt, and sat down behind the radioman, who had his set tuned into the British Armed Forces Overseas Radio. It was playing American jazz. Handing Lovett a set of earphones, the radioman said, "Listen to this. Louis Armstrong plays the best trumpet solo going on 'One O'clock Jump.' "

Lovett, something of a jazz aficionado, listened a moment. Then he said, "It's fine music, but that sounds to me like a Fletcher Henderson arrangement of 'Tuxedo Junction,' and I'm certain that's Erskine Hawkins on trumpet."

The radioman raised an eyebrow. Lovett listened a while longer, then returned to his seat in the plane's center section. When the record ended, the radio announcer disclosed that it had indeed been a Fletcher Henderson arrangement with Erskine Hawkins on trumpet, recorded in 1939.

The radioman banged his fist on his table and snorted, "That's the first time I ever saw anybody from Washington on this plane who knew anything about anything!"

Lovett was celebrating his fifty-sixth birthday eight years later on September 14, 1951, when the Senate confirmed Truman's appointment of him as Secretary of Defense. Sworn in three days after that, he was then instructed to "make yourself available for the press" and went to a conference room full of bleachers and klieg lights.

"I always photograph like something the cat dragged in," warned Lovett. While news photographers snapped a rash of intimate, candid camera shots, Lovett bantered, "I want you to get a picture of Clark Gable and put my name under it. Otherwise, if you use my picture, you'll make recruitment fall off."

After about forty-five minutes an aide came in, and said "Mr. Secretary, you're due at the White House."

"That's enough," Lovett told the photographers. "Any more and you'll scare every mother in the country."

Outside the room, waiting for the elevator that would take him to his car in the Pentagon's basement garage, he watched as two photographers backed out of the conference room, dragging a footlocker full of their gear. He heard one mutter, "You know, that old bird wasn't kidding. He really is a homely old bastard."

On his way to the White House, Lovett told the story to his limousine driver. Sniffed the loyal chauffeur, "I don't think that's so funny."

He may not have been the handsomest official in government, but all his other credentials for holding high office were impeccable. His judgment was highly regarded. The intellectual equal of Forrestal, his background and extensive government experience were cut in the Forrestal pattern as well.

"The goverment has spent more money training me than they have on any other man," he commented after his appointment. Certainly, very few people had been trained as much.

Son of a Huntsville, Texas, judge, Lovett learned to fly in 1916. He became one of the Navy's first pilots, and joined the Aerial Coast Patrol organized on Long Island, New York, by first Army Assistant Secretary of War for Air Trubee Davison. He went to France as a naval ensign pilot in 1917, won his French wings, established a U.S. Naval Air Service Transition Flying School that fall. Then, assigned to the Royal Navy Air Service in England, he piloted flying boats on North Sea submarine and convoy patrol until January, 1918.

After flying Royal Navy night bombers in raids on German submarine pens and marshaling yards in occupied Belgium and France, he became a crusader for the bombing business, convinced the Navy sufficiently to be ordered to set up the first naval bombardment squadron. For that achievement, coupled with showing what the unit could do flying night bombers out of France, Lovett was awarded the Navy Cross and promoted to lieutenant commander.

He also found time to complete the requirements for a Bachelor's degree from Yale (1918). Lovett returned to the United States in 1919 and took postgraduate courses at Harvard Law School and the School of Business until 1921, when he became a clerk in the National Bank of Commerce in New York. Eventually, he built his career up to a full partnership in the Wall Street banking firm of Brown Brothers, Harriman, and Company, also becoming a director or trustee in a handful of railroads and insurance companies. With all his business activity and additional philanthropic work, he maintained his aviation enthusiasm and kept abreast of European commercial and military aviation developments during annual trips abroad.

In 1940, Army Secretary Stimson, impressed with Forrestal's work for Navy Secretary Knox, asked him "if there are any more up there on Wall Street like you." Forrestal named Lovett. On December 19, Lovett resigned all his business connections, obtained leave from his philanthropic and educational interests, and became Stimson's special assistant.

The following April he was appointed Assistant Secretary of War for Air. Still a disciple of air power, he was a major influence for acceptance of this new kind of military striking force by top Washington leadership. With typical modesty, however, he handed the credit to others—Marshall among them. At the first George Catlett Marshall Memorial Dinner in Washington in 1960, Lovett said: "One of General Marshall's most unusual attributes, and one I think added a great deal to his stature, was his recognition of the fact that nature never stands still and that change is, indeed, one of the primary laws of life. His receptiveness to new ideas, for example, in the use of air power and in the

Marshall Plan, was made easier by this philosophy. He was not burdened with the attitude of mind which regards any change as a threat to the established order, or vested rights, which must therefore be automatically, even blindly, resisted."

Like Forrestal in the Navy, Lovett was tied up primarily in procurement and production during the war. He cajoled aircraft manufacturers into pooling their plants and experience in constructing long-range bombers and was a key authority in approving the start of the B-36 development.

During that period, Lovett's friendship with Marshall began building. The military head of the Army Air Corps was General Hap Arnold, a jovial, impatient man, who led by personal example. At the beginning of the war, Arnold pushed for Air Corps independence. Marshall persuaded him to wait until after the war ended, promising that he would then help sell the idea.

As civilian head of Army's air arm, Lovett was involved in all these dealings and also became deeply embroiled in Marshall's relationship with Secretary of War Stimson, Lovett's boss. "Marshall had tremendous respect for the aging statesman. To save as much burden as possible," said an aide, "Marshall started going to Lovett for virtually everything."

One of Lovett's attractions for Marshall was his wit, which could temporarily deflect, for Marshall, his grief over the tragedy of American losses overseas. Lovett found the same solace in Marshall. More than a decade later, he said of those years: "His attitude toward the Army, I often thought, approximated the worried affection you see when a mother, on a street corner, with her very dear, small son beside her, sees him rather vaguely step off the curb into a street filled with speeding traffic. She reaches down, snatches him by the arm, yanks him back onto the sidewalk, hands him a resounding whack on his dumb little head and, while he howls at the top of his lungs, she bawls him out for having scared the living daylights out of her. In many things the 'Old Man' felt compelled to do, there was definitely that attitude. And in it, I found comfort and delight."

Lovett resigned at the end of 1945 to return to Brown Brothers, Harriman. When Marshall took over the State Department in 1947, he asked Lovett to be his Under Secretary. Lovett agreed, left that post when Marshall left in January, 1949, returned again to private business, and had been back with his firm less than two years when Marshall once more asked him to join the government—this time as Deputy Secretary of Defense.

Lovett had broken ground for a new home the day before. He left it and his Brown Brothers, Harriman desk on twelve hours notice. He scarcely saw his new house again until after it was finished. Korea had provided impetus, but Lovett returned to Washington primarily because Marshall had asked him to.

"I loved that absolutely magnificent man," Lovett said later. "There was none finer, more dedicated or with more ability."

"He and Lovett were the perfect combination," said Marshall's aide, Jim George. "Lovett was the best description I've ever seen of an alter ego. Every morning, he would put his coat and hat on the conference room table, spend the next uninterrupted half to three-quarters of an hour discussing daily and long-range problems with Marshall. That was all the guidance he needed."

Pat Carter, head of Marshall's executive secretariat, adds: "It was one of the finest mutual-admiration relationships I've ever seen. There was respect going in both directions. Their minds were very much alike. Their motives, intent and dedication were identical. There was never any question about who was boss, never any question in Marshall's mind that the job would be done by Lovett as Marshall wanted it done when Marshall was out of town. Everyone knew when Lovett took a decision, that was Marshall's decision, too."

In only one instance, apparently, was that understanding challenged.

Lovett approved a March, 1951, draft call of 80,000 men for the Army—which promptly protested that it would have no place to put that many draftees and did not have enough uniforms and rifles to outfit them. Lovett answered, "You'll have to. We'll have to build up like that to get them overseas."

The main problem was the Army's bookkeeping system, which counted as inventory only what was in possession of the Technical Services (i.e., the weapons in Ordnance Corps, the clothes in Quartermaster Corps, etc.), not what was in the combat divisions or their depots and bases. Without mentioning that he knew that fact, straight-faced Lovett told the Army he would get them some help.

"Then he and McNeil put on quite a show," chuckled one

observer. The Marines, they said, had some extra pairs of shoes they could release.

The Air Force even had some old Army uniforms Joe Collins (Army Chief of Staff) could have. Collins' sense of humor didn't stretch that far. He went to Marshall.

Marshall had a habit, when being briefed, of folding his arms and sitting stern-faced, staring without comment while he absorbed all of what he was hearing. "You couldn't tell whether he was agreeing with you or not," said one officer.

When Collins finished, Marshall told him, in essence, that when Lovett made a decision, it was Marshall talking.

Collins answered, "Thank you very much. I believe we can do it." They did, by pulling inventory out of the division depots and issuing to the draftees "not five of everything but two of everything."

Over the years, Marshall had already acquired a measure of the military leadership in Defense, the capabilities and limitations. He never had quite that easy a relationship with the civilians and left a great deal of that contact up to Lovett. While Marshall attended daily briefings with the Joint Chiefs and the President, Lovett, with a heavy delegation of responsibility, handled the Pentagon's internal administration, the budget, and the procurement programming.

One additional asset Lovett brought to the Deputy Secretary's office, according to a close observer, was "his tremendous rapport built up, especially in the war years, with the air frame and engine industry people." In 1950, Truman wanted full mobilization in the United States for war, not only to stamp out the fire burning in Korea but also to prepare for the one expected to ignite in Europe. Taking a longer-range look at the future, Marshall suggested that revving the military engine up to full power one year, shutting it off two years later, and revving it up again a few years after that might ruin the military industrial base, its supply stockpiles and pipelines, the continuity of military training—indeed, the whole military posture.

Instead, Marshall proposed that the United States maintain a preparedness level higher than in the past but somewhere short of all-out rearmament. He visualized a kind of national "minuteman" force, alert enough and strong enough to handle "police actions," capable of quick expansion. Truman and the Congress reluctantly agreed to Marshall's program. The task of executing the details of that scheme, particularly setting up an industrial base that could convert rapidly to munitions production, fell to Lovett.

One help: there was no budget ceiling. Defense spending, which had run $11.5 billion in 1949 and $11.9 billion in 1950, climbed to $19.7 billion in 1951, doubled to almost $39 billion in 1952, peaked at $43.6 billion in 1953. Thus, the Services, although they still harbored some differences, were reasonably compatible. (The Navy, for instance, building a convincing case in Korea for its theories of flexible, integrated fighting capability, said it had never really objected to unification—only to unification as practiced by Johnson.) As long as there was a sound military justification for some Service proposal, there was no open bitter controversy.

The only ceiling was set by Lovett's good sense. And he owned large amounts of that. His mind, Pentagon leaders soon learned, was keen and quick. He had "one of the finest memories for great detail, for facts and figures, that the Pentagon had ever dealt with." One aide, Marine Corps General Carey Randall, said, "He could soak up information very rapidly, retain it all for long periods of time."

The Defense Secretary's staff was growing much larger by then, losing much of the personal family tone of the Forrestal era, but its members had learned a lot and knew where to get information when Lovett needed it. He got substantially better staff support than any of his predecessors in the Pentagon front office. Still, one budgeter marveled, " 'Uncle Bob' had a built-in calculator for knowing just what he was committing himself to. He had been in the banking system so long he could add up in his head what kind of expenditures he had approved; and his figure would be within one-half a per cent of the correct total even though it might take his staff two days to add it up precisely to see if he was right."

Lovett's life as an international banker paid off in one other respect, as well. Where Marshall "had a genius for making a man think the program he was on was the greatest project in the world," Lovett "had a faculty for getting people to do what he wanted without ordering it."

"He was the smoothest negotiator you've ever seen," said one general who had felt the brunt of that talent. "He'd spent his life negotiating loans. In the Pentagon he negotiated, but he always got his way."

There was, however, one aim that he and Marshall and Truman and a host of other backers only partially realized: improvement in military manpower strength. In 1945, Marshall had written: "It is impossible for a nation to compensate for the services of a fighting man. There is no pay scale that is high enough to buy the service of a single soldier during even a few minutes of the agony of combat; the physical miseries of the campaign, or the extreme personal inconvenience of leaving his home to go out to the most unpleasant and dangerous spots on earth to serve his nation." In 1950, when he moved into the Pentagon, Marshall announced that he was setting up a new position, the Assistant Secretary of Defense for Manpower, Personnel, and Reserve Forces. He told Lovett he was amazed such an important area had not been granted that kind of attention before.

When the Secretary called for candidates to head the new staff office, Eisenhower quickly suggested Mrs. Anna Rosenberg, giving as her main credential the highly effective job she had done for him in that same field when Roosevelt sent her to Europe during the last year of World War II. Marshall asked Lovett what he thought of the idea.

"It is either going to be a stroke of genius or the biggest bust of your military career."

Marshall jotted a note to Mrs. Rosenberg in longhand, asked her to consider the job. She accepted, and was put in an office next to Marshall's. "Six times as big as McNeil's," said one disgruntled employee, "it was big enough to hold a dance in there." It could be reached only by walking through the outer door to the Defense Secretary's office. "It made her post appear as important as hell."

When she arrived, Marshall continued to call everyone by his last name—except Anna. She was one of the few people who had unlimited access to Marshall twenty-four hours a day. Unlike the other Pentagon workers on her level, she gave no sign of being dazzled at the sight of the Great Man, would burst into his office any time the urge, or a problem, moved her. Summed up one Pentagon observer in retrospect, "Anna thought straight, and talked like a man. She jangled her jewelry a bit, but she put a capital 'p' in 'personnel.' "

She almost didn't get the chance. When Truman asked Marshall to serve, he told the General there would (for a change) be no politics in Defense. Marshall could appoint whomever he wanted. (It was quite a while before any Democrats were picked, as it turned out, after Anna.) Taking Truman at his word, Marshall named Anna without telling Truman until later. That annoyed some of the White House staff, who thought Marshall had gone too far. They were inclined to be cool toward Anna, anyway, because they believed she had waited until the last minute to back Truman in 1948. When Senate hearings were called to confirm the appointment, White House staffers gave her little backing and let it be known they would have no objection to a full-blown investigation.

The hearings got out of hand. Volatile Washington was being needled at the time by an anti-Semitic pamphlet called "Common Sense." Probably making Thomas Paine spin in his grave, it purported to expose the "international Jewish conspiracy." In addition, Senator Joseph McCarthy was just cranking up his inquiry into Communists in government. A Communist spy with the same name as Anna Rosenberg's husband, Julius, had just been convicted and sentenced to death. Casual newspaper readers confused the two, unrelated families. As Anna, herself, said later, "I was Jewish, an immigrant, had been a pro-labor worker, and was a woman. What could have been worse?"

Senate hearings on her appointment were allowed to drag on and on. Still, she kept her sense of humor. During one exchange, a Senator asked her, "How close are you to Stuart Symington?"

Anna, who was related to Symington by marriage, answered, "Senator, if I were any closer, it would be a public scandal."

It was not all banter. Hate merchants spread charges that she was a Communist sympathizer. Marshall was outraged. Eisenhower, Bernard Baruch, Nelson Rockefeller, "everybody you ever heard of who was head of anything," were called to Washington to support the appointment. Finally, after three months of questioning, Anna Rosenberg was confirmed as the first Assistant Secretary for Manpower by voice vote. Immediately, she started pushing what had long been a Marshall dream, universal military training.

UMT had been called for by Marshall at least as far back as World War II. After the war, he had really rolled up his sleeves on it, actually doing more work for it than for unification. To him, UMT would be, he said, "clear evidence to the world" that the United States did not propose to abdicate its responsibilities in the face of the rise and spread of Communism. Johnson, supporting him, once told Congress, "The greatest deterrent in the world to Russia would be the fact that you can mobilize 10 million men overnight who have had UMT."

Truman backed the idea and kept presenting Congress with appropriation requests to start UMT. But Congress shunted the money off to other Defense projects. Politically, the idea was dynamite.

When Anna Rosenberg translated Marshall's objectives into a new program for 1951, it came out relabeled Universal Military Training and Service. The idea was that everybody, including the infirm, would serve in some capacity. The training would boost national physical fitness. Every citizen would be a part of the militia, a modern-day minuteman. This immediately caused an uproar. Churchmen preached that the government was trying to militarize America. Educators lectured that the schools would lose tuitions. After several months of hearings, a well-watered-down version of Marshall's UMT program was defeated on Capitol Hill by a narrow vote. The project was shoved into a quiet corner and kept there.

But, if Anna failed at UMT, she succeeded in grand style with many other projects. She set up a Defense Advisory Council on women in the Service, had them constantly asking the question, "Aren't there a lot of men doing the kind of work women could do?" Marshall subscribed enthusiastically to that idea and approved all appointments to officer rank for the ladies—although his reasons in some cases weren't exactly cold logic but, according to some staff members, more along the lines of, "Oh, yes, I remember her. A very good-looking woman."

The Assistant Secretary for manpower also set up a committee to inspect training camps to find out "how our boys are being treated." Just the establishment of the committee helped. Trying to find out where the committee would visit next, the Services quickly learned that the schedule was one of the Pentagon's most closely guarded secrets. The net effect was that training camp facilities were improved everywhere, just to avoid some Service installation getting what, predictably, would be a well publicized black eye from Anna. She charged ahead successfully on a proposal first advanced by the Air Force to integrate the Services. Negroes were soon serving alongside white men in combat units. "We found," said one of Anna's assistants, "that on the firing line they were very friendly. The further they got away from the front, the worse the idea of integration got."

She exposed manpower problems that had heretofore been buried in the Services. One was that the Services were sending mediocre talent to duty in the Office of the Secretary of Defense. Top officers were grateful for escaping a chore they were certain would prevent their being promoted. In Anna's end of the business, Personnel, at least, they began receiving the promotions.

Her office also delved into the utilization of manpower, prodded by "a fellow named Lyndon Johnson who would be on the phone at about 6:30 every morning, pestering us for using engineers as janitors, etc." Another complainer was Eleanor Roosevelt, "although hers were mostly the basket cases."

A key Rosenberg contribution was to make the Services, for the first time, justify their manpower requirements in relation to each other. She proposed to the Secretary of Defense that he make them accept equal proportions of 1-2-3-4 categories of proficiency. Until then, the Army had generally received the dregs of the draftee and enlistment groups. Manpower saw that each man brought into the military was rated on education, income, and health—having learned from graphs of those three main elements that a man topnotch in one or two was likely to be just as strong in the others. The Air Force and Navy objected, fighting over how much of a ratio each should be granted in each category. Marshall said it was a fine idea and signed the procedure into an order.

While Anna was giving the Secretary of Defense a closer hold on the manpower business than he had ever had before, what earned her the tremendous amount of press coverage she received in those days was the human side of her operation. Paralleling her earlier performance in Europe, she traveled extensively, went to Korea to check the barracks, the showers, the kitchen menus, and make sure "our boys are comfortable." Hard-bitten old combat veterans choked, but that didn't faze Anna. She returned from her Korean trip with a pile of names, sent personal notes to wives, mothers, and sweethearts telling them she had seen their boys in Korea.

The Korean conflict was a very unpopular war. World War II veterans sent to stave off defeat until recruits could gain experience had left dismayed and distraught families at home. Anna's well-publicized Korean trip told every wife and mother across the United States that a compassionate "one of their own" was running Pentagon personnel. The word spread: "If you write Anna, you get an answer." The women of America wrote, as many as two or three thousand letters a day, messages like, "My husband was a clerk in World War II. From the GI bill, he has a PhD in biological chemistry now. But the Army still has him working as a clerk. Can you help?"

"Every one," Anna decreed, would receive an "individually typed, personally signed letter." A big correspondence panel was set up. Anna talked her way into meetings of the Joint Chiefs and ordered them to pay attention to the effort and not try to manufacture form letters. Nor could anybody kid her about living conditions of the troops. From her travels, she had seen for herself. She followed up by inspecting each letter personally, convinced the generals she meant business by scratching big "X's" through their first few cold mundane attempts, and sending them back for rewrite with a pointed "This doesn't answer the question!"

All these programs meant long hours. In the office at 7:45 every morning, Anna worked a full day six days a week, and usually part of the time Sunday. She was in the office until nearly midnight at least four times a week, and on weekends took over the Defense Secretary's kitchen to feed her staff.

She never left the office if "Uncle Bob" was still there. And Secretary of Defense Robert Lovett was usually there—working a seven-day-a-week schedule himself. He had come down to the Pentagon from New York just to help out Marshall, with no intention of staying. He accepted the promotion to Secretary because Marshall had asked him to, because of Korea, and because the United States was just a little more than a year away from national elections. It was tough enough finding a man to be Defense Secretary under normal circumstances. Finding one who would be willing to, and capable of, taking charge for only a year would have been impossible.

When Lovett moved one door down from the Deputy's office to Pentagon command, he brought with him a simple-sounding three-rule formula for success:

1. Know your job.

2. Let people know how important they are and work hard for what you agree with them is needed.

3. Praise them when they're right and chew them out when they're wrong.

Like Marshall, he had an aversion to the limelight and avoided speech-making. (Friends in his native Texas once trapped him, however. They asked him to return home to address a civic group. He answered quickly, "I'm sorry, but I'm busy that day." They countered, "But we haven't picked a day. You pick it.")

Also, like Marshall, he had an abiding affection for the military man, and, like Forrestal, he knew intimately the unglamorous business end of the Defense operation. But, unlike Forrestal, Lovett could ease the long, tiring hours of digging into detail. His diversions were not those normally expected of a Wall Street banker.

Besides discovering with some astonishment the boss's devotion to good jazz, stodgy Pentagon employees were a bit shocked one day to learn that Lovett's enthusiasm for sports cars had led him to checking a new one out by tooling it back and forth across a bridge near the Pentagon. The staff soon learned, as well, that he considered the week a major success if he managed to sneak away from work for a while on a Saturday afternoon to go to a movie.

He would be criticized later, in some circles, for not doing much while he was Secretary of Defense. In fact, there wasn't much of a really lasting nature he could do. From the gloomy picture national opinion polls were painting of Democratic prospects in the election, there seemed little likelihood they would be in office after November, 1952. Lovett knew quite well, as he said, that "you don't bend the massive Defense organization sharply. It will turn only in gradual shifts." Thus, his mission had about it a good deal of the flavor of a holding action.

So, by then, did the Korean fighting. The month before MacArthur was fired, U.N. forces had retaken Seoul and by June, had driven a short distance north of the 38th parallel. There, they had drawn a battle line and stopped. At the end of June, Soviet U.N. delegate Jacob Malik proposed a cease-fire. Acting on Washington's instructions, General Ridgway, on June 30, broadcast a suggestion that the Allies and the Communists meet to discuss an armistice.

Talks started on July 10 at Kaesong and were transferred to Panmunjom in October.

On the battlefield, the next two years of fighting would be known as the "Battle for the Hills," after the geography that controlled valley supply routes in the area. Vicious battles raged over what became household words in the United States: "Old Baldy," "Pork Chop Hill," "Heartbreak Ridge," "T-Bone Hill," "White Horse Mountain," "Siberia Hill."

The effort to rescue Greece from Communist aggression had taken eighteenth months. The Berlin airlift lasted fifteen months. The Korean conflict had begun to look as though it might be endless. What it meant had been spelled out by Marshall during the MacArthur hearings.

Of the military men, he had said: "What our troops have done has really been magnificent. Thank goodness a few of them are now coming back and they will return in much larger numbers beginning the end [of May, 1951]; but we have small choice at the moment in the matter; and what we can do is appreciate to the full the heroism, the endurance, and the skillful fighting that those men are doing for us."

Of their successes: "We have filled the hospitals all over China with wounded. On one section of the front, left of our line in Korea, the Chinese attacked with thirty-four divisions. Twenty-six were pretty largely chewed up just after four days of fighting and only eight to ten remained to be committed to action. . . . In the same three months, our losses have been greatly reduced."

Of the steps to a cease-fire: "The method was to inflict the greatest number of casualties we could in order to break down not only the morale but the trained fabric of the Chinese armies." He contended that the United States was destroying China's "best trained armies, [forcing them] to negotiate without enlarging the struggle. [This course of action] also [will] retain our needed allies, particularly at the United Nations council table, and build their confidence in our leadership in this delicate matter—the first real test of American leadership in the Cold War."

The test was not one that sat very well back home. Truman's unannounced and virtually undefended, but very real, policy—the "purgatory of limited war," historian Trumbull Higgins called it—was onerous to a nation that liked clean-cut, uncomplicated victories over oppression.

In the November, 1950, elections, at the height of the panic over losses in Korea, Administration candidates had been driven from Congressional office by those who had campaigned for stronger measures against Communist China and less kowtowing and economic aid to Allies, especially in Western Europe. The U.S. voter-taxpayers, who had been led to expect gratitude from Europe, were instead under pressure to change the nation's ways. They demanded "a thorough housecleaning" in the State Department. For a clincher, as one writer noted, they pointed to "the enormous public debt that had been built up in twenty-five years of Democratic leadership during depression, war, and paying for European recovery."

Nearly 80 per cent of the nation, according to polls, harbored a growing suspicion that Truman's operation was rotten with incompetence and even disloyalty. The same polls showed Truman on his way out. "Voters didn't like his methods and were dubious about his objectives," said one columnist.

It was the first major election since the Republicans had broken an agreement to back the Democrats on foreign policy. It was also the first chance since the fall of China, the end of the U.S. atomic monopoly, and the start of a "police action" that threatened to turn into a major war, for members of the American public to voice an opinion. Their public spokesman had been MacArthur—which accounted, in large part, for his popularity when he returned to the United States after Truman fired him. In the summer of 1951, many people were still angry about that act.

It did little good for Secretary of State Dean Acheson to point out that U.S. handling of the war was serving its political purpose; that the enemy had sustained enormous losses "they can't gloss over"; that "the Chinese Reds have betrayed a long-standing pledge" to their own people to demobilize; and that the broken promises of social and economic improvement were "reflected in the sharp increase in repressive measures and propaganda."

Of the friction and frustration in the country, perceptive (but already much maligned) Acheson said: "Our name for problems is significant. We call them headaches. You take a powder and they are gone. These . . . pains are not like that. They . . . will stay with us until death. We have got to understand that all our lives danger, the uncertainty, the need for alertness, for efforts, for discipline will be upon us. This is new for us. It will be hard for us."

Previous emphasis on maintaining an air atomic attack superiority had left few resources to be spent on more conventional, limited-war arms. The rush to correct that shortage, which now seemed plainly a mistake, meant demanding more than normally would have been asked of some who believed they had already served more than enough. It created confusion, unwanted changes in accustomed ways of living, a gray world of half war, half peace. People took as villain a foreign policy that, because it was being negotiated almost day by day, seemed to be built on expedience, not plan.

From experience, Lovett could sympathize with State Department officials in their unpopularity. "They are always in the position of putting up the other side in the formulation of national policy." He accepted their belief that time was on the side of the United States, if the Western Powers could remain united, contain further Communist expansion, and preserve the *status quo* of military power. Besides, while the whole United States deplored the Korean conflict and debated the point of it, the nation hardly noticed changes that were being discussed openly inside the Pentagon—changes that markedly affected Lovett's view of what needed doing.

The Secretary of Defense cannot afford to spend too much time taking care of what's going on today. Tomorrow must be his major concern. Turning the ponderous, slow-moving Pentagon toward the future must be done each day—or Defense machinery will not be available when it is needed.

As a Marine once told lawyer Francis Matthews when he was Navy Secretary: "The thing you don't understand is the military time-space equation. When you call your New York stockbroker from your Omaha office, you assume five minutes after you hang up that you own the stock you told him to buy. What you've got to realize is that if you order a Marine division to Hawaii right now, nothing is going to happen for sixty days. Transportation has to be arranged. Supplies, equipment, and men have to be assembled. You don't decide now for what you want now. You decide now for what you want two months from now."

The entire Department of Defense is that problem multiplied several times in size, complexity, and delay—with the needs for research and development added. Lovett's principal tool for steering the monolith was the budget. Said his Deputy Secretary,

William Foster, who had a government background much like the Secretary's, "In development and control of the budget, Lovett was superlative."

His frame of reference was reflected in his annual report in 1952:

> We must try not to buy too much equipment which may be made obsolete by weapons now in the development stage. . . . At the same time, we cannot fight today's battles with tomorrow's weapons. We have to strike a balance between the two. We cannot count on the bold new developments always working out, and we cannot afford to arm our troops with paper promises. We must, therefore, bring the most careful judgment to bear on the selection of weapons for production.

With the technological revolution reaching a high pitch by then, what Lovett had in mind was an array of hardware that made Buck Rogers' comic strip equipment seem not fantasy but fact. It ranged from such things as a radio-guided, 250-mile-an-hour antitank weapon the size of a golf ball to atomic engines and nuclear bombs capable of destroying as much as a 100-square-mile area. Military laboratories were developing chemical, bacterial, and radiological warfare agents. A host of missile programs were begun—some designed to carry an atomic warhead as far as 2,000 miles. The intercontinental *Atlas* ballistic missile, which had been started in the late 1940's and then abandoned, was started up again. Says Foster, "We started it with our left hand while fighting Korea with our right."

It was a grim era in Defense history, but Lovett's personality was a perfect antidote. Serious and reserved with visitors, for the staff he eased the rugged stresses with the salve of humor. "He was warmhearted, fun-loving, a raconteur," they recall. He was a close friend of humorist Robert Benchley and himself "a great mimic. He would have made a wonderful actor." A secretary who was in the office remembers, "He could say more with a quip than most people could say in a three-page memo."

Sharp enough to return from a committee meeting and relate all that had happened in detail, he had a habit, delightful to the staff, of recounting what had been said, who was sitting where, by caricaturing people at the conferences—"First, that bulldog down there said . . . and then this crowing rooster over here said . . ."

He enjoyed as much as any of these sessions his budget negotiation meetings with the Navy. Navy Secretary Dan Kimball and Chief of Naval Operations Admiral Fechteler were each deaf in one ear. Seated according to protocol, each man had his bad ear turned toward the other. The result was that they had to discuss strategy in a loud whisper, audible to everyone in the room. Thus, Lovett knew before they even told him when they agreed to "settle for half now and get the rest next year."

During one such parlay, they outlined a request to Lovett for $200 million in overhead costs as part of their shipbuilding funds. Lovett didn't want to talk to Congress about "administrative overhead," told Kimball he was reminded "of the story about the guy who ran a brothel in Texas. As he prospered in his one-story cottage, he kept adding more and more one-story wings on the building. When someone asked him why he didn't build up instead of spreading out, he said, 'I'm trying to hold down the overhead.'"

Lovett believed that giving Congress too much detailed information only encouraged it to pick the budget apart. It could result, in this case, in getting approval to build ships but being turned down on hiring enough people to build them—particularly among economy-minded Congressmen who considered "overhead" another word for "sin." The Navy reworked its budget and buried that unavoidable cost by allocating a portion of it to each of the ships in the program.

Unlike the autocratic Johnson days, Lovett's tour was marked by reasonableness. Once, negotiating his Operations and Maintenance (housekeeping and equipment repair) funds with Lovett, Air Force Chief of Staff Vandenberg confessed, "I'm sure our people don't know what they're talking about on what is needed. I don't think your people know, either. Let's split the difference and we'll watch it closely as we go along." Lovett accepted the proposal—something no other Secretary would have done. (The final cost for that year was more than Lovett's budget people originally wanted to give but less than the "negotiated" figure.)

One of Lovett's most significant contributions to long-range Defense strength was to establish firmly the preparation of a coordinated Defense-wide budget. Forrestal had started that coordination. Johnson had tabled it, in effect, with his sweeping arbitrary decisions placing temperamentally autonomous and mutually jealous Services under Truman's pre-Korea budget ceiling. Lovett, also, with considerable help from McNeil, lopped billions off military money requests. One such appeal for funds totaled over $100 billion. Lovett chopped it in half and with his talent for negotiation kept the Services reasonably happy over the huge slash in their "absolute minimum requirements."

With his effective technique, he was able to dig down to the roots of Service budgets, uncovering the assumptions on which requests were based. He insisted on seeing not only the final total but the figures that showed how it was reached. "We're not questioning your assumptions," he would say to the military, "We just want to know the basis for your decisions." This technique enabled him to cut through the sacrosanct air of "absolute minimums" accorded these expert military opinions by the time they reached the generals. If, for instance, the Army said it must have 10,000 tanks, Lovett's staff would go ask the second lieutenants who had compiled that total where the tanks were going to be used—and find out 10 per cent of them were scheduled to sit on parade grounds.

The Services were humming with war and expansion, buying "new" (mostly World War II vintage) weapons. And a general or a chief of staff in war is never criticized for having too much. But even in Korea there wasn't enough time, money, or matériel to go around. The build-up had to be orderly.

Adding to the problems of the build-up was the explosion in technology, the increasing complexity of weapons. Said Lovett, "We are progressing from piston engines to jets, from visual operations to radar, from certain types of artillery to rockets, from piloted aircraft to guided missiles, from World War II explosives to atomic warheads." Although the new hardware was much more effective (for every F-86 jet fighter shot down over Korea, the Chinese Communists were losing nine Russian-built MIG-15's), the cost was much higher. In the airplane business, for instance, 27 times more direct engineering man-hours were required to design a modern fighter than the 42,000 man-hours for a World War II fighter. Work devoted just to aerodynamics jumped 120 times in the ten years from 1942 to 1952.

"With more man-hours to be paid at the higher wage rates of postwar years," said Lovett, "it is inevitable that the end product is going to cost more whether it is a modern airplane, ship, tank, or any other major weapon." Finally, he said, the Defense Department shared the burden of "maintaining a level of civilian economy to keep this country healthy, so that in our efforts to prevent war we do not do permanent damage to the system which supports our way of life."

All these problems had been around the Pentagon for some time, but, said Foster, "War intensifies everything about tenfold." Some of the decisions, with the larger national interest in mind, should properly have been made by the Joint Chiefs. But the Chiefs were not given this opportunity in 1952 any more than they had been in Johnson's era.

As a result, both Marshall and Lovett saw the need for further Pentagon reorganization. But neither one wanted to rock the boat while the Korean fighting was going on.

On November 18, 1952, Lovett sent a long letter to Truman containing recommendations for improving the administration and operation of the Defense Department. Truman "not able to make peace," said newspaper columnist Walter Lippmann, "because he was politically too weak at home and not able to make war because the risks were too great overseas," had had his dilemma solved by the voters two weeks earlier when they swept the Democrats out of office, swept President Dwight Eisenhower and the Republicans in.

Lovett's letter was supposed to be handed to the new President when he arrived, to be read in private. That way, if the President didn't agree with some of the suggestions, he wouldn't be under pressure to adopt them. But, in violation of what the Secretary of Defense had understood was to be its confidential nature, the document was released to the press on January 8, 1953, as both Truman and Lovett were leaving office.

In the letter, Lovett pointed out that the opinions expressed were personal, not the results of a properly coordinated staff study, and were set down only to give "my successor a running start on certain problems." He prefaced his thoughts for improvement with the following praise:

> The quality of our professional military officers and the permanent civilian staff [which provides about the only continuity in the overall establishment] is remarkably high. It compares very favorably with any large industrial organization of its approximate size, complexity and wide range of functions. I have great respect and

affection for our professional military men and having had an opportunity of seeing them both at the council table and in the field, I know of no country more fortunately situated in this respect than ours.

Then, warning that "unification is necessarily evolutionary," he spelled out changes he believed advisable, noting that, in the event of war, "an essential job of the Secretary of Defense and his colleagues, both military and civilian, will involve 'distributing shortages' among Army, Navy, and Air Force." He added, "Based on past experience, these shortages will involve manpower in bulk and critical occupational specialty; matériel in all its forms; land, water and air transportation; communications facilities; funds; industrial and military facilities and so forth."

And, he argued, in the event of war, present authorities provided the Secretary by the National Defense Act "will prove to be inadequate" simply because the main one, dollar control, becomes especially weak when the shooting starts.

Another of his contentions was that the "legal beavers" were still at work, in abundance as they always will be, examining every comma in the legislation to find a way of side-stepping orders and doing as they pleased. Calling for clarification of the Secretary's "direction, authority and control" in relation to requirements written in the law that the three Military Departments be "separately administered," he pointed out that in the supply, warehousing, and issue business particularly "certain ardent separatists occasionally pop up with the suggestion that the Secretary of Defense play in his own back yard and not trespass on their separately administered preserves."

He called the authorities, or lack of them, in the Joint Chiefs "one of the principal weaknesses of the present legislation," adding that the same lack also affected the Munitions Board and the Research and Development Board. "It is clear," he wrote, "that overall 'civilian control' is essential and that it is fundamental to our form of government. Yet, civilian judgment must be based on adequate military advice given by professional military men in an atmosphere as free as possible from Service rivalries and Service maneuvering."

Observing that the President, the National Security Council, the Secretary of Defense, and the three Service Secretaries should not, in his opinion, attempt to conduct military operations and should avoid hampering the military in carrying out their specialized functions, he said that they still clearly needed "proper military advice"—a commodity that, he implied, was hard to find.

> By their very makeup, it is extremely difficult for the Joint Chiefs to maintain a broad non-Service point of view. Since they wear two hats, one as Chief of an Armed Service and the other as a member of the Joint Chiefs, it is difficult for them to detach themselves from the hopes and ambitions of their own Service without having their own staff feel it is being let down by the Chief. Maintenance of an impartial, non-partisan position becomes increasingly difficult in times of shortage of either men, money, or material. In fact, it is remarkable that the form of organization currently in being has worked so well and it is, I think, a tribute to the quality of the individual involved.

Out of unfounded fear over possible creation of an "Armed Forces General Staff," he added, "we have succeeded in making the Joint Chiefs of Staff a sort of clearing house for papers instead of having them occupy their rightful position and instead of leaving them adequate time for their great responsibilities."

They should, he said, concentrate on their Joint Chiefs duties, either by delegating all their individual Service responsibilities to their Vice Chiefs or, if necessary, by separating themselves from their Service ties and acting solely as a Combined Staff of senior military men. Said one aide, "I think we place too great a burden on a man with this two-hat thing."

The Joint Staff, Lovett claimed, faced the same quandary. Its junior officers had to consider their future careers and promotions in the separate Services. "It is not unnatural, therefore, that they should from time to time become the advocate of their own Service's point of view. There is, furthermore, a natural temptation to indulge in the indoor sport of 'back-scratching.'" He proposed that this Joint Staff, revamped to give it a military-civilian composition, be made the Secretary of Defense's staff, be held responsible only to him, and receive its efficiency ratings and promotions from him.

He called for the setting up of unified commands reporting to the Secretary of Defense "with the advice of the Service Secretaries and the Joint Chiefs." He said the Secretary should, in effect, be the Deputy of the Commander in Chief, the President. He said the Munitions and Research and Development Boards, with their built-in legislated rigidity, should be abolished and replaced by an Assistant Secretary of Defense's office for each of the two functions. He said there were far too many levels of headquarters in the various Services, in his opinion, "thus adding to the overhead and inevitably causing delay. Furthermore, each headquarters sets up a chain reaction of demands for housing, transportation, etc., thus adding to the cost.

"I have a similar feeling about the number of committees . . . a very contagious virus which has the unpleasant characteristic of rapid reproduction."

The problem of protecting official secrets, first mentioned by Forrestal, was, Lovett said, still of cardinal importance and he named as one of the great hazards to national security "the apparent inadequacy of existing legislation to protect this country against traitors, spies and blabber-mouths."

He raised the bugaboo of UMT again, suggesting: "One of the most promising areas of reduction of cost lies, in my opinion, in keeping the standing military forces to a minimum to protect against disaster while having immediately available a basically trained reserve. The only satisfactory method of accomplishing this desired result, that I am aware of, is through a system of Universal Military Training and Service."

Finally, he noted that the organizations of the Army, Navy, and Air Force were all different, that the responsibilities and authorities of their Chiefs of Staff differed, and that much of their operation was still what it had been before unification. He called for a "thoroughgoing study" to pull out the best from all three and set up a single organizational pattern.

> As an indication of one area in which modernization and improvement appears to be needed, consider the 'technical services' organization in the Army. There are seven—Corps of Engineers, Signal Corps, Quartermaster, Medical, Chemical, Transportation and Ordnance. Of these seven, all are in one degree or another in the business of design, procurement, production, supply, distribution, warehousing and issue. Their functions overlap in a number of items, thus adding substantial complications to the difficult problem of administration and control. . . .
>
> It has always amazed me that the system worked at all and the

> fact that it works rather well is a tribute to the inborn capacity of teamwork in the average American. . . .
>
> A reorganization of the technical services would be no more painful than backing into a buzz saw, but I believe that it is long overdue.

Lovett concluded that another person in his job with different work habits might disagree with all this. Regardless of that, he announced, "I will do my utmost to see that my successor is fully briefed and I will gladly hold myself at his disposal for any assistance I can give in making his take-over of responsibilities smooth and effective." When Lovett left the Pentagon, he had spent fully a third of his working years in public service. The first ninety days after his departure he spent rehabilitating a physique that had been strained repeatedly for years. Then, when he finally returned to Brown Brothers, Harriman, he found, "I began sweating out the frustrations of the railroads which are not at all unlike the military in the problems and entrenched interests they face."

His government work, both in the Department of State and Defense, had been punishing. Its peak pressures had come when he would testify all day long on Capitol Hill and have to do his office work far into the evening. Yet, "even then," he reminisced, "that period of my life was happier than any I have known before or since."

VIII

Charles E. Wilson

[JANUARY, 1953–OCTOBER, 1957]

IN 1945, General Dwight Eisenhower said that unification could give the United States a more efficient combat force with only 75 per cent of the manpower required by separate, autonomous military Services. In 1952, he argued: "Such unity as we have achieved is too much form and too little substance. We have continued with a loose way of operating that wastes time, money, and talent with equal generosity. With three Services in place of the former two still going their separate ways and with an over-all defense staff frequently unable to enforce corrective action, the end result has been not to remove duplication but to replace it with triplication. . . . Neither our security nor our solvency can permit such a way of conducting the crucial business of national defense."

On defense issues, his Republican campaign pitch for the Presidency that year against Adlai Stevenson was almost identical to Democrat Truman's program in 1949. But enough people thought they saw a difference that the man Marshall had said couldn't be elected received over 33 million votes—more than any previous Presidential candidate in U.S. history.

If he won, Eisenhower had promised the voters, he would go to Korea to see the war at first hand. That promise brought a smirk from Democratic politicians, but to the voters in an unhappy nation "it was better than sitting home doing nothing." The President-elect was scheduled to arrive in Korea on Thanksgiving. Combat forces at one stop decided to order turkey and trimmings for him. He didn't arrive. They went ahead and ate. Told he was due in that evening, they ordered and ate Thanksgiving dinner again. As they finished, they were notified he would be in the next day. A bit weary of cranberries and dressing by now, they gave it one more try. He didn't make it that day either.

When he finally arrived in the Far East on December 2, Eisenhower had with him the sixty-two-year-old president of the General Motors Corporation, Charles Erwin Wilson. (Two Charles E. Wilsons ran giants of U.S. industry in that era. "Electric Charlie" headed the General Electric Company. "Engine Charlie" had worked for General Motors more than thirty years and had been its chief executive officer since 1940.)

Eisenhower had met Wilson several times during World War II, knew his reputation as one of the ablest big corporation executives in the United States. After the 1952 election, he called Wilson at a Business Advisory Council meeting in Georgia, and asked him to be Secretary of Defense, reasoning that Defense is the biggest procurement and management job in the world, and, as an aide said, "Anyone who can run General Motors can run anything."

Short, stocky, with a ruddy complexion and white hair, "Engine Charlie" had an almost paternalistic warmth about him the Pentagon found surprising. Said one staff man, "There is no harder school of rivalries to get to the top of than at General Motors. I can recite how such a friendly man got to the top, but I can't understand it." Added Carey Randall, still in the Pentagon front office from Lovett's time, "Charlie Wilson had every human kindness you could imagine."

Ohio-born, a 1909 electrical engineering graduate of Carnegie Institute of Technology, Wilson worked for the first ten years after graduation for the Westinghouse Electric Company, designing its first automobile starting motors and handling its radio generator and dynamotor design/development for the Army and Navy during World War I.

General Motors hired him in 1919 to be chief engineer and sales manager in the automobile division of its subsidiary, Remy Electric Company. By 1925, he was Remy general manager, and he was made president of GM's newly organized Delco-Remy division a year later. His work directing the design and highly profitable sales of a whole new, diverse product series earned him a GM vice-presidency in 1928.

During the next decade, he played a key role in GM's purchase of other companies to expand its range of corporate activities and, at the same time, build up its automobile parts and accessories business. Also given continually increased responsibilities for GM labor relations and production planning, he finally became GM executive vice president in 1939. In 1940, when William Knudsen took a leave of absence to direct Roosevelt's industrial war mobilization effort, Wilson was appointed acting president. He dropped the "acting" from his title when Knudsen resigned all his GM connections a year later.

In the next four years, Wilson directed a production force that, by war's end, was churning out military hardware at the rate of $10 million worth a day. GM's $12 billion contribution to the war effort included almost one-fourth of all tanks, armored cars, and airplane engines built in the United States, nearly half of all the machine guns and carbines, two-thirds of all the heavy trucks, three-fourths of all Navy diesel engine horsepower. Wilson even organized an aircraft division out of some of his East coast plants and made several thousand aircraft for the Navy.

Understandably, Wilson was often asked by the military and Congress for advice on proper war allocation of industrial resources and manpower. Just before one summons to Washington, he broke his leg while ice skating and had to make the trip on crutches with his leg in a cast. After finishing testimony on Capitol Hill, he struggled down the long flight of steps outside the Capitol building and stopped to rest while his chauffeur went to get the car. He sat down on the bottom step, stretched his cast-covered leg out in front of him, and laid his crutches at his side. It was unseasonably hot in Washington that late winter day. The president of General Motors took his hat off and set it bottomside up beside him. A passing lady tourist, touched by the sight of the tired homey-looking character in the slightly misshapen double-breasted suit with a cast on his leg, spied the hat and tossed a quarter in it.

His trip to Capitol Hill in January, 1953, had no such comic highlights. Some Democrats, swamped by the tide of Eisenhower popularity, were trying to "prove" that the voters had elected a "big business" White House. Wilson owned thousands of shares of GM stock. He had more GM stock and cash bonuses due him in the next few years. His wife, Jessie, also owned some GM stock. When the Senate Armed Services Committee, still headed by Georgia Democrat Richard Russell, called hearings on his nomination, those stock holdings made Wilson a natural political target.

Noting that General Motors was a major military supplier, the committee registered dismay at the "obvious" conflict of interest if Wilson took over the Pentagon. They ordered Wilson to dump the stock—or his appointment would not be approved. Heavy smoker Wilson, cigarette ashes fluttering down the front of his dark blue pin-stripe suit, slouched in his chair, looked around the luxurious, oak-paneled committee room, gazed up at the massive, ornate chandeliers, and announced, "The trouble with you men is you just don't understand the problem."

The committee would have been less incensed if he'd hit them in the face with a wet glove. Congressmen rarely put up with anyone lecturing them in their own workshop. What's more, these old Senate campaigners had heard their first military testimony from a general named MacArthur who had brought along an aide named Eisenhower. They hardly needed any instruction, they thought, from a newcomer. Worse, this august body of senior legislators had never before heard such effrontery as that phrase, "You men." Their dignity was offended.

Charlie Wilson had struck out on the first pitch. For a week, the committee banged away at him. Wilson kept refusing to unload his stock and finally complained, "I really feel you are giving me quite a pushing around. If I had come here to cheat, I wouldn't be here."

Countered Russell, "I'm sorry you feel that way, Mr. Wilson. I am not trying to push you around, but I have my responsibilities, too."

Blunt, outspoken Charlie Wilson shot back, "I understand that. But I am just human, and I am making a great sacrifice to come down here. If there was a nice clean way . . . to sell everything, and put it into government bonds, I would do it. But the [tax] penalty is too great, gentlemen, and I do not know why you ask me to do it."

Would he be able to make a decision adverse to General Motors when he was in Defense, they wanted to know. The question was loaded. It came in the midst of a discussion on the crash Korean War contracts Marshall and Lovett had let to build munitions plants designed to be easily converted later to peacetime uses. Proud of the fact that, at GM, his people, without help from public funds, already had built many multiple-use production lines, which made cars in peacetime but could be switched quickly to tanks in an emergency, Wilson was in a free-enterprise frame of mind.

He answered that corporations ought to make their own plans to serve the country without waiting for the government to prod them. And he added, "For years, I thought what was good for the country was good for General Motors and vice versa."

Democrats—newly elected Senator Stuart Symington and Capitol Hill powerhouse Lyndon Johnson among them—broadcast that remark as having been, "What's good for General Motors is good for the country." Quixotic puritans and patriots across the nation reacted violently to such blasphemy. Wilson was never able to live down that deliberate misreporting of his remark. It smirched his whole tour in Defense.

Because of that experience, moreover, he could never quite accept the fact that he was working for Congress as well as the President. But, on January 22, after the whole subject had been blown up to ridiculous proportions, he knuckled under and agreed to sell the stock. On January 23, his nomination as Secretary of Defense received unanimous approval.

In effect, Wilson had tried, and failed, to overcome one of Washington's double standards. Elected officials can steer government business to their constituent industries—and, during campaign speeches, even brag that they have done so. But they demand of the executive branch of government more purity than was expected of Caesar's wife.

After this episode, Eisenhower said, "I have found that some of our Senatorial friends are so politically fearful . . . they carry the meaning and intent of the law . . . and court interpretations [on government standards of conduct] far beyond anything that could be considered reasonable.

"The likely eventual result is that sooner or later [Presidents] will be unable to get anybody to take jobs in Washington except business failures, political hacks, and New Deal lawyers. All of these would jump at the chance to get a job that a successful businessman has to sacrifice very materially in order to take."

In the next four years, Wilson's Congressional relations gradually improved, said one wit, "from atrocious to poor." His image in the press more or less kept pace. Wilson enjoyed press conferences, held them on what approached twice-a-month frequency, and often backed up that unprecedented performance by inviting correspondents to lunch. Nor did he hide behind that frustrating, for reporters, official shield of "This is off the record."

After the gross distortion of his "What's good for General Motors" quip, delivered in closed Senate hearings, he told his public relations staff, "Whenever we put our foot in our mouth hereafter, we're going to do it on the record." Even a close family friend on the *Detroit News* was no longer permitted to call him at his Bloomfield Hills, Michigan, home to talk business "off the record."

Newspapermen loved him. Though he often rambled around the subject, as he did in Capitol Hill testimony, he had a saying for every situation. To the delight of writers and to the Pentagon's chagrin, "He could put his foot in his mouth easier than any Secretary of Defense we've ever had," a staff member said.

One theoretical merit of his frequent press conferences was that reporters heard all about a problem all at once. Supposedly, this free flow of information would keep the press from blowing up something out of all proportion to its merit. But reporters describing complex subjects, meeting deadlines, limited by available news column space, can and often do summarize. Their stories sometimes read considerably at odds with what a Defense Secretary thought he was telling them.

Once, discussing research and development, Wilson properly pointed out that he didn't think the U.S. Government should take over from private enterprise and finance with tax dollars all the basic research done in the nation. "I mean, finding out why the grass is green, things like that."

"Research and development" had already long since become something akin to a new world crusade in America and had been tagged the fountainhead of future U.S. security. Wilson's afterthought comment reached headlines as: "Defense Secretary Against R&D Spending. Says He Doesn't Care Why the Grass is

Green." Wilson suddenly looked like an insensitive engineer standing in the way of progress.

Much later, he really dropped a bomb when he told the press he would like to increase the size of military Reserve forces and finance the move by cutting back on National Guard size. The Guard wasn't much of a fighting force, anyway, he said, adding that some Korea-bound Guard units had taken as much as a year and a half to get ready to go, which seemed a little long to him. Besides, he noted, relatively mild Guard service was being used as an escape hatch from compulsory active military duty. The National Guard, he summed up, is full of draft dodgers.

Since Hawaii and Alaska were not yet in the Union, there were only forty-eight state governors to scream at him for impugning the patriotism of their private armies. Next day, the White House issued a statement that sounded like a denial of Wilson's claim. Asked at his next press conference what he thought of the White House not backing him up, Wilson answered, "I don't know about them. The White House is not my dunghill."

A press aide blanched, then mumbled at his boss, "If those reporters ask for facts, I can prove the Guard is a bunch of draft dodgers, because they are. But how do I prove the White House is a dunghill?"

Such stories about Wilson were proof to many Pentagon workers of the justice of their ten-year-growing aggravation with a press corps whose outstanding talent, they believed, was for inaccuracy. And Wilson could have made a fairly strong case against the Fourth Estate if he had cared to. He did not.

His wife did. She got her opening when a reporter made the mistake of asking her if she could confirm that her husband's loose tongue had alienated him from the White House. Jessie Wilson lost her temper. For the next few minutes she berated that reporter and every "false, malicious, misleading" thing he represented. His listening compatriots dutifully reported the incident in their next editions.

A few days later, Mr. and Mrs. Wilson, on their way to their Florida ranch, were offered a lift by Eisenhower as far as Augusta, Georgia. As they walked toward a wall of reporters on their way to the Presidential plane, Wilson smiled at his wife, suggested to the President, "Let's walk Jessie out there in between us so she can't say anything to get us in trouble."

Congress and the press were not Wilson's only headaches. A much more substantive problem lay in the unique role carved out for him in the Pentagon. His chief military adviser was his boss, the general in the White House. "Ike made all those basic military decisions," pointed out one Wilson aide. And, like Roosevelt in World War II, easily accessible Dwight Eisenhower kept direct pipelines open to the Joint Chiefs. Understandably, Wilson deferred to that group on purely military matters. He took his instruction on politico-military matters from a Secretary of State Eisenhower considered without peer, John Foster Dulles. Thus, Wilson's job was simply to run the business end. He was, in essence, what Pentagon job descriptions said the *Deputy* Secretary of Defense should be.

Such a position need not necessarily be untenable. But Wilson, himself, created additional occupational hazards by flying in the face of predictable military peacetime behavior. "Wilson organized the operation," said comptroller McNeil, "to give managers and commanders considerable latitude with just enough checks and balances so they didn't get crossways to the boss."

He didn't mind a little inter-Service competition. In fact, he encouraged it. Like Forrestal, he believed, at least initially, that Defense should not be set up like a pyramid with the Defense Secretary sitting on top. Rather, the Pentagon would work best and make the correct moves more often if it were a collection of counterbalanced, coequal professional specialists. The object of such a confederacy was to provide earnest and intelligent opposition to allegedly good ideas from any one group of experts.

"The process," said McNeil, "will improve an idea even if it is adopted. And it will weed out the ideas that look great today and silly a year later."

Wilson's role in this competitive turmoil of "purposeful conflict" was, as he saw it, to pick the right people for pivotal posts, then sit back as a judge dealing only with those problems subordinates could not resolve among themselves. Forrestal had cautioned, "There still remains the imponderable element—which provides the synthesis for all the specialties—namely, *management*, which is the ability to handle people, to select leaders and to exercise judgment."

Delegating authority to virtually autonomous divisions, which were allowed even their own independent design engineering staffs, had worked with impressive success in Wilson's ten-year command of General Motors. But at GM there is a profit-and-loss statement to gauge continually how right who is in doing what. The military, in peacetime, have no profit-and-loss measure. They have to use a patchwork substitute called "policy guidance." Its basic arithmetic is the budget allocation. Its payoff is national prestige and major policy influence for the military department whose arguments are most convincing. With no war to provide battlefield proof that one opinion is more right than another, the debates can, and do, go on without end.

The whole idea of delegated authority had not worked for Forrestal in an almost identical environment five years earlier. Wilson thought it would for him. One important reason was Eisenhower's promise that no new top Defense official, military or civilian, would be appointed until he had first earned Wilson's approval. With that promise, and the luck of timing, Wilson became the first Secretary of Defense who really got to name his own first team.

Forrestal had inherited his team, was unhappy with at least one of them, and suspicious of them all by the time his mental illness became pronounced. Johnson and Lovett would just as soon have replaced some team members they were bequeathed—although, in Johnson's case, three (Sullivan, Denfeld, and Symington) were forced out more because of the power they represented than because the Secretary lacked confidence in their ability.

By the fall of 1953, the Joint Chiefs were almost all entirely new faces. Only General Lemuel Shepherd was a holdover, having been appointed Marine Corps Commandant in January, 1952. Tours of all the old Korean war chiefs had ended by August. Matthew Ridgway moved in from his Far East command to replace J. Lawton Collins as Army Chief of Staff that month, at the same time Admiral Robert Carney took over Fechteler's job as Chief of Naval Operations. Admiral Arthur Radford, who had fought hard against unification five years earlier and battled even harder against the B-36 in 1949, had had a complete change of view about the military future by 1953, according to Eisenhower and Wilson. In August, he replaced Omar Bradley as Chairman of the Joint Chiefs, staying until just two months before Wilson left in 1957. General Nathan Twining was named Air Force Chief of

Staff in June, 1953, and later replaced Radford as Chairman of the Joint Chiefs.

One of the hurdles to smooth, efficient Pentagon performance is the difficulty of holding on to high-level civilian political appointees. Far too often, just as they begin to learn what they are supposed to be doing, they resign. Under Wilson, the record was mixed; at times, title-shuffling in the Pentagon front office seemed a little like a game of musical chairs.

Wilson's first Army Secretary, former textile executive Robert Stevens, stayed two years. Former Michigan Governor Wilber Brucker, who had been Wilson's General Counsel for a year, took over, fell in love with the Army, and set a record for Secretary longevity by serving until January, 1961.

Wilson's first Navy Secretary, Robert B. Anderson, served just fifteen months, then became Wilson's Deputy Secretary, stayed another fifteen months until Eisenhower made him Secretary of the Treasury. Anderson's Navy replacement, Charles Thomas, had spend six months as Under Secretary in 1953 and then another nine months as Assistant Secretary of Defense (Supply and Logistics). He headed the Navy until March, 1957, when Navy Under Secretary (for four years) Thomas Gates moved up.

In the Air Force, former Chrysler corporation executive Harold Talbott had served two and one-half years, would probably have stayed longer if he hadn't been spotted using Air Force stationery for personal correspondence promoting a private company in which he was a partner. Assistant Secretary of Defense (Research and Development) Donald Quarles replaced him in 1955, stayed until named Deputy Secretary of Defense in 1957, and was replaced in turn by four-year Air Force Under Secretary James Douglas.

Wilson didn't fare so well on continuity with his alter egos. His first Deputy Secretary, Roger Kyes, brought by Wilson from GM, was around for fifteen months. His replacement, Anderson, stayed another fifteen. The new man, Reuben Robertson, had been Vice Chairman of the Advisory Committee on Business Organization of the Department of Defense, headed by former President Herbert Hoover. Robertson stuck it out eighteen months until Quarles moved up in May, 1957. During that same four-year stretch, Wilson swore in a total of twenty-six different assistant secretaries. Not counting Comptroller McNeil, who stuck for the full term, each of Wilson's key staff offices got a new man to run it approximately every sixteen months.

How long they served, how much experience they gained, and, therefore, how much their full talents could be brought to bear on Defense problems were important to Wilson's effectiveness in running the store. As he left, Lovett had advised Wilson to utilize the executive secretariat he and Marshall had relied on so heavily. Urging Wilson to use promotion and prestige incentives to obtain sharp people for manning that group, he said, "You'll need top talent to provide these final audit and protective services."

However, Wilson let the executive secretariat lapse into disuse, feeling, for a long time, that the Services with their own highly motivated men could be convinced they should work cooperatively. Two years, almost to the day, after he had told his staff the Services would get along because "I have handpicked the Secretaries," he reluctantly admitted, as had Forrestal, that persuasion did not appear to be enough. For example, one of "his boys," after discussing with Wilson what he knew would be an unpopular order to his own Service, said, "I agree with your thinking, Charlie. But please, order me to do it, in writing, so I can go back and face my own people, again."

In spite of such incidents, Wilson maintained a large faith in people and tried consistently to delegate responsibility to others. (Even in his personal business, he believed in delegating. Shortly after taking office, he gave power-of-attorney to his top military aide, whom he'd barely gotten to know.) He was hard not to like. Compared to the shell of aloofness his four predecessors had retreated behind with visitors, Wilson warmed almost immediately to everybody. He was very considerate of those closely associated with him. And, "He loved to travel," the staff soon discovered, "but almost solely just to meet new people." He felt the same about his walks around the Pentagon. His predecessors had had their hair cut in the privacy of the office. Wilson preferred walking down to visit the public barber in the Pentagon shopping center. "He just wanted to find out what us commoners thought," said one.

The staff soon learned that he and his large family (three boys, three girls) were a devoted clan. Said the sergeant assigned to handle his routine needs, "More than once I got a call from Mrs.

Wilson telling me, 'He has to go to the White House today. Would you make sure his shoes are polished?' "

Apart from being Secretary of Defense, he ran a dairy farm in Michigan with one son. With a son-in-law, he owned a beef cattle ranch in Florida, and he had a plantation in Louisiana. A walking file cabinet, he carried personal business papers in his coat, always hauled around two briefcases. One was full of routine, unclassified Defense reading. The other was crammed with livestock information. "He was the guy," smiled one aide, "who decided what bull would service which cow."

"He was happiest," claimed an assistant, "wearing a windbreaker and an old pair of boots, stomping around the farm. He gave me quite an education in livestock."

Because the Services soon found out they could always appeal their committee disagreements, Wilson's "purposeful conflict" routine meant plenty of problems jumping up to his level. These problems, in turn, meant long hours. "But Wilson didn't mind working all night," said McNeil. "Neither had Forrestal."

Wilson counterbalanced the grind by taking two or three weeks off occasionally. "You'd need that long," said one of his budgeteers, "for the projects he left you. And by the time you were getting through, he'd be back to stir up some more."

"The only criticism I ever heard of him," said Randall, "was that he was too patient. But he never believed in jumping the gun. When he was handed a problem, he liked to amass every bit of detail. He'd talk even to the working troops who made up the briefing charts. He'd quiz people for hours, days, even weeks. He lost all track of time in these discussions."

Nor did he think he had to go hunting snarls. "He felt almost anything, if it occurred at the right time, would inevitably force its way clear to the White House without any help from him," a top assistant said. His case in point was the Army enlisted man who, in 1957, killed a Japanese woman who was gathering spent ammunition on a rifle range outside Tokyo. Japan wanted a trial in its own courts. U.S. policy was that military men on active duty would be tried only in U.S. military courts. The relatively insignificant-looking, but potentially explosive, international incident was, of its own accord, being considered by the highest echelons of Washington just hours after it happened. (Wilson, Dulles, and Eisenhower spent days thrashing out a solution, finally agreed to let Japan try the man. He got a three-year suspended sentence and was returned to the United States.

While he was in office, the Services could hardly blame Wilson, any more than they could blame Forrestal, for not having given them the chance to thrash out differences on their own. Even before he was sworn in, Wilson had begun touring the world to meet all the three- and four-star officers he could, to talk to them, size them up, let them size him up. In the Pentagon, although he stayed out of their meetings, he mingled with the Joint Chiefs themselves almost constantly. (Radford tallied fifty-nine such meetings in one month with one, a few, or all of them.) They had standing invitations to join him for lunch.

He organized annual meetings of all three-star officers, and up. "It was a kind of educational thing," said one who attended. "There wasn't really any new policy that came out of these, just a tremendous exchange of information with the opposition."

In the same format, he set up annual sessions of the Joint Chiefs' civilian counterparts. Called the Joint Secretaries Conference, it was held at the Quantico, Virginia, Marine base a few miles south of Washington "so they'd be close to the Pentagon in case a fire flared up." Beyond all these scheduled meetings, Wilson let it be known he would see anyone in the military anytime and would let a man stay as long as he wanted trying to thrash something out.

Just as they couldn't complain about Wilson's availability when they had to get decisions, the Services could hardly squawk, as they had in Forrestal's time, about lack of guidance. Quoting, for public effect, George Washington's "To be prepared for war is one of the most effectual ways of preserving peace," Eisenhower had spelled out his basic military platform in 1953. Its highlights: the United States would never, on its own initiative, start a world war, and, therefore, its arsenal must be huge enough to withstand a first attack and still retaliate decisively; a nuclear war would be so catastrophic that forces must be designed primarily to deter war rather than to win it; military forces must be kept continually modernized to correct the U.S. fault of beginning tomorrow's war with yesterday's weapons.

In addition, Eisenhower had said, "Defense policy must take into account the need for a system of alliances" suggesting that allies ringing the Iron Curtain would provide their own local security, especially in ground forces, while the centrally located, highly productive United States would supply mobile reserves, particularly in sea and air power. Finally—and the catch, as the Services soon figured out—"national security was not just military but economic strength as well."

Eisenhower had heard of an ammunition shortage during his Korean trip. The shortage was the result of a budget opinion in Washington overriding a command judgment in the field. It was good proof of Lovett's contention that control of money can be one—but should not be the only control—a Defense Secretary has.

In spite of such lessons, Eisenhower announced, as Truman had before him, that the government would be put back on a pay-as-it-went basis. Pointing out that Washington had spent less than its tax collections only four times since 1930 (in 1930, 1947, 1948, and 1951), Eisenhower emphasized the tie-up between military and economic strength by ordering his Secretary of the Treasury to attend all National Security Council meetings. In practice, the principal difference between Eisenhower's program and Truman's was that Eisenhower set the budget ceiling higher.

As a well-trained military officer, Eisenhower made heavy use of formal staff organization and procedure. His NSC meetings, for instance, were big operations, held twice a week or more often. (According to Washington Democratic Senator Henry Jackson, the whole effort was overorganized.)

In 1957, Wilson insisted that, during their nearly five years together, Eisenhower never once told him, "You have only so much money for Defense and you'll have to cut your military efforts down within it." But the implied promise to spend whatever is necessary for security has always, in times of relative peace, meant lots of different things to different people. What three independent military departments consider necessary always adds up to a good deal more than Presidents or even Secretaries of Defense consider necessary.

Eisenhower's flexible ceiling soon acquired considerable rigidity. He pounded in the first nails himself. Within a balanced budget, he said, military forces would rate a slice of funds based on which of their functions were most important to fundamental military policy. The priorities came out, in order: nuclear retaliatory or strike forces; forces deployed overseas; forces to keep the sea lanes open; forces to protect the United States from air attack; last, and not much more than least, the Reserve forces.

In other words, the paramount Pentagon missions were to be greater emphasis on deterrence, on improving the delivery and destructive power of nuclear weapons, and on air defense capability. This "new" program had begun to be formulated during a ten-day cruise on the Navy's luxury yacht, the *Sequoia*, in the spring of 1953 by the new Chiefs of Staff–elect. In six months, they would be responsible for carrying it out.

Labeled the "New Look" (the same tag used that year for the fashion in women's dresses), the program implied more revolutionary changes than it actually contained. Eisenhower's New Look was, in fact, only Truman's air-power doctrine with the price forced higher by more advanced, more expensive technology. It did introduce one new feature. Truman had kept postponing what was called the "year of maximum crisis," because the Pentagon kept falling behind schedule getting prepared for it. Eisenhower announced that in the future, "No predicted critical danger date could be taken as decisive in Defense planning."

Examining the New Look, each Service wanted to know, "What's in it for me?" Wilson picked up Eisenhower's budget hammer and pounded a few nails into the flexible ceiling himself. After the President reminded the Services that he was giving Defense a total budget three times larger than it had ever been before in peacetime, Wilson began what the White House euphemistically termed "a reallocation of resources among the five prime functional military missions."

Predictably, the Army's new money requests were chopped first, although the cuts seemed more rugged on paper than they were in fact, since the Army still had a surplus of several billion dollars left over from Korea. With a demobilization drop from 1.5 million to 1 million men between December, 1953 and June, 1955, the Army's spending allowance also plummeted from a high of nearly $13 billion to $7 billion. Navy and Marine manpower size in the same period went from 1 million to 870,000 and the Navy's fiscal year 1955 budget (July, 1954 to June, 1955) fell $1.5 billion from the previous fiscal year's $11.2 billion. On Eisenhower's priority shopping list, over half the new Navy funds were earmarked to be spent on Naval aviation.

Air Force manpower climbed from 950,000 in 1953 to 970,000 in 1955. The Air Force budget climbed in fiscal 1955 to $16.4 billion. By fiscal 1957, it was spending half the $36 billion total Defense budget—five times what it had had to spend in 1950.

Throughout 1953 and 1954, the Army grew sadder and sadder, and the Navy got edgy. Tensions started rising again. As Carey Randall summed up: "In the field there was little problem. The element that resisted any kind of control was right in Washington. The squabbles rose out of competition for the dollar."

Anticipating trouble, Ohio Senator Robert Taft (the "Mr. Republican" Eisenhower had beaten for the Presidential nomination in 1952) warned in 1953, "I have no confidence whatsoever in their [the military leaders] judgment or their ability to break away from recommendations they have made in the past." Eisenhower had already gone to work on that possibility.

One of his first executive orders in 1953 set up the President's Advisory Committee on Government Organization, informally titled the Rockefeller Committee, after its chairman, Nelson Rockefeller. It was a driving force in analyzing, reshaping, and pushing nine reorganization plans for 1953 originally put together by the Budget Bureau's office of management and organization. Plan No. 6 covered the Defense Department. It drew heavily on recommendations left by Robert Lovett the year before. Exploiting a power of the Presidency provided by Congress (that Presidential reorganization plans automatically become effective within sixty days after submission to Congress, unless disapproved by concurrent resolution of both Houses), the Rockefeller Reorganization Plan No. 6 was sent to Congress for approval on April 30, 1953.

Annoyed that the White House had used reorganization-plan powers rather than formal legislation to request the changes, Congress spent most of its time arguing that point of etiquette rather than the substantive changes themselves. Plan No. 6 went into effect on June 30. It abolished the various Boards, transferred their work to the Secretary, and authorized him to appoint a General Counsel and eight Assistant Secretaries to cover separate pieces of the total Defense business—i.e., research and engineering, manpower, comptroller, supply and logistics, properties and installations, international security affairs, public affairs, and health and medical (that mainly to placate the American Medical Association lobby). Dubbed "vice presidents," these assistants, backed in each case by staffs numbering anywhere from 50 to as many as 350 persons, gave the Secretary of Defense far more horsepower for detailed investigation of Service activities than he had been able to command with just three assistant secretaries.

The Secretary also gained authority to appoint a Service as *his* executive agent to run a unified command or other Defense-wide project. Until then, the Joint Chiefs had been naming one of *their* members to such tasks. Since that Chief, whoever he might be, had reported directly to them from his own Service, the effect had been to cut even the Secretary of his own Service out of the picture.

Along with these changes, the Chairman of the Joint Chiefs was given control of the Joint Staff and its director, a control Omar Bradley had maintained before by sheer force of personality. The Chairman was also given the right to approve Service appointments to the Joint Staff, meaning that he could now keep the Services from dumping any deadwood there, as they had been doing. Seemingly unimportant in itself, this control had significance as the start of the trend toward centralization of military authority in the Joint Chiefs' Chairman. He moved one step closer to heading, for the Secretary, a truly unified military staff, one step closer to being the main contact between the separate Chiefs and their President, their Defense Secretary, and their National Security Council.

Gaining these powers did not mean that Wilson could perform instant miracles. As one result of the reorganization, the Secretary of Defense was supposed to be able to do more with less people. Yet, even after abolishing the cumbersome board and committee structure, combining similar or related functions among his new staff offices, streamlining procedures, clarifying responsibilities, and reassigning some activities to the military departments, it still took almost his full tour in office for Wilson to shave his immediate staff down from 3,100 military and civilian personnel to 2,400.

Because he concentrated on internal management, Wilson was running only a part of the Defense organization—when in fact, at his level, foreign policy and military plans, and their budget support, should be inseparable. But, if he deferred to Eisenhower and the Chiefs on military matters and to Dulles on politico-military affairs, he deferred to no one on getting the most for the money. His greatest contribution to Defense was based on his talents as a production expert. "He always had trouble understanding the military operation, but in the area of procurement he had forgotten more than most guys knew," said one official. Besides telling military buyers how to negotiate contracts with industry, Wilson used money as his main weapon for program support and as a policing vehicle in running the business. "He was always concerned with lead time, programming, budgeting, just about everything McNeil was interested in."

To McNeil, "Money was where all the programs came together. We tried to use it to point up problems that needed solving." Once given the military program by the White House, "the dollar is about the only common denominator to measure effort and gauge progress," he said. "All you have to know is whether costs are running somewhere in line with original estimates."

"Wilson knew enough about production," added a general, "that we all felt we could take his advice." In one case, the Secretary cut delivery lead time on certain aircraft types from thirty months to between sixteen and eighteen. "By the time he left," a procurement expert said "the way the Air Force was bragging about it, you'd have thought they dreamed it up."

With Wilson's experience in business and McNeil's in Defense, after a couple of years working together, they made a good pair. Between them, they knew what the Services were doing in Defense, knew, as one observer put it, "where the bodies were buried." In effect, McNeil became Wilson's general manager and, as such, exercised more influence than he would admit—at least, publicly.

Both men understood the importance of lead time. As one budget officer explained:

> The Services would yell when we'd lop $5 billion off their money requests each year by shaving a little, for instance, off each of that rash of new missile developments they were always starting. But Wilson knew if the Services started say twenty projects they claimed would cost $2 billion total, the real cash outlay any given year, assuming they stayed within estimates, was not going to be more than say $1.8 billion total.
>
> We just took some of the cushion out before they began. You can always count on three or four projects falling behind and not finishing the race on time.

Wilson did not mind a little inter-Service competition when hardware developments were still in the testing stage, but he was death on duplication when new weapons reached the far more expensive production line. From his GM experience, he was convinced that a certain element of competition tends to promote excellence. "The problem," said Randall, "is not that competition existed, but when do you cut it off?" The pressure on him to be right when he answered that question didn't rattle him particularly. He agreed with Truman, who had said, "If you can't take the heat, stay out of the kitchen." In typical engineer fashion, he would listen to a set of figures and, "Then," according to a frequent observer of his routine, "all of a sudden, out would come his slide rule and he'd start asking questions."

The flaw in his running of the Pentagon was not with his slide rule. The trouble was that the Services didn't view money quite the way Wilson did.

Just before the 1952 national elections, the United States had set off a hydrogen bomb more powerful than even the scientists had expected. To military technologists, the new bomb meant a potential revolution in weaponry. Now, enough destruction could be housed in a light enough warhead to make sense of intercontinental ballistic missile programs, shelved in 1949 as "impractical." Shortly thereafter, the Army revealed it had built an anti-aircraft guided missile that "could destroy an entire bomber fleet with one atomic explosion."

Less than two years later, Russia began her own series of H-bomb tests. Whoever developed an intercontinental ballistic missile (ICBM), engineers told the Pentagon, would be able to hurl halfway around the world in thirty minutes the same devastation at less cost than it would take a bomber four hours to deliver. Washington launched crash programs to get such a weapon before the Communists did.

With only slightly less crusading zeal than they'd shown warring over control of the A-bomb in 1949, all three Services in Washington fought for pre-eminence in the missile business. They all had read the Eisenhower priority shopping list. They knew where the money and influence lay. This new Cold War contest was being fought in the laboratory and factory, not on the battlefield. Industry, particularly in aircraft, missiles, and parts of the electronics field, became almost a part of the military. Literally billions of dollars were at stake. More to the point, this new technological revolution was fogging up roles and missions. The Army called the ICBM "artillery." The Air Force said it was "simply an unmanned aerial delivery system." (The Navy was willing to go along with either label, because it could properly use the weapon, no matter what it was called.)

Science had been interfering with clean-cut descriptions of separate Service roles and missions for a long time. Even in 1947, the subject of roles and missions was so touchy it was left out of the National Security Act. Instead, it was enunciated in a supplemental Presidential executive order—for one reason, to preserve a flexibility the Pentagon might need to meet changing military situations in the future. Another reason for that move had been that the Services could not agree on what their separate roles and missions should be—mainly because none of them wanted to give up any possible claims to the then new hardware.

Forrestal's first session with the Chiefs at Key West hadn't clarified much about roles and missions. Neither had later Forrestal and Johnson meetings at Key West, Newport, and in West Virginia. A Wilson-sponsored meeting at Key West in 1953 didn't alter the situation much either, although, like Forrestal, Wilson took the Chiefs there "to get away from the phones and find out what they really thought."

By 1954, technology had shaken up the military environment even more—to a degree made clear in an Eisenhower remark that "The expression 'Tried and true' has been replaced by 'If it works, it's obsolete.'" The roles-and-missions paper that had looked all right to the Army in 1953 was dismaying in 1954. The Army had already been put down one notch by the priorities listed in Eisenhower's military platform, and then even more by the big budget cut they had been handed. (A few of the Washington Army's more superficial thinkers even began charging, in private, that their old leader was being hard on them just to avoid the accusation of favoritism toward his former Service.)

By 1955, the Services had long since turned to the press, as they habitually did, to state their independent cases, try to undermine Secretarial decisions. For a while, Wilson thought the flurry of articles was mainly the result of a higher-than-normal Pentagon collection of bright generals and admirals surrounded by bright young officers, all of whom wanted to write by-lined magazine articles. At first, he asked them to stop voluntarily.

"You ought to be too busy to sit around writing magazine pieces," he said. "Surely, you don't do it for the money." That remark was meant to smoke out the ones who were doing it for the money. The articles continued to crop up. Finally, he had to order the practice stopped. That controversial directive—a "gag," the military predictably labeled it—was one of the first signs that Wilson's honeymoon with the Pentagon staff was over.

The Army's main gripe in that rapidly developing missile era was that it was coming out a poor third in the Pentagon, although its missile experts, headed by former German citizen and V2 rocket scientist Wernher von Braun, were building the best hardware. The bitter Pentagon in-fighting over that point finally jumped into the open in the spring of 1955. Ridgway, who was retiring, anyway, got permission from Army Secretary Stevens to write directly to Wilson, denouncing the Wilson treatment of the Army.

A copy leaked to *The New York Times* was printed as an exclusive "open letter." Wilson saw it in the paper on his way to Quantico to the annual Joint Secretaries Conference. "Who's he writing to, me or the press?" Wilson snorted. "I can't deal with all his ideas on my way to Quantico."

Asked immediately by newsmen if Ridgway's blast would reopen the roles-and-missions directive of 1953, Wilson quipped, "I don't like to rehash old problems. It's like trying to make birth control retroactive." (The *Reader's Digest* picked up that comment, printed it, paid him $10 for it.)

Ridgway poured more fuel on his flame with a series in *Life* magazine. Wilson and Eisenhower were both shocked and disappointed. Wilson had never made a decision with which the majority of the Joint Chiefs hadn't agreed. Why, he challenged, should he be blamed for Ridgway's failure to convince them of the Army point of view?

One loyal Wilson aide said angrily, "As a field commander, Ridgway was fine. But a Chief of Staff has to go around selling people. That takes a different kind of talent than directing forces in battle. What Ridgway found out in the Pentagon was that you can't give an order there and expect to have everyone fall dead."

Ridgway was not the only Pentagon executive fighting Wilson. As the missile competition became more heated, Wilson got to feeling that the Services were all keeping two sets of books, one for him and one for themselves. He learned, for instance, that the Air Force had been working for eighteen months on the *Thor* intermediate range ballistic missile (IRBM for short) before they had an appropriation for it.

Such a move had been fairly easy to make. Total funding for missile development was huge. The field was virtually brand new and riddled with unknowns. On some projects, technical delays were causing a slow-down in planned spending rate. "They simply shifted money off lagging programs onto ones that could use it right away," said one budget expert.

What bothered Wilson most was that the Services always seemed to find the money for what they wanted to do, but never seemed to be able to for what he wanted. Part of his frustration: "You tell them not to do things—and they do them anyway."

In late November, 1956, he issued a "clarification" of the 1953 roles-and-missions directive. Prompted mostly by the inter-Service money competition and development duplications, the clarification was an attempt "to improve coordination," and set up a better balance of intra-Service effort. It mirrored the White House policy guidance the Services all, supposedly, had accepted. The military saw the "clarification" affecting their whole existence—which it did.

In the preamble, Wilson announced that whatever weapons were assigned a Service in peacetime were not necessarily the only hardware it would be permitted to use in war. He also advised that just because one Service developed a piece of equipment, it didn't acquire proprietary rights to the operational use of that equipment.

Then Wilson ticked off who could do what. The substance was that the Army's ability to roam was restricted. In future, Wilson said, the Army (which was rapidly replacing the Air Force it had lost in 1947 with a new one) would not be allowed to operate a fixed-wing aircraft heavier than 5,000 pounds or helicopters weighing more than 20,000 pounds. That order pretty well limited Army pilots to flying light observation planes. Airlift of Army combat units and supplies into the battle area was to be an Air

Force, not an Army, responsibility, Wilson ordered. So was close air support.

The Army could handle short-range, point-to-point air defense, but area air defense was the Air Force's problem, or the Navy's if air defense was ship-based. Army missiles could have a range of no more than 200 miles. IRBM (1,500-mile) missiles, when operational, would be fired by the Air Force, or by the Navy if ship-based, but not by Army either way. And ICBM's (5,000 miles) were aerial delivery systems, not artillery, which the Air Force would command, too.

After another six months of Pentagon pushing and shoving over Wilson's "clarification," the squabble finally welled up almost to the proportions of the "Revolt of the Admirals." National headlines went to banner size in June, 1957, when an Army colonel in the Von Braun arena was courtmartialed for allegedly handing missile secrets to newspapermen. His defense, reminiscent of 1949: he was supporting his argument that the Army knew more about the missile business than the Air Force.

Wearily, Wilson reiterated his 1956 criteria on who was responsible for what in hardware. By then, he had become the first Secretary of Defense to stay with a President for his full four-year term. The unceasing pressures were beginning to tell. Although most of the United States did not know it yet, he and the rest of the Pentagon knew they were in the midst of a missile race with Russia. Believing that, under the circumstances, his nation might not survive an error in judgment by its Defense Secretary, Wilson handed in his resignation. At a small dinner, he told friends, "I'm leaving because I found myself making decisions from fatigue."

Unfortunately for Wilson's score card as Defense Secretary, the Services apparently did not begin to recognize until he was leaving that their arsenal needed a great deal more in it than the weapons of nuclear holocaust.

IX

Neil McElroy

[OCTOBER, 1957–DECEMBER, 1959]

WHEN THE PRESIDENT OF Procter & Gamble, six-foot four-inch Neil Hosler McElroy, stood next to short Charlie Wilson, they didn't seem to have much in common. But physical differences aside, they were a good deal alike. Each had run for a decade the top U.S. company in its field. Engineer Wilson's GM was building nearly half the cars on U.S. highways while salesman McElroy's P&G was producing half of all the products used to clean the cars, the people in them, and most of the clothes the people wore. (Each year, went one mystical computation, P&G "sells enough bars of Ivory Soap alone to give everyone in the world four baths.")

Generally credited with making P&G the leading merchant of cleanliness, McElroy was called "the nation's number one soap salesman" in a 1953 magazine story, which said, "he belongs to the new breed of scientific salesmen who base their selling not on emotional appeal but on facts and figures." Like Wilson, he wore conservative clothes, was methodically thorough, enjoyed traveling a lot to meet new people, and had a quick smile he used often.

Born in Berea, Ohio, sixty miles from Wilson's birthplace, he was raised, like Wilson, by school-teacher parents who advised, "God will provide if you will get out and scratch." Tough minded even then, he used to hold his breath if he didn't get his own way —until his equally tough-minded mother cured him by throwing a pan of cold water in his face. He worked in a can factory, then a laundry, shoveled snow, mowed lawns, had $1,000 saved by the time he finished high school.

Like his two brothers before him, he won a scholarship to Harvard, where he organized a dance band to help pay his way through (he played piccolo and piano). He earned a B average in economics, was substitute center on the basketball team and president of his club, became adept at staying up all night winning low-stakes bridge and poker games. Graduated in 1925, he returned home to Cincinnati for the summer, and got a $100-a-month mail clerk's job in P&G headquarters. He planned to go back to Harvard Business School in the fall, but he never made it.

Being mail clerk meant "I was supposed to open and read everybody's mail. It's one way of finding out what's going on." Hard-working and ambitious, he got his chance to move up when his advertising department boss began missing work often to tend a sick wife, leaving him in charge. "It was the kind of situation bound to lead to the hothouse development of a man—or break him completely."

Promotion manager by 1929, he stayed with P&G thirty-two years, climbing successively from manager of advertising and promotion to director and vice president of advertising to vice president and general manager. He was named company president in 1948. Long before that, he had convinced top management that the way to keep fast-growing P&G growing even more was to have it compete with itself. The company was virtually a collection of separate entities, each with its own boss. Like Wilson at GM, McElroy saw competition pay off. Three years after McElroy reached the top, P&G owned 40 per cent of the U.S. soap market, pioneered in and grabbed off 69 per cent of the new (in 1951) detergent field.

Though prosperity kept P&G in continual hot water with Washington's antitrust bureaucracy, his check-and-balance organization produced a batch of new cleansers (Duz, Tide, Joy, Cheer, Spic and Span, Shasta, Drene, Ivory Snow). To sell them, P&G became one of the country's biggest advertisers, spending roughly $15 million a year on newspapers and magazines, another $30 million on network radio and television. The bulk of it financed "soap operas."

Under fire from do-gooders for supporting "such trivia," McElroy answered, "The problem of improving the literary tastes of the people is the problem of the schools. The people who listen to our programs aren't intellectuals. They're ordinary people, good people, who win wars for us, produce our manufactured products and grow our food. They use a lot of soap."

Wilson and McElroy seemed at odds on only one major point. Unlike Wilson (or his Pentagon reputation, anyway) the president of P&G nurtured his internally competing operation with a strong dose of exploratory research. A high six out of every hundred employees worked on the research end of the business. McElroy was proud of the results and noted, when he became Secretary of Defense on October 9, 1957, that 70 per cent of P&G's income that year was from products that had not existed twelve years earlier.

His drive carried him well beyond the office. Cincinnati's top joiner, he belonged to local and national civic organizations that ranged from the National Citizen's Council for Better Schools through the Cincinnati summer opera to the Rockwood Historical and Philosophical Society (a Cincinnati executives' poker club). As chairman of the 1955 White House Conference on Education, he impressed Eisenhower with his sharp mind and ability to make things happen. Once, he raised on the spot $50,000 in pledges from thirty top Cincinnati businessmen after they had listened at a McElroy-arranged luncheon to an Eisenhower appeal for aid to education. At one meeting of the Education Conference, McElroy arrived early and was introduced for the first time to the score of other Conference members called into Washington from all over the country. Then, he walked them into Eisenhower's office and introduced each one to the President without flubbing a name.

In early July, 1957, he was vacationing in Arizona when Eisenhower's special assistant Sherman Adams reached him by phone and asked him to take over the Pentagon. McElroy said he would think about it. He called P&G, put some people to work exploring a possible leave of absence and the possible effect on his stock options, his investments, and so on. After several trips to Washington talking to Wilson and others in Defense, McElroy called the White House on August 6 and accepted the job, with the condition that, if P&G dropped its handful of Defense contracts to avoid a conflict of interest, he would take a leave of absence from the company rather than quit. Eisenhower agreed. McElroy said he would serve just two years. Eisenhower granted that condition as well.

McElroy finally moved up from head of the nation's twenty-ninth largest corporation to become boss of the world's biggest business simply because he couldn't refuse. He took over an organization that paid as much for one nuclear submarine as P&G's entire $67 million net earnings, an outfit whose operating costs for just ten days equaled P&G's 1957 net sales of $1.156 billion. As it had been for Wilson, the move was expensive. It cost McElroy a 92 per cent cut in his $285,000-a-year salary.

The day of the announcement, humorists in the Ft. Myer, Virginia, officers' club, insisted that Wilson's only advice to McElroy was, "Now remember, don't ever say 'What's good for Tide is good for the country.' "

Out at P&G, comments were more serious. "Just as he remembers names and faces," pointed out a P&G official, "Mac remembers facts, and woe be to anyone in the Pentagon who doesn't remember that Mac can remember every damn thing he ever saw. He can look at a page with hundreds of figures on it and get to the source of any error. He has the same ability to detect a flaw in an argument."

Three weeks after McElroy told Eisenhower he would take the Defense Secretary post, Russia announced it had successfully launched a "super-long-distance intercontinental multistage ballistic missile." The ICBM, they said, "flew at a very high, unprecedented altitude . . . landed in the target area." On October 4, McElroy was at the end of a month-long, worldwide tour of U.S. military bases. He was having dinner at the Army's Huntsville, Alabama, ballistic missile center when rocket scientist Wernher von Braun was called from the table and returned grim-faced in a few minutes to announce that Russia had just successfully placed a satellite in orbit around the earth. McElroy's whole Pentagon career had been charted before he was even sworn in.

The following month, the Communists put up a six-times-heavier *Sputnik II*. The 1,118-pound capsule carried a live dog. Although it was the animal that got public attention, the launch told U.S. missile experts they were much closer to a neck-and-neck race with Russia to build an ICBM than they had thought. The power necessary to push a half-ton payload into orbit was the power necessary to push an ICBM off the ground. Russia was still some distance away from being able to hit the United States with a missile attack. But the subtle difference between military security and space satellites was largely lost on the general public, shaken and suddenly clamoring to know "What's happened to us?"

Congress accused Defense Deputy Secretary Donald Quarles of head-in-the-sand complacency when he insisted, "The military significance of this particular phase of the [missile race] competition has been exaggerated."

To a rattled Free World, blessed with the infallible perception of hindsight, such talk was clear proof that national security had been victimized for years with what one writer called "a track record of error which any fool should have been able to avoid."

"How can you exaggerate the military significance of a test by Russia of an intercontinental ballistic missile?" Congress demanded of Quarles.

He answered: "You can exaggerate it by failing at the time to take into account all of the other factors . . . our very great manned aircraft striking power at that time, and the fact that . . . what we know about [the test] does not entitle one to believe that they have, either had at that time, or will have in the near future, a striking power based on this kind of development."

But, the "important thing to note," he added, was "the rate at which they have moved forward . . . this is a challenge to us it is very important for us to meet."

The reaction to that statement was violent. Explaining why he did not want to talk about *Sputniks*, he said, in a later speech: "You will understand my reluctance when I remind you that so far no one in the Administration has succeeded in saying anything about them that the critics didn't tear to pieces."

Quarles also volunteered a bit of sound advice markedly like Marshall's advice to the nation in the early stages of World War II. (Indicative of the changing times, the advice a general gave in 1939 came from an engineer eighteen years later.) Said Quarles: "I find in the existence of the first satellites no cause for national alarm. In this respect I am disagreeing with many people who have been saying, 'Let's beat them. Let's put up a bigger satellite. Let's shoot something farther.' And 'Let's reorganize.'

"In this present technological competition it is imperative we not be sidetracked from our prime security objectives by extraneous or irrelevant issues. The overriding objective of our present effort must be to maintain adequate military forces in being—adequate to deter military aggression or to defeat its purposes if our deterrent should fail.

"After all, we are facing the very real threat of existing Communist armed forces. Russia alone has more than 170 divisions; her western satellites have another 70; and the Communist Far East around 200—a grand total of around 440 divisions. When we add to this the Communist-bloc combat aircraft strength of more than 25,000, including the most advanced types, and her 500 submarines we see a very formidable capability.

"We must not be panicked or pushed into any sudden dispersion of effort which would scatter our talents and resources in an unprofitable or wasteful manner. We must not be talked into 'hitting the moon with a rocket,' for example, just to be first, unless by doing so we stand to gain something of real scientific or military significance."

Quarles' opinions deserved more than the flat Congressional renunciation they got. Engineer Quarles had, in a sense, grown up close to the missile business. He had worked for Western Electric Company since 1920, studying theoretical physics on the side. During World War II, Quarles concentrated on military electronics and radar for the company. Both fields were important to military missile studies going on as early as 1942. After the war, he worked on missiles for Western's Bell Telephone Laboratories. Then, in 1952, he became president of Western's Sandia Corporation making warheads for the Atomic Energy Commission.

Appointed Assistant Secretary of Defense (Research and Development) in 1953, he was named Secretary of the Air Force in 1955 and boosted to Deputy Secretary of Defense in 1957. He knew as well as anyone that, for all the publicity they receive in the last few months of testing, new military weapons do not spring full-blown overnight. (The B-17 bomber, for example, had taken ten years to develop, the B-29 and B-36 nearly as long.)

He was aware that, until 1952, all three Services had concentrated most of their energy on developing a conglomeration of small missiles and rockets, ground-launched to hit aircraft, fired from aircraft to hit other planes, fired from aircraft to hit ground targets. Why, Congress demanded, had the United States "ignored" what Russia clearly had not—the development of a 5000-

mile-range intercontinental ballistic missile? The facts, Quarles tried to explain, were that a three-year, $2.3 million study into the feasibility of making such an ICBM had died in 1949 because there were too many unknowns. Could a guidance possibly be made that would steer the missile accurately to a target 5000 miles away? Could a warhead be designed that wouldn't be burned to ashes by friction on re-entering the atmosphere from airless outer space? Was there a power plant big enough to boost the whole vehicle up to speeds of 17,000 miles per hour, which was the initial momentum required to lob it halfway around the world?

But the biggest question, until 1952, was pinned to the warhead. To throw a one-pound bomb several thousand miles would take about 200 pounds of launching missile. The first atomic warhead weighed 9,000 pounds. Constructing a 1.8 million-pound missile to haul it was, compared to using a bomber, not only frightfully expensive but militarily risky. Said one expert, "The idea of being able at a reasonable price to hit anything halfway around the world with any military effect seemed about like trying to hit the eye of a moving needle with a limp thread."

As a result, military long-range missile research centered mainly on unmanned aircraft with a bomb-tipped, short-range missile mounted on the nose, a rocket in the tail for takeoff, a jet engine to fly it to target. The Air Force worked on two such aircraft, the Navy on one. Then, in 1952, the technological dam broke.

That year, the United States exploded the first hydrogen bomb. It generated more power than even its developers had anticipated. Further tests the following spring indicated that the "wasteful, inefficient idea" of developing an ICBM now seemed to make a lot of practical sense. By February, 1954, a Strategic Missiles Evaluation committee had reported to Wilson that the Pentagon would soon have a thermonuclear bomb lighter but more powerful than atomic warheads; that guidance, re-entry, and other ICBM headaches could be solved in a few years; and that the ICBM and the H-bomb should be married as soon as possible.

Quarles, who had left Western Electric five months earlier to work for Wilson, endorsed the report nine days after it hit his desk. Management machinery was set in motion to accelerate ICBM development. The Air Force organized a Western Development Division in California and gave its commanding Brigadier General Bernard Schriever a hand-picked team of 400 officers.

Within months, his operation involved seventeen major contractors, 200 prime subcontractors, thousands of suppliers, in all nearly 90,000 persons hunting answers for what was now called the *Atlas* ICBM.

At least part of the financing was to come from cutting out all the duplications in smaller missiles. In mid-1953, Wilson had ordered a Service review "to standardize" on one missile in each category "for production and use by all the military departments." The only problem was that all the Services had jumped into the missile business eagerly when it began, but when it came time to choose the type to cancel none of them could make the tough decision.

While that argument was going on between Wilson and the military, the Pentagon started buying insurance in ICBM's. To guard against Russia being already well along in ICBM work, Defense began an intermediate range (1,500-mile) missile project. It could be finished sooner than *Atlas* and, deployed overseas, filling the security gap until *Atlas* was in operation. Target date for completion of the ICBM was late 1958, of the IRBM early 1957.

By November, 1965, Wilson had approved buying even more insurance. A *Titan* ICBM development had begun. In the IRBM field, Wilson ordered the Army to build the *Jupiter* and the Air Force to exploit *Atlas* experience to develop the *Thor*. The Navy was told it would fire the *Jupiter*, too, which, to the Navy seemed sheer insanity. All these missiles were fired by hypersensitive liquid oxygen fuel. Heat from just one cigarette could ignite a missile carried on shipboard and obliterate the whole boat.

Within a year, the Navy had convinced the Pentagon that it (a) should put IRBM's in the huge new nuclear-powered submarines and (b) use nonvolatile solid propellant missile fuel, which, though less well researched, was Navy's only practical answer. The Pentagon agreed. In 1946, Navy's *Polaris* became the third IRBM development going.

The reason for all these project duplications: with so many engineering unknowns in rocket engines, guidance, nose cone reentry, etc., each project would take slightly different approaches to the problems. The idea was to increase the chance to avoid delays if one proposed technical solution on the drawing board turned out to be no good when tested. (Overlapping as the projects seemed, the duplication was not, at that, much insurance. With just one major problem to solve, engineers on the Manhattan project in 1940 tried four different ways to unlock the atomic bomb secret before they finally found a key.)

Wilson had organized a Defense Ballistic Missile Committee to coordinate inter-Service project efforts, and see that technical knowledge as it developed on one program was distributed to the others. He named a special assistant for guided missiles so IRBM/ICBM work didn't bog down in Washington red tape. Each Service named one, too, for the same reason. The Cape Canaveral test facilities, rudimentary in 1954, began to look, said one reporter, "like a high-class, chromium-plated amusement park."

The White House gave these missile programs highest priority. From 1946 through mid-1953, the United States had spent nearly $3.5 billion on all missile work, but only $7 million on IRBM/ICBM projects—less than the money spent in those years to support the farm price of peanuts. Spending on IRBM's and ICBM's jumped to a one-year total of $14 million in 1954, jumped again to $161 million for the fiscal year ending in June, 1955, reached $515 million the following year, and soared to $1.365 billion for the twelve months ending in June, 1957.

All this spending was wreaking havoc with Eisenhower's attempts to balance the Federal budget. But he knew he had no choice. Whoever got ICBM's in sufficient numbers first would change the world balance of power. Weapons like the crossbow, the musket, and the machine gun had each taken decades to revolutionize military strategy and tactics. The ICBM was doing the same thing in less than eight years. In 1945, a scientist had said, "Can you imagine what an atomic bomb in Hitler's hands *first* would have meant in World War II?" The same thinking, applied to Russia, fit missiles.

As some awareness of the missile race leaked out to the general public, Washington, at least, picked up a tendency to jump after any new Russian announcement—and usually in the wrong direction. The results for Defense leadership were aggravating distractions. Both Quarles and Wilson seemed convinced, in 1956, that these distractions were just what the Communists wanted.

One such diversionary fuss started with a 1955 May Day celebration in Moscow, when Russia flew what appeared to be her counterpart to the B-52 over the Kremlin. By mid-1956, with national elections warming up, Democratic Senator Stuart Symington launched a Senate investigation into the state of U.S. air power. His committee's allegation was that the Republican administration had allowed the United States to fall behind in bomber strength. The "Bomber Gap" looked like a budding campaign issue.

Air Force Secretary Quarles tried to take some steam out of the inquiry by arguing, "In 1959, the B-47 with tanker support will remain the largest force of intercontinental bombers in the active inventory." Moreover, the United States already had 60 B-52's and would be building approximately 500 more within the next two years. With the worldwide sprawl of bases from which these bombers took off, he said, "no aggressor can reasonably expect to knock out" such a force on the ground and thus avoid retaliatory devastation. Besides, the so-called Tactical Air Command aircraft were not just common old fighter planes. "They can carry A-weapons the effect of which is huge indeed."

Added Air Force Chief of Staff Nathan Twining: Even if Russian bombers attacked, which he thought unlikely in 1956, "our present-day fighters would have no problem with them." Furthermore, he said, how many bombers the United States built was not decided by how many the Russians had. Rather, what bombers the United States needed was determined by what it would take to get through Russian anti-aircraft defenses with enough bombers left to destroy all strategic targets.

But, fretted the committee, hadn't Strategic Air Command's General Curtis LeMay warned that the Russian *Bison* was comparable to the B-52?

Wilson replied, "I don't like to, you know, quarrel over words, but comparable according to the dictionary means capable of being compared, and General LeMay said they were comparable and he is correct because they are both heavy jet bombers, and they are comparable.

"They are capable of being compared. But when you compare them, you find that our B-52 is superior, and also I will say this: that if the situation was reversed and their *Bison* was as much better than our B-52 as our B-52 is better than their *Bison*, we would all be greatly worried."

The Senators could not be calmed. First, Washington Senator Henry Jackson (whose home state was headquarters for the company building B-52's) stabbed at Wilson with, "Isn't it a fact that we knew or should have known, in light of the [Russian] atomic explosion in August, 1949, that they would be building long-range, modern jet bombers to deliver the bombs they were manufacturing? Isn't that an assumption that our leaders should have made at that time? I do not understand why you indulge in the assumption they were building a defensive air force."

The transcript of the hearing continued (Wilson cutting in first):

"That is what they are doing."

"Well, but you discovered later that you were wrong, that the intelligence estimates were off, and you know that is a fact?"

"No."

"Suddenly didn't we discover on May 1, 1955, with this huge [actually, perhaps thirteen in number] Soviet fly-by of *Bison* bombers, that we had miscalculated on the production of intercontinental jet bombers [by] the Soviets?"

"I am sure that the Soviets showed us purposely about all they had."

Back across the Potomac, Defense was moving very close to its missile answers. In September, 1956, a *Jupiter* test vehicle was fired. It rose 680 miles, traveled 3,300 miles down the Cape Canaveral firing range at a maximum speed of 13,000 miles an hour, and hit where it was aimed. During the same time period, the Air Force had learned how to make a warhead that would not burn into ashes as it re-entered the atmosphere.

Confidence picked up in U.S. ability to be ready in time. The Pentagon started chopping off insurance programs. Four small missile projects were dumped after a total of $276.8 million had been spent on them. One Air Force airplane-missile, the *Navaho*, was scrapped after costing $679.8 million. Pentagon top management could see its way out of the woods. With *Jupiter*'s success making duplication unnecessary, *Thor* became the odds-on favorite for cancellation in the IRBM field. Whispers started that the *Titan* ICBM would follow.

By then, at least one gravy-train was running. "Industry was really wasting money on overtime," complained one Pentagon official. "So were labor unions, going on wildcat strikes to get their way. They put a gun to our heads, but what could we do? It didn't seem to make any difference to them that this was a race for national survival we were in." Wilson clamped restrictions on the use and abuse of overtime.

Then *Sputnik I* went up.

The next day, October 5, Defense officials knew from the electrified public reaction that "We'd have been lynched if we had tried to cancel anything. It would have been political suicide."

Four days later, Neil McElroy was sworn in. His honeymoon in office was not just with the Pentagon but with the whole United States. He looked good taking control, in part, at least, because the nation badly wanted him to look good. Not since George Marshall had a change in Defense authority stirred such hope. And not since Louis Johnson had an outgoing Secretary been hit so hard for what he'd done.

Inadvertently, Wilson had stated why the year before. In a press conference probing for his opinion of Air Force–Army infighting over control of missiles, he had noted, "A good bit of discussion now is over what you might call paper missiles, the things going on down in the future. Now some of our missiles are out of that category, but others are not. They are just things that we think we will have X months or years from now, and you can always get a bigger argument when you haven't got the facts."

The Congress, the public, and the press, in October, 1957, were quite willing to give him an argument. Some of his flip press conference remarks came back to haunt him in retirement. Once, Wilson had cautioned on research and development, "as the field broadens, we must be more selective." Still, he added, R&D spending from 1954 through 1957 was two and a half times larger than it had been in the pre-Korean period. Moreover, he told a reporter, the military was spending $5.2 billion on R&D in 1957 compared to $3.4 billion in 1955. "That's a lot of money to spend on research, young fella," he said.

After *Sputnik*, newspapers again quoted the remark, using it as proof of Wilson's negative attitude toward research and his "shortsighted" reason for chopping $1 billion out of Service R&D requests in 1957. They overlooked the fact that practically all the slashing had been on projects other than ICBM's. When McElroy restored, on October 28, $170 million in basic research funds, an anxious America called it major progress that corrected one reason for U.S. failure in the space business.

Even when McElroy said a decision was against his better judgment—but he was going ahead anyway on the urging of his military experts—Congress and the public nodded approval. Since mid-development of the ICBM, the Air Force had been working on what it called the "concurrency concept." Basically, that meant scrapping the standard routine of waiting until a weapon had been proven in testing before starting to train operators, build launch pads, buy and store spare parts. Instead, to be off at a run, training and stockpiling of parts and construction of launch facilities all were in production while the missile was still being tested and modified.

A month after he took charge of the Pentagon, McElroy warned of the concept: "This is being done for one reason only . . . to buy time . . . I feel confident we are going to be questioned 12 months from now, when the atmosphere may very possibly have changed, as to why this seemed like the right thing to do. . . .

"I regret . . . these urgent programs cannot go through . . . the normal kind of testing and development which would let you make a decision that would be tighter.

"We have moved [into production] on *Atlas, Thor, Jupiter,* and *Polaris* ahead of the completion of the research and development phase of the programs. [That] is not the basis on which people would move in industry. At least, I would not have moved that way in my former connection with industry."

The rush was all right with the U.S. public, which was even more worried about U.S. security in 1957 than the Pentagon had been in 1954. Influential columnist James Reston in *The New York Times* noted that there had been in the past "no analysis of the threat of Soviet technological gains, or disorder in the Pentagon, or the need for a more sympathetic Government attitude toward men of brains, or the need for stronger leadership at the top that [had] not been available to the White House for years."

In its second cover story on Neil McElroy, in January, 1958, *Time* magazine assured its readers: "In the masculine Pentagon world, McElroy is a man's man: he can be a two-fisted bourbon drinker, barely manages to suppress a lifelong passion for shooting craps, has a short-fuse temper and can use four-letter language that does not spell T-I-D-E."

That, thought a frightened Free World, ought to take care of the inter-Service bickering over command of missiles that was allegedly another of the causes for U.S. space failure.

On October 18, McElroy lifted the overtime restrictions on top priority programs. On October 30, the Defense Science Board was enlarged to twenty-eight members from civilian life "to assure the swifter application of scientific research results to military matters." Five days after Russia successfully launched *Sputnik II* (with a dog in it), the Army was brought into the satellite business with top priority: Army officials would orbit *Explorer I* in no more than ninety days. (Eighty-four days later, on January 31, they succeeded. But by then, the psychological war with Russia had already been lost.)

On October 12, 1957, Defense issued a revised policy on basic research amounting essentially, said one spokesman, to "correcting past Army and Air Force shortsightedness in not giving widespread recognition to its men with a special interest in and competence for R&D."

On October 15, Defense set up a new Director of Guided Missiles. The press promptly called him a "Czar," and McElroy promptly said he wasn't. McElroy sent a note to the Services saying he wanted to "assure you of my constant availability to assist in any way the resolution of problems you may encounter."

On November 25, Lyndon Johnson called the first Senate committee hearings on why the United States was behind in the missile-space race. The House announced that it also would investigate. Two days after that, McElroy said both *Thor* and *Jupiter* had come so far down the road they would be produced for deployment overseas, and he added he was organizing an Advanced Research Projects Agency, manned by the "best brains in the Services," to handle projects, viz. space and anti-missile missile work at first, until they were well enough developed to be turned over to a military department. His implied reason was to gain tighter control over how the Services exploited, or failed to exploit, modern technology in the embryonic stages when its combat value was still unclear.

Lyndon Johnson enthused, "More decisions have been made in the Pentagon in the last six weeks than in the last six years."

Wrote a normally complaining columnist, "It begins to seem possible that the soap industry has miraculously given this lucky country a first-rate Secretary of Defense."

Both comments were a little wide of the mark. McElroy didn't plan any more than Wilson had to rule Defense with an iron, autocratic hand. "His concept of the job," said one P&G assistant, "was not going down there to be bright as hell on everything military. He felt you can't expect a man to step out of the soap business and become an expert in missiles in three weeks."

But, said Carey Randall, "I never saw a man whose learning curve was faster. One month, plus a few meetings in Washington, and he had a grasp of what was going on." McElroy had demonstrated his ability in the course of an early Johnson committee session when Symington introduced a letter he had written to the White House shortly after *Sputnik.* It was filled with detailed questions about the whole U.S. defense program. The letter had been referred to the Pentagon and had arrived the day before McElroy did. McElroy had discussed the lengthy reply, prepared in detail by various Pentagon staff members, before he signed it and sent it to Symington.

Symington had this letter, together with an eleven-page analysis of it, stuck underneath papers containing an incredible number of questions the Senator intended to ask McElroy. When Symington's turn came during the January, 1958, committee meetings, he started on his questions one afternoon at 4 o'clock. He was about halfway through the list when the hearings adjourned at 6:30.

The Johnson committee lawyer collared a McElroy assistant as the party was breaking up and asked, "Why on earth didn't Secretary McElroy explain that the letter was written just after he had taken office? He could have referred the questions to Quarles this afternoon and let him answer them."

The long-time McElroy worker replied, "You don't know McElroy. If he signs something, he knows what's in it, is prepared to defend it, and accepts it as his own."

Congress was still impressed with him the following spring. During House Appropriations committee hearings in April, 1958, on the fiscal 1959 Defense budget request, Congressman Dan Flood finally interrupted the pointed, detailed quizzing of McElroy with, "You are an extraordinary fellow. I have listened to my distinguished colleagues work you over for about three hours. They haven't put a glove on you. They never put a glove on you in the last three hours and they are not amateurs."

"Maybe they weren't trying, Mr. Flood."

"Oh, they were trying! Never mistake that. They tried. It is amazing. You are an amazing fellow."

The Pentagon thought he was a little amazing, too, at first. One small reason was having to keep a fresh chocolate cake in the

Pentagon mess for him. He had the unsettling habit of calling for a piece of it at breakfast time. "I figure eating cake in the morning doesn't hurt the waistline," he explained.

When he first moved into the Pentagon, he had four telephones on his desk: the white phone hooked up to the White House, the red phone tying him to all military command posts worldwide, the regular Pentagon phone, and a personal phone on his private home number at the Sheraton Park Hotel annex. He took the home phone out after the first month, simply because he was too busy to make any personal calls and was not using it.

Like several of his predecessors, he read voraciously, often getting up at 6 A.M. to pour through *The Washington Post*, *The New York Times*, and *The Wall Street Journal*. In the office by 8 A.M., he left at anytime from 6 to 8 P.M., taking a big briefcase of papers home to read. (Once, he walked in on a little [5′1″] TV repairman, who looked at the bulging valise, looked up at McElroy, and asked, "Getting a little behind in your work, maybe?")

In spite of staff efforts to cut down on the number of his social obligations, he accepted a lot of invitations to evening parties. He went, when he would rather have stayed home, partly because he felt he had an obligation to go and partly because he liked to mix with people. His Saturdays were spent in the office except when he announced, "Not this Saturday. I'm going to a Business Advisory Council meeting."

"He loves to talk business with businessmen," said a friend. "He gets his relaxation out of that—when he's not playing tennis."

In the office, he was "friendly, considerate, a kind of public relations type," to many of the staff—except when someone made a mistake. Because he put a great deal of confidence in what subordinates told him, an error passed along to him usually meant he would be tripped up in public. Then, back in the office, the jaw would set, the blue eyes would harden and he would warn, "I was embarrassed by that. I don't like to be embarrassed."

"You didn't make mistakes around him very often," said an aide, "or you just weren't around anymore."

He kept Wilson in the Defense sphere for a while, more out of concern for Wilson than because McElroy felt any real need for his advice. "He spent quite a little time with Charlie when he first came to Washington," said a friend, "and developed an affection for him." For two years or more, Wilson's wife had wanted him to leave the Pentagon. "McElroy didn't believe Charlie really wanted to leave the job at all."

Wilson apparently had caught, or McElroy felt he had, the same bug that had bitten most of his predecessors. "After most of them got a taste for the infinite difficulty of the job, they acquired an infection, a kind of malaria about it," philosophized one Pentagon hand. "It's the result of dedicated men dealing with life and death matters at the top and leaving undone work at the bottom when they depart."

"After swimming at breakneck speed for five years, Wilson had suddenly turned into a quiet backwater," said a McElroy aide. "McElroy just knew Charlie must feel kind of lost. He called Wilson every so often for a while, especially when he was about to do something that might look like reversal of a Wilson decision."

And the new Secretary worked even harder to take care of Congress. Indeed, in his first several months in office, Congress didn't let him do much but testify. The Johnson committee demanded big chunks of his time. So did Vinson's House committee, forcing him to repeat much of what he was telling Johnson concurrently. The reason for all this work of McElroy's was neatly put by Vinson in January, 1958, when he asked, "What can Congress do to accelerate the entire missile program . . . besides appropriate money?"

The answer was "Not much." The rest of the lengthy inquiries were spent in fretting over how well the United States was advancing. For much of the next two years, McElroy appeared before a raft of committees on both sides of the Hill: Appropriations, Foreign Affairs, Space, Preparedness, Government Operations, and special subcommittees. One aide, who tried in vain to cut out some of the duplication, said, "Committees called when there was really no need for him to be there. They were only out to establish their prestige, or get some press coverage."

Outside his immediate office staff few knew what trouble McElroy took to prepare for one of these quizzes. A first appearance meant a prepared statement. In the case of the Armed Services or Appropriations Committees, it could run from twenty-five to forty pages, loaded with hard facts and plans. McElroy had to be prepared to explain or defend every word, every shade of meaning, as well as the specific program he wanted approval for.

To warm up for the questioning, McElroy used an old Navy

trick, the "Murder Board technique." Staff assistants would play the part of Congressmen and grill him in the office. "The tougher subordinates could be, the better the boss liked it," said one of them. Once on the Hill, questions could be tiring and picayune. Work would pile up back in the Pentagon. Nerves would wear thin.

Said one member of the "Murder Board": "A man thoroughly on top of his job is pretty well prepared to defend his recommendations. But when you consider the broad scope of his responsibilities, and the fact that many Congressmen are more interested in precise reasons for closing a base in Alabama or refusing to build a new armory in Potato Junction, and when you realize that many think they would derive political benefit for their party by finding ways of using the Secretary's statement to embarrass him—you get some idea of the preparation required."

Roughly three hours were spent on homework for every one hour McElroy spent in testifying. And hours on the Hill weren't short. In the thirteen working days of January, 1959, for instance, McElroy was talking to Congress for all or part of ten—a total of thirty-nine hours on the Hill.

Like his appearances as a witness, the series of goodwill breakfasts he started in the Pentagon for Congressional leaders were full of risks. "Naturally," said one man who attended some of these breakfasts, "every Congressman and Senator brought up his own pet subject or project and pressed McElroy for some promise or commitment." A White House special assistant once commented to one of McElroy's men, "Whether you know it or not, your boss has been walking on eggs all morning—and never cracked a one."

Behind the palaver, Congressmen weren't above trying a little horse-trading. Eisenhower had reluctantly approved an Air Force bid to start development of a supersonic bomber, the B-70. "We did it primarily because we didn't want to give up on the future of aviation," said one Pentagon official. "But we didn't regard it as a weapon, not with long-range missiles coming along."

Air-power–minded Congressmen didn't care for such an attitude. Even Pentagon politicians shuddered when one Senator asked the Navy, which was seeking more *Polaris* money, "Admiral, how can I back you on *Polaris* if you won't back me on the B-70?"

The Pentagon shuddered again when, because of some "strange-looking objects" spotted flying over Moscow, pressure was put on McElroy to get an airplane powered by nuclear energy flying early. He was almost prodded into trying to fit a nuclear engine into a B-36. Less erratic experts talked him out of it, convincing him the aircraft would be a militarily ridiculous white elephant.

In spite of such agitation, Congress basically gave McElroy considerable leeway, consistently pushing more money at him than Defense asked. When he wanted to close a base or not build a veteran's hospital down the road from one that was already practically empty, his hand-shaking diplomacy kept Congressmen in a mood to negotiate. (On one point, however, they were adamant: "The only place where it's imperative you spend the money we appropriate is to keep the National Guard at 300,000 men.")

With billions pouring into missiles, Congress wanted an "equitable distribution of contracts to industry on the basis of geography"—and voting precincts. McElroy refused. If the Pentagon started diluting pure Defense need by trying to take care of surplus labor, depressed areas, and all the nation's other problems, he explained, not only would it seriously weaken Defense but also destroy the people's confidence in what they assumed were military efforts to buy the best security available.

So great an emphasis did McElroy place on—or have placed on him by—the need to keep in close touch with Congress that his aide's appointment calendar listed nontestimony days as "Free." That sarcasm had a certain grain of truth in it. He had indicated early in his two-year Pentagon tenure that the organization would enjoy a lot of internal freedom.

In January, 1958, Congress asked him if he had had an opportunity really to get oriented in the Defense Department.

Answered McElroy: "Even Charlie Wilson, who had been there for almost five years, did not feel as if he was fully oriented. . . . As to how long [before] I could know enough . . . to make decisions, a man coming in there has some very able support . . . General Twining [Chairman of the Joint Chiefs] as an example. Secretary Quarles is another . . . McNeil and Gates and Douglas and Secretary Brucker and so on.

"These men have been in the Department for a considerable period of time. They are capable. So it isn't that I am so extremely well oriented—although I worked pretty hard at it, and the times have worked hard to get [me] moving pretty fast, too—but that the protection of the country lies in the fact that the organization supporting the Secretary of Defense is a strong one."

There was a flaw in that thinking, as Forrestal and Wilson had learned.

Some years later, a McElroy aide said: "He went down there with the idea his major job would be to develop in these military leaders a sense of being good businessmen in these times as well as good combat commanders. He had the feeling when he left that he was never able to get it across.

"He was accustomed to dealing with business operations where you have vice presidents for various departments. If the vice president for sales doesn't like a proposal, a discussion is held. He presents his case and the problem is hassled out. Then the President says, 'OK, we'll do this.' From then on the vice president of sales breaks his back to make it work. He's a management man.

"Not so in the military. In the Joint Chiefs, when a Service takes a view, from that point on, that Service does everything it can to continue to sell its views. State Department does the same thing. All his life, a private citizen is shifting allegiances, but in the military they instill in the man the opinion 'This is the greatest Service there is, and you can't be *really* sure unless, for instance, the Army has its own fighter aircraft.

"The Services really have a lot of very effective ways to get their way. Publicity programs, reserve organizations, companies that benefit from the contracts all can put on pressure, particularly with Congressmen. So can the Service friends who are columnists, the Services' own Congress liaison officers, their military associations. You do resist, but you can't resist everything."

Adding to what jaded Pentagon veterans considered rather routine conflicts, McElroy had to answer for space research. That task was not very pleasant. Sitting off in a corner of Canaveral when McElroy became Defense Secretary was a stovepipe project known as *Vanguard*. It was supposed to fulfill a promised U.S. contribution to the International Geophysical Year: launching a satellite sometime in late 1957 or early 1958. Afraid that there might not be enough technical talent in the United States to keep that promise and build ICBM's, too, the White House had decided any help *Vanguard* got would have to be what was left over from missile work—which meant not much.

But after *Sputniks I* and *II*, *Vanguard* was rushed to readiness—and, on December 6, 1957, blew up on the launch pad, its pointed nose cone looking, said one reporter, "remarkably like a dunce cap." In January, Eisenhower asked Congress for a $1.27 billion addition to the fiscal 1958 budget to disperse SAC bombers so they weren't such attractive targets, to further accelerate the ballistic missile programs, and to build an attacking-missile radar warning screen across northern Canada. (The first *Atlas* missiles sat out in the open and took hours to fuel up for firing—frighteningly defenseless against an enemy ICBM's ability to drop on them from halfway around the world in thirty minutes after firing.)

Said McElroy gloomily, "We have no definite proof [the Russians] are ahead but we are proceeding on the assumption that they are."

Said one observer later, "It will probably be years, if ever, before we can gauge our total loss in Free World stature, after that one *Sputnik* launch."

In 1956, Defense had been criticized for asking $20 million to launch *Vanguard*, "a frightening waste of the taxpayer's money for a scientific game." In 1958, it was told the $110 million it had spent on the program by then was "a horrible penny-pinching obstruction to progress."

Wernher von Braun said he had told the Pentagon he could put a satellite up in 1956, and Defense officials had turned him down. Congress demanded to know why. He had, the Pentagon agreed, but he had also said it would cost a three-month delay in developing the *Jupiter*—and, in 1956, Defense didn't want to take that risk with national security.

By 1958, encouraged by Navy's *Polaris* success, the Air Force was at work on a solid propellant ICBM called *Minuteman*. The Army turned that direction, too. Although the Army had accepted the roles and missions agreement in 1953, when its longest missile would travel only 200 miles, anyway, it had begun objecting as early as 1954 when it found out *Jupiter* would be able to go much farther, and it was still objecting in 1958. Smarting from an Air Force attempt, which McElroy denied, to put Army's von Braun team of missile experts on the Air Force payroll, the Army named their new solid-propellant-fueled missile *Pershing*. The reason, claimed an Army colonel privately, "We figured if we called it that, the Air Force wouldn't touch it with a ten-foot pole."

Congress wanted to know, from Joint Chiefs Chairman Twining, why the Pentagon insisted on holding the Army to within a 200-mile missile range. Hadn't it seemed just as stupid to the Air Corps when Secretary of War Woodring limited bomber development to a 300-mile range prior to World War II?

Answered former Air Force Chief of Staff Twining dryly, "It was not a very popular decision."

But the 200-mile limit stayed in place. By 1959, as McElroy had predicted, agitation started against Defense waste on duplicate and triplicate missiles. Trying to sort out which ones ought to go, McElroy moved slowly and was charged with "letting the organization run him more than he runs it."

"I do think . . . the people of this country also look to us, as they particularly do sometimes when the Russian is quite gruff as he is at the moment, to be sure that the decisions we have taken have not been too hasty, and have been made with consideration of efficiency as well as rapid moving forward," he told Congressional questioners.

But they remembered a lot better his answer when they asked why, in 1959, he didn't choose between the *Nike* (Army) and the *Bomarc* (Air Force). Wasn't one anti-aircraft missile enough?

"This is one area where we have not done very well in making a decision," he said. "It would not bother me if you held our feet to the fire and forced us . . ."

To Congress, that was a public confession of vacillating indecision. McElroy's main problem, said one Pentagon expert, "I don't care how fast a learner you are, you just can't move this organization much in two years."

McElroy knew a lot about research and management. He was out of his element in the military. Lacking any real background, he relied on subordinates and found to his chagrin that only a few officers had the nonpartisan breadth of view and the courage to tell him what they really believed rather than what their Service ambitions dictated. Result: the advice from his experts in the separate military departments had him swinging back and forth between conflicting points of view or sending a question back to the Joint Chiefs for "clarification." What military decisions were being made were coming, in the final analysis, from civilian scientists and budgeteers.

Said an aide, "McElroy faced an appalling situation where each Service wanted all the missiles and lots of everything else and it was almost impossible to get any real guidance."

He once asked the Services, in frustration, "How do you expect me to make these decisions?" This necessity should hardly have surprised him, however. Wilson had once had to call the Joint Chiefs in, when the missile controversy was first heating up, and ask them all to swear allegiance to their Commander in Chief. "The way the military departments can undermine a Secretary's job is amazing," said an observer of all this, "and always has been."

By 1959, the credit for McElroy's beefing up of Defense research went either to engineer Quarles or to the claim, "That would have happened, anyway." The look of his performance in office was warped out of perspective by a general public misconception about what was happening in Defense. Out of that difference between what was and what the country thought (with some Congressional help) came an additional vote against McElroy.

His intelligent decisions, particularly in missilery and aviation, looked negative. He went slow on supersonic bomber development because missiles had made its value seriously questionable. He resisted terrific pressure to litter the landscape with *Atlas* missiles, knowing they were already outdated by new ICBM's coming off the drawing boards even before *Atlas* was in operation. He asked less and spent less than the Congress kept trying to throw at him. In essence, if he failed at anything while in office just twenty-six months, it was failure to live up to Forrestal's first advice, "You not only have to do a good job, but the public has to be convinced you are doing a good job."

A Defense Secretary rarely sees his plans come to fruition in his own time. What needed doing, and how well McElroy did or did not do it, was fuzzy until well after his successor had taken office—and by then the soap company president was almost a forgotten man in the Pentagon.

X

Thomas Gates

[DECEMBER, 1959–JANUARY, 1961]

As science had increased the complexity of weapons, it had also increased the pressure for highly skilled troops to operate these new weapons. Defense could no longer afford to enlist the bulk of its manpower from the ranks of men too ignorant to do much except drive a truck or fire a rifle. Yet, college graduates, leery of military regimen and unimaginative routine, were uninterested in working for pay scaled to a ditch-digger's ability. To add to the Pentagon burden, what specialists Defense did snare, and spend from five to ten years training, were grabbed up by higher-paying weapons manufacturers. "We were becoming the biggest vocational training school in the United States," said one personnel officer.

Nearly every Defense Secretary had asked the Congress, which maintained a tight control over these matters, to modernize the rules, regulations and pay of both military and civilian Defense people. The theme, stated specifically by Lovett and underscored by Wilson, was to emphasize talent through promotions, cutting down the routine handing out of raises to men merely for serving time. McElroy shook a lot of Congressional hands trying, largely in vain, to push through Wilson's legislation.

Few objected to the obvious logic. But practical application ran into roadblocks. Entrenched officers on promotion boards found it hard "to give some kid with half my years in Service a promotion it took me five years to get." Nor could the Congressmen, who had acquired much of their own Capitol Hill status through longevity, bring themselves to feel much enthusiasm, especially since, to them, any pay raise for Government workers was political anathema.

Congress' view of this threat to military preparedness and internal Pentagon efficiency was a good deal shorter-ranged than that of the military leadership, which had to deal with the problem. Called on the Congressional carpet over U.S. bomber strength, in 1956, and again over U.S. missile strength, in 1957, Deputy Secretary of Defense Don Quarles said both times, "No weapon would contribute as much to (military) effectiveness as would a solution to our problem of attracting and keeping qualified people." Congress accused him of trying to change the subject.

Other Defense headaches came and went as the nature of military threats changed, but the search for good people was constant. The talent hunt was just as rugged at top management levels. "We literally dragged people into these jobs they didn't want," said Carey Randall.

The Defense General Counsel was regarded, next to the head of the Justice Department, as the top legal office in Government. Other than the Treasury Secretary, no Government official had more fiscal responsibility than the Defense Comptroller. "These aren't training jobs," said Randall. "They're proving jobs. You handle one of these and you can handle anything."

Once there, few of the top executives knew what it meant to relax. After one died at his desk and an assistant secretary in Personnel died of a heart attack, McElroy ordered everyone to take yearly physical examinations. "We don't want to know the results. Just call when it's done." (The examinations led to the discovery that a Chief of Staff and a budget expert had cancer. One of the men, it was said, would probably have been dead in six weeks, but for the test.)

Quarles was a good example of what the Pentagon was lucky enough to hire for comparatively little money. His promotion to president of Western Electric's Sandia Corporation in 1952 was his first real chance in thirty years' hard work to begin making a big salary. A year later, at fifty-nine, he had given it all up to become Assistant Secretary of Defense (Research and Development). "He lost $250,000 he couldn't afford to lose," said a friend, "when he accepted that job."

Member of several engineering groups, holder of more than one doctorate, he played a decisive role in directing the crash missile programs. During Congressional investigations into alleged U.S. missile-space failures, committees tended to excuse new Defense Secretary McElroy from the tough questions. They verbally crucified Quarles for this "sad state of affairs which," said one interrogator, "stank in the eyes of the Lord."

Quarles' answer was, "I feel we are ahead in electronics. I feel we are ahead in atomic weaponry. I feel we are ahead in many branches of aviation, but I do not include the particular area of earth satellites, which isn't, incidentally, a military area." As he knew it would, that factual answer merely incensed committees already on edge, anyway. Such talk had a hollow political ring for a nation that could hear the "beep" of an enemy satellite flying overhead.

After one particularly venomous session, an embittered McElroy assistant snapped, "The miracle is that we can get anybody to come down here. You go looking for guys who can move in fast and be helpful right away. You're apt to find them in some of these new research companies springing up. They're ex-professors who aren't wealthy but can finally see the money coming. We tell them to divest themselves of all their stock. Then, when they've done all this, we heap all this abuse on them."

Capitol Hill wasn't Quarles' only battleground. He was, for McElroy, "a crucial man who gave tremendous help, particularly on the scientific and technical questions." He worked endless hours. Even Pentagon employees used to such things were nonplussed when he came to a staff party one Christmas Eve, had a drink, shook hands all around, and was back at his desk by 7:30 P.M. "Don Quarles was just a bear for work," said one aide. "You couldn't make him take off."

McElroy finally went to him and said, "Don, I've never suggested rank between us and I won't again but I am today. You are to take a vacation." Quarles managed to stay away a few days. But some weeks later, the heavy unrelenting schedule collected full payment. On the morning of May 8, 1959, a heart attack killed him. Before the day ended, Eisenhower called Navy Secretary Tom Gates and told him he would have to take Quarles' place.

Gates, who had served in the Washington grind almost six

years, answered, "No, I don't." But he said he would think about it. His resignation as Navy Secretary had already been accepted by the White House three months earlier. The Navy had a farewell dinner planned for him. He was still around only because his replacement, Under Secretary William Franke, had come down with hepatitis. "This is not the job to take while sick," Gates had told him, "I'll stay on another month until you're well."

The week after Eisenhower's call, Gates took a Sunday cruise on the Navy's executive yacht, the *Sequoia.* He stayed up playing cards all night while aides needled him with, "You won't take it because you don't think you can handle it."

On Monday, he had a White House appointment at which he was to give his answer. As he dressed to leave home, his wife asked, "What are you going to say?"

"I don't know."

He finally accepted the chore because "I couldn't think up any good reason why not." With the exception of Lovett and Quarles, no Deputy Secretary had ever been better trained. Like Lovett, he had a banker's background. The only child (his mother died when he was born) of a University of Pennsylvania president, Gates graduated from Penn in 1928 and joined an investment banking firm. A partner by 1940, he was also director in a handful of corporations. Like McElroy in Cincinnati, Gates in his hometown Philadelphia was an active citizen, holding one office or another in everything from the Philadelphia Child Guidance Clinic to the Community Chest.

A Naval Reserve officer in World War II, he was picked to set up a Naval Air Intelligence School in Norfolk, Virginia. There, he used his commanding officer's rank to write his own ticket to combat duty in the Atlantic. "All I did was to write out orders 'FROM the commanding officer,' 'TO the commanding officer.' Naturally, they were approved."

Sent to the Pacific in 1943, he was back in Europe for the invasion of southern France in 1944, and was back in the Pacific after that for the Philippine liberation and the battles for Okinawa and Iwo Jima. His performance earned him one Bronze Star and, in lieu of another, a Gold Star.

After the war, he became an investment banker again. "I was flabbergasted," he said later, when Navy Secretary Robert Anderson called him in the midst of a business transaction in 1953, and asked him to be Under Secretary "for a year or so." But Gates was fairly easy to convince.

"It was so deeply rooted in his natural instincts about what a good American should do," said one Pentagon executive, "that I doubt if he thought twice about refusing."

Promoted to Navy Secretary in 1957, he believed the move up would be easy, but "It was the move I understood least," he said afterward. "The experience was a tremendous asset, but I found the front man's job is completely different from the businessman's job." The toughest task, he found, was making choices on how much to spend keeping the fleet ready to fight and how much to allocate to build more modern hardware. "This balancing was the most challenging part of the job."

He and then Chief of Naval Operations Arleigh Burke developed a close partnership while hunting for the answers and often lost all track of time—a preoccupation their wives soon found they had to adjust to.

Working late one night, Gates suddenly jumped to his feet. "My gosh, Arleigh, it's 8:25, and I was supposed to be at some damned fool black tie dinner at eight."

Burke, who was hosting the dinner, answered, "Well, you know, I have an idea it's *my* damn fool black tie dinner you're talking about, and we're both late!"

On his last day as Navy Secretary, Gates's staff gave "Our Hero" a "Big Daddy" award for "asking nasty questions, doing battle with the admirals, and [while he listened to their pleas] straightening paper clips day after day to throw in the wastepaper basket."

Gates noticed a big change when he moved one door away from McElroy's office. "When you sit there," he said, "you're all by yourself. You don't belong to anybody. In Navy, I was always being briefed and helped and argued with. In DOD* in the first week, nobody called on me at all."

By 1959, Gates had a good line on how the two Defense Secretaries he served under had operated. "It was very easy to work for both of them, really," he said.

Wilson "was gregarious, a tremendous worker. He was more

* Technically, "DOD" stands for the entire Department of Defense. In common military parlance, however, it is shorthand talk for the Office of the Secretary of Defense.

interested in efficiency and organization than in foreign affairs. Time meant nothing to him. You never knew when you went to see him whether you'd be there a half hour or three hours. He'd explore over and under and around a problem and in between. He was a sort of philosopher, too. I was devoted to him, loved the old boy, to tell the truth."

McElroy "has one of the quickest minds. He must have an IQ of 1000. It was a cinch being deputy to Mac. He traveled a great deal and tended to leave running the store to me." Gates also learned McElroy was a determined man and "rarely changed his mind once it was made up." Among other things, that meant McElroy resigned when he said he would, at the end of his two year's promised service.

On December 2, 1959, Gates took the oath of office as seventh Secretary of Defense. Tall, dark-haired, he was fifty-three, looked years younger, had a habit of cocking his head to one side when he walked, and of expressing both favor and scorn with just one word, "Fabulous!" Among top military officials, "You start with 'terrific' and go on from there describing that guy," was the general opinion. "He's tops in all categories."

"From thirty feet away, he looks as dignified as white tie and tails," said one man, "and from three feet away he is as unassuming as your next door neighbor."

"I ran the office entirely differently from most people," said Gates. "I picked the kind of men who were young and modern and bright as hell to be my aides. I shared my innermost secrets with them. I wanted in privacy their frank opinions. I never cared who got my hat or my airplane ticket [an aide's usual chore] and I can get into a car by myself.

"I didn't always do what they said, but they were very helpful as a sounding board. I know in at least one case it hurt the man's career to do it."

Typical of the payoff was the education he got from one aide after a Service general had briefed him on an alleged personnel problem. Said the aide, "Boss, that guy's lying to you; not on purpose, but he is. Here's the real situation . . ."

Like Wilson and McElroy, Gates was affable. He had a quick smile and an ability to laugh at the pressures. "They give us such nice offices," he once told the staff, "because they never let us out of them."

"He was a great one for everybody doing things together," said a secretary who had been with him since Navy days. "He took us all to an Army-Navy football game once, for instance."

To Gates, this human relationship was basic. "The Pentagon runs a high percentage on emotion," he said. "Families are uprooted. Assignments changed. There is rumor, gossip. It is so important to pay attention to morale." It was often his first thought even in major policy decisions. In late 1960, when the U.S. balance of payments reached serious proportions, Eisenhower told Gates to cut down on the number of troops permitted to take their families overseas, and to order troops already there not to spend as much personal money on the local economies. Gates agreed—but asked that Eisenhower's written order be directed to all Government employees abroad. Since most overseas employees were military, anyway, it wouldn't make that much difference in dollars, but it would make a great deal of difference in morale, he said. The President overruled him.

Gates did not earn his high Washington reputation just by being a nice guy. Like the other Eisenhower Defense Secretaries, "He was not impulsive but once he made a decision, it stood." He had shown a willingness to make tough choices—a rarity among military department leaders. At the height of the missile race, for example, when the Services were fighting to keep alive every project they had, Navy Secretary Gates canceled two missile programs and a flying boat development. The Navy had spent $680.4 million on them, but Gates was convinced the onrush of technology had made them obsolete.

Later, he recalled "When we were debating going ahead with *Polaris*, we knew in operation it would conflict with Air Force strategic targeting and it would fall in the Defense Secretary's lap. We called industry together on Christmas Eve for a rundown on 'Can we build it?' I violated the whole Navy organization, but this was an important weapon. You can't fool around with differences of opinion."

Believing he would be Defense Secretary only until a new President was elected in November, 1960, few expected Gates to do much more than caretake. He surprised everybody. "It's a terribly difficult job. I went to work at it. I didn't really think about the lame duck business."

The main plank in Gates' Defense platform he had pounded

home the night the White House called to ask him about becoming Deputy Secretary. He had been reached in Philadelphia where, as Secretary of the Navy, he was making a speech—one he had put a lot of work on because he thought it would be his last. In a general Pentagon atmosphere of controversy, it was a rare exercise in Defense statesmanship and, as events of the next few years would corroborate, a masterpiece in perception.

Pointing to the increasing Communist creation of limited wars, chaos, and disorder, "of their attacks against weak spots especially in rising new and uncommitted nations," he advised in part:

> The deployed fleets of the Navy, together with their embarked and ready Marine landing forces, are the Nation's most evident and effective response to these tactics. [These forces] must maintain a capability to use either nuclear or conventional weapons to the controlled degree necessary to achieve the objective. More funds are required for this purpose. More accent on its importance is needed. This support will have to come from the elimination of certain very expensive mass-destruction, single-purpose weapon systems which [currently] have a priority of claims against our national resources.
>
> The Joint Chiefs continue to struggle with divided opinions as to emphasis to be placed on various systems; and the Secretary of Defense continues to struggle handicapped by traditionally divided Service opinions. The kind of constructive, objective teamwork that enabled us to win wars would help him.
>
> I believe the Navy should put its contribution to the Nation's general war deterrent primarily in missiles based under the seas. This, except for warning and reconnaissance, would place the carrier forces in the business of limited war where they excel and, in fact, are the best and often the only practical way to handle such a situation. . . .
>
> As we explore space, delve under the ice and the oceans, live with the startling advances of science, and share the work of command and foreign policy, our officers must be scientists, economists, ambassadors, as well as sailors. This can never be accomplished with the short tours of duty or the constant rotation systems we have followed in the past. More education, stability and expertness is a certain requirement for the future, and equality of career opportunity must accompany it.

There was ample evidence in the world to support Gates's theme. Lovett had once advised the Pentagon, "Good judgment is usually the result of experience, and experience is frequently the result of bad judgment." By the spring of 1960, the United States had acquired plenty of Cold War experience. Since before Gates had come to Washington, a world in turmoil had been probing for U.S. weakness from an almost uncountable variety of directions.

President Eisenhower had hardly been elected in 1952 when MacArthur called and laid out again the war plan that had cost him his command. It included use of atomic weapons to decimate China's industrial base and transportation facilities; a pincers invasion from both sides of Korea along the Yalu River by 400,000 Chinese Nationalists with two Marine divisions in the lead. If necessary, bombs would be dropped to make a radioactive area in North Korea to prevent the Communist army from escaping up the middle.

The object of this offensive was to destroy the Red Chinese military force and end the war-making capability of the People's Republic of China. Otherwise, MacArthur predicted, Korea would degenerate into a permanently divided nation sitting on a shaky truce, Red China would eventually grow to oppressive military power, Southeast Asia would be lost to Communism; Japan would become a Communist satellite, and Asia "will be lost forever as a Western ally."

Truce talks had been stalled for several months on technicalities. In the spring of 1953, Eisenhower got Red China back to the negotiating table by announcing, "The United States cannot stand forever on a static front . . . Small attacks on small hills would not end this war." He relieved the 7th Fleet of its role as referee in the Formosa Strait, saying, "It is ridiculous for the United States to be defending Communism from the Chinese Nationalists." He increased military aid to the South Korean army and hinted at the Panmunjom truce table that, unless there were sudden progress, the United States "intended to move decisively without inhibition in the use of weapons including atomics" and without trying to confine hostilities to Korea. In essence, he threatened to use MacArthur's plan.

On July 27, 1953, the Communists signed an agreement to let an international armistice commission settle Korea's problems. Troops of both sides withdrew behind a two-and-a-half-mile buffer zone stretched across the peninsula. In the three-year war, the United States had spent $15 billion to supply nearly half the 800,000 U.N. troops and had suffered nearly 140,000 killed and wounded.

The quavering U.N. registered "grave concern" over U.S. reports that 38,000 U.N. military and South Korean prisoners had died during the war from Chinese and Russian Communist torture, starvation, and murder. Four years later, the United States threatened to halt peace talks unless Red China stopped violating the truce by, among other things, sending troops on forays across the buffer zone. Twelve years later, pointless, periodic diatribes were still being heard around the Panmunjom truce table.

These alarms were only a beginning, not an end. By the time Gates became Secretary of Defense, there had been eighteen undeclared wars fought in the world in fourteen years. Power struggles, political coups, and assassinations—most of them caused or exploited by Communists—had plagued a long list of poor, newly independent countries. While the U.N. fought in Korea, France fought in Indochina a war that had begun with Communist guerrilla insurrection as early as 1946. After defeated French forces signed a truce in 1954, dividing the nation up into Laos, Cambodia, and North and South Viet-Nam, Communist rulers in North Viet-Nam started infiltration all over again into South Viet-Nam and Laos, as they had tried to do in Korea.

Red China bombed Nationalist-held islands just off the mainland near Formosa. Eisenhower forestalled an impending invasion by alerting the 7th Fleet again and obtaining from Congress an unprecedented war-waging right to send troops "as he deemed necessary" to defend the area.

World Communist leader Joseph Stalin had died in March, 1953. Eisenhower commented, "The world knows that an era ended. The Soviet system shaped by Stalin and his predecessors was born of one world war. It survived with stubborn and amazing courage a second world war. It has lived to threaten a third." The American President asked the new Russian leadership for an end to the arms race. His message, much like George Marshall's in accepting the Nobel Peace Prize later that same year was:

> This world in arms is not spending money alone [to live] a life of perpetual terror and tension. It is spending the sweat of its laborers, the genius of its scientists, the hopes of its children.
>
> The cost of one modern heavy bomber is this: a modern brick school in more than thirty cities; [or] two electric power plants, each serving a town of 60,000 population; [or] two fully equipped hospitals; [or] some fifty miles of concrete highway. We pay for a single fighter plane with a half-million bushels of wheat. We pay for a single destroyer with new homes that could have housed more than 8,000 people.

The United States, he said, is ready "to dedicate our strength to serving the needs, rather than the fears, of the world. I know of only one question upon which progress waits. It is this: What is the Soviet Union ready to do?"

Russia, it seemed, was not exactly sure until after at least one execution and a banishment or two, which left Nikita Khrushchev in charge of the Kremlin. He started a vitriolic denunciation of Stalin's "terrorist tactics" and called for world peace talks in Geneva. However, it gradually became clear that Communist talk of peace masked war action.

While Eisenhower offered the world an "Atoms for Peace" development program and offered Russia as "Open Skies" mutual aerial inspection of military bases, there were revolts, riots, coups, assassinations, and violence in countries around the world. Much of the terror was clearly Communist-inspired or manipulated. By 1957, Khrushchev was telling the United States in a TV interview from Moscow, "Your grandchildren in America will live under socialism." (Later, he rattled his missiles with the threat "We will bury you.")

In this period of ever-growing tension, other changes had occurred. Said Neil McElroy in 1958, "Technology has galloped." U.S. scientists were probing the heights and the depths. Jet fighters were capable of such speeds they outran their own ammunition, as one proved when it was hit and shot down by its own cannon-fire during target practice on an East Coast firing range. The first U.S. nuclear-powered submarine, the *Nautilus*, spent a record-shattering ninety-six hours submerged traveling under the North Pole ice cap. Three B-52's flew nonstop around the world in forty-six hours. A Navy fighter-bomber set a new altitude record of 98,560 feet and was topped days later by an Air Force fighter climbing to 103,395 feet. The Army developed an atomic antiaircraft guided missile which, it was claimed, could destroy an entire bomber fleet with blast effect alone. And the Army flew the first nonstop transcontinental helicopter trip across the United States.

The National Aeronautics and Space Administration was organized to put more power behind U.S. space research efforts. It soon announced plans to put men in orbit and on the moon. The Army set up a Strategic Army Corps (STRAC) of 50,000 paratroops ready, it said, to fight a limited war anywhere in the world on only hours' notice.

Gates walked into an office that was under pressure from all sides. The Army wanted $15 billion more than the budget it was then receiving to start a five-year modernization program. It pointed out that Russia's armies already were well equipped with second- and even third-generation hardware while 70 per cent of U.S. matériel was of World War II vintage or older. The Navy wanted to build an all-nuclear-powered fleet, to strengthen antisubmarine defenses against Russia's 500-submarine force (Hitler had started World War II with only about 125 subs), and to build more *Polaris* submarines. The Air Force, like the Navy, wanted more modern fighters and also wanted more ICBM's, supersonic bombers, and jet cargo planes to haul Army's STRAC.

There were technological pressures to push a wide spectrum of new hardware developments, combat-readiness pressures to buy lots of what was already proven, and political pressures to buy more of what was already obsolete. "It's remarkable," said one observer, "that we haven't compromised the security of the country in all these things."

Adding to the rest were economic pressures. The United States had come out of World War II assuming that science had made war cheaper. It had not. Inflation, continually increasing military administrative overhead, and the mounting costs of military retirement benefits were partly responsible. The complexity of equipment added new costs. While hardware firepower soared, so did its technical sophistication. And that is expensive. A World War II bomber had cost $600,000, a B-52 over $7 million. A World War II submarine had cost $4.7 million. Its nuclear-powered offspring cost ten times as much. The $55 million aircraft carrier of 1945 cost, with nuclear power, $360 million fifteen years later.

Although the military experts were being chastized for permitting "bomber gaps" and "missile gaps" to develop, they had long since turned their attention to preparedness for limited wars.

Said Arleigh Burke: "Planning for what may happen short of general war is considerably more complicated than planning for all-out war, which is a relatively clear-cut proposition. It is far more difficult to visualize situations complicated by unpredictable political and economic factors, situations to which there is hardly a clear-cut, easy solution. It is extremely difficult, for example, to think through a future Korea, or Indochina, a Formosa, or a Middle East.

"It is this danger of limited war, of little aggression, of aggression by proxy, of political subversion, of the piecemeal loss of free peoples, that is of most concern to the Free World confederation today."

A humorist in the Defense procurement business commented, "With headaches like these, is it any wonder that each year we buy $120,000 worth of aspirin and $1 million worth of tranquilizers?"

Hampered by a held-down budget, however, the limited war build-up that most Pentagon leaders agreed was needed had taken a back seat to missiles. Hardest hit was the Army, which was aggravating its own problem by spending a large share of its funds on missiles, anti-missile missile developments, and thousands of its own Army-piloted aircraft. To stand a chance against Russia's massive 175-division, 2.5-million-man army, General Maxwell Taylor (Army Chief of Staff from 1955 to 1959) wanted a huge increase in U.S. Army size, as well as the modernization program. To grant it all would have meant spending each year as much on the Army, in effect, as the $18 billion or so being spent on the Air Force.

The Joint Chiefs told Taylor, basically, that he would receive no more money and that he should cut manpower, using the funds saved to boost firepower, including planned employment of tactical nuclear weapons. Said Wilson, "Our basic defense policy is based on the use of atomic weapons in a major war and . . . the use of such atomic weapons as would be militarily feasible and usable in a smaller war. In other words, the tactical nuclear weapons, in a sense, have now become conventional weapons. There is no such thing as a nice, easy-going war."

Taylor took his case to the people. He wrote a book called *The Uncertain Trumpet* (one incensed Pentagon official promptly retitled it *The Uncertain Strumpet*). The gist of Taylor's book was that the unresolved contest in the Joint Chiefs was leading to confused indecision, and the full threat to U.S. security was being shabbily tackled. His key point: the huge U.S. atomic power had not been enough to keep the peace as "evidenced by the many forms of limited war which have occurred since 1945. If we are to cope with lesser situations, we will need considerably more than the atomic retaliatory force."

Part of Taylor's difficulty, it turned out, was that, like Ridgway in the missile arena, he was being whipsawed. In front of him were Joint Chiefs who didn't believe he was giving enough credit to the other Services' limited war contribution. Behind him was his own staff in near rebellion from being, it thought, always third in line when the money was handed out.

Whatever the squabbles really cost the Army, they did precipitate one Washington move. Three months after McElroy took office, Eisenhower told him to reorganize the Pentagon. Said one wit, "Obviously, the Russians beat us to the punch on *Sputnik* because we were not organized properly and had all this bickering." The main effect of most Government reorganizations is psychological. At least, they give the country a notion Washington is doing something.

Predictably, McElroy's shake-up, passed by Congress in 1958, increased the stature of research and development. The Act set up a Director of Research and Engineering. He was to rank third in Pentagon command, behind only the Secretary and his Deputy. Most important, he was to receive all research and development funds appropriated by Congress, and he, in turn, would distribute these funds to the Services. "Putting that $6 billion R&D budget under DOD control," said Gates later, "has meant a tremendous change."

On the other side of the shop, in combat operations, McElroy took an effective swipe at a stumbling block Lovett had warned of six years earlier. Here, "a phrase, 'separately administered,' had been interpreted by the Services since 1947 as giving them the right to refuse the Secretary information in certain areas," said an aide, "and to regard overall supervision of certain phases of their activity as an intrusion into their private operations."

McElroy cited several examples to Congress. The Capitol Hill reaction cost the military dearly. The Joint Staff was reshaped to be a real military staff for the Joint Chiefs and the Secretary. The Secretary not only received the right to assign roles and missions, but combat commands now reported directly to him (through the Joint Chiefs, if he preferred). The military departments, in effect, were removed from combat command channels and left only the requirement to supply forces with equipment and trained manpower.

The underlying significance of these changes was that Congress had put in writing one more vote for centralizing authority in the Secretary of Defense. But there was no altering the fact that the organization was still being run by people. "No wizard machine or chart exists which can give solutions where such intangibles as judgment, knowledge, determination and leadership are concerned," said one Defense critic.

One man who knew that probably better than anyone else in the Pentagon was Wilfred McNeil. Defense Comptroller since creation of the Department in 1947, he and his office were generally recognized thirteen years later for having been the main instrument of military unification. Every Secretary had faced the hurdle of wondering just how much of a tyrant he had to be to coerce the Services into moving in a coordinated direction. Contenders for resources can't help being parochial.

Even within the military departments, this parochialism exists. (When heat was turned on the Air Force to deploy *Atlas* missiles, Air Force General Curtis LeMay countered it with, "I don't want to hear we should buy more ICBM's from the people who make them. I want to hear it from the men who will have to use them.") In his own office, a Defense Secretary can see the effects of narrow vision. Engineers want more money for research and development; Personnel wants more for people; supply experts ask more for hardware already in production. As one budget executive described it, "Everybody else works on their own problems. The Comptroller works on the Secretary's problems."

A rear admiral and chief Navy disbursing officer in World War II, McNeil had later become Forrestal's financial expert. The limits of his budget responsibility he drew from the guidelines of the first Budget Bureau Director, Charles G. Dawes. When he took office in 1921, Dawes had said that if Congress decides it wants garbage on the White House steps, "it would be our regrettable duty, as a Bureau, in an impartial, nonpolitical and nonpartisan way to advise the Executive and Congress as to how the largest amount of garbage can be spread in the most expeditious and economical manner."

In practice, under Forrestal's guidance, McNeil had developed that philosophy into using money as the principal tool to guide top management planning, the primary control over Service activity, and the chief means for measuring in one place separate Service progress against plans.

Leery of McNeil's Navy training when he took office, Louis Johnson had said, "I don't think you and I are going to get along, but will you stay another thirty days?"

"If you disagreed with him," McNeil said of Johnson later, "either you got fired because he thought you were trying to undercut him, or he loved you. He was autocratic at first because he felt such an absolute necessity to centralize authority. In his last few months, he was no longer so arbitrary, or when he slipped into that habit, he could be spoken to frankly. By then, he was actually doing a pretty good job."

So was McNeil, apparently, because he was still around when Wilson arrived and was, in fact, acting Secretary of Defense for more than a week while Wilson argued his confirmation with the Senate. "Thank heaven, there were no crises then," he said afterwards. Under Wilson, there was virtually nothing done that McNeil didn't have a hand in. "He was," said an assistant, "Wilson's general manager, his counterbalance against the contenders."

"We always got 110 per cent support from all the bosses," said McNeil. "We were criticized a lot but we didn't worry as long as the boss was happy. We had less trouble from the senior generals and admirals who understood very well what they could take from the economy without getting hurt or causing an over-reaction. We had more difficulty with some of the top civilians, and, of course, from those colonels who always want to fortify the moon." (After one such middle-management, financial soul-searching in McNeil's office, a story circulated through the Pentagon that the colonels who lost were suggesting, "Let's get some aircraft company to make him an offer. It's worth $200,000 a year to get him out of there.")

A product, like Gates, of the Navy's checks-and-balances organization, McNeil firmly believed that Service competition, "if you keep it from running amuck," provides strong motivation. So did Wilson, McElroy, and Gates. McNeil's best example hit the headlines when the first *Polaris* was fired successfully from its underwater launch platform, the submarine *George Washington*, in July, 1960, more than three years ahead of its original schedule.

"No weapon system ever built was so complicated or had so many problems as *Polaris*," said McNeil. "They couldn't even tell the missile guidance which way was straight up. Yet, *Polaris* was into production faster than the Army's new M-14 rifle." Competition against Army and Air Force to build a better IRBM was, he believes, at least part of the reason.

Another reason was money support from the top. "*Polaris* is one of the few projects ever undertaken in or out of Government where there was no attempt to sweep dirt under the rug. The result was development of a mutual trust between the project office and top management which cut out a lot of the higher-level inclination to waste time and overhead funds reviewing their requests."

Although McNeil resigned a month before Gates became Secretary, Gates inherited the Comptroller's staff of seasoned, fact-finding talent. This staff was not Gates' only back-up. He pulled close friend Jim Douglas in to be Deputy Secretary. Like Gates, Douglas had been around seven years, first as Under Secretary, then as Secretary of the Air Force. The military hadn't met as tough a pair of supervisors since Marshall and Lovett.

"We had a real advantage," said Douglas. "Every once in a while it occurred to me, as I listened to a Service briefing, that I had heard all these arguments before—even helped devise some of them. This time-in-Service also helps in knowing who to contact for what you know are authoritative answers—an advantage a new man doesn't have."

But for all the bright men behind him, Gates was clearly the man in charge. "He asked the Chiefs of Staff to work on the Defense Secretary's job and let their Vice-Chiefs run the Departments," said one aide. "None of them knew what he was talking about—so he showed them."

Gates closed the long-standing gap between civilian leaders and military advisers by resurrecting a Forrestal technique. "Instead of waiting for the papers to come up before he started asking questions, he jumped in the pit, took off his coat, and really slugged out an issue with the Chiefs," praised one assistant.

Until Gates made that simple move, the arms-length relationship between the military and civilians had hampered intelligent decision-making. Almost by tradition, Joint Chiefs advice had consisted of something like "(a) this is the problem but these solutions are not feasible; therefore (b) this is what we should do, Sincerely . . ."

Complained one veteran, "It didn't help the Secretary one damn bit. He didn't know what they had in mind when they stated the problems, which usually had a lot of politics and economics and Service ambition underneath them; and he didn't know how much any of these factors affected their conclusions. There's rarely any such thing as purely military advice, and Gates knew it."

In spite of meeting with the Chiefs once a week for "the stirring of the soup," as one observer put it, Gates didn't abuse his authority. "I saw to it that everyone, particularly the Chiefs, had their innings. They have leadership problems of their own. They can't afford to lose face with their own people. It's worth taking the time to listen before you do something, even when you know at the outset what you're going to do."

He found his methods created great loyalty to him. "I had little problem on adverse decisions. And when I did, I didn't have the end runs to Congress ['legalized insubordination,' Eisenhower had called them] and the press leaks."

One example was his decision to set up a joint strategic targeting group in Strategic Air Command headquarters. With *Polaris,* Navy had re-established itself in the strategic power business. After a month-long personal study, Gates concluded the targets picked for it had to be coordinated with those selected for the Strategic Air Command. Gates' decision to have a unified group do that coordinating met with immediate and strong opposition from Arleigh Burke. Navy officers could see themselves losing control of their new weapon just as the Army had lost control of *Jupiter.*

Gates encouraged Burke to appeal the decision. He did, for upward of five hours in the White House. After Burke had expressed all the blunt, outspoken complaints he could think of, the decision stood—and Burke sent a wire to the entire Navy.

He would support the decision, he said, and the rest of the Navy was not only to support it but to send Navy's best people to fill billets in the new joint planning group.

Said Gates, "If I had made that decision three months sooner, and not listened to objections, all hell would have broken loose."

His work with the Joint Chiefs also cleared up a lot of back papers "that had been lying around quite a while." For one, "In about twenty seconds I decided Navy would be responsible for military activity related to Africa. That decision freed up thirty-two position papers that had been written arguing over who should. With that many on such a relatively minor subject, you can imagine how many more they had for complicated questions."

One of his two most important tasks, he believed, was to stop the proliferation of divided opinions and make the Joint Chiefs assume more corporate rather than separate Service responsibility. "I wanted to end the arguing and get on with it."

The other chore he spent a great deal of time on was the international situation. He began meeting with the Secretary of State in the office Sunday afternoons, hammering out differences of opinion between foreign policy and military planning. He worked hardest at it after an aide told him, on one subject, "There's no point debating that. State has already decided."

He snapped back, "Who do you think I work for, the Secretary of State?" The world was no quieter in 1960 than it had been in the previous seven years. There was civil war in the Congo, rioting in the Union of South Africa, Belgium, South Korea, Laos, and Italy. A planned Eisenhower-Khrushchev summit conference fell apart when the Russians shot down a U.S. U-2 reconnaissance aircraft over their territory. Japan canceled a proposed Eisenhower visit in the face of Communist-led rioting against his planned trip.

The United States clamped an embargo on shipping to Cuba except for medicines and food when Fidel Castro's government turned wholeheartedly to Communism. And in November, 1960, U.S. ships were patrolling the Caribbean after both Guatemala and Venezuela had asked protection against Cuban invasions.

In the Pentagon, Gates, who wasn't supposed to be able to do much in only a year, had done and was doing a great deal. He worked as hard on internal efficiency as he did on the Joint Chiefs. Following up the 1958 Reorganization Act, he asked his General

Counsel for a rundown on what administrative changes he could make. The answer was a list of about twenty major alterations. "One or two needed Presidential approval and a couple needed Congressional blessing, but to my amazement, seven-eighths of them could be done just on my order."

With glowing praise from Congress, he set up a Defense Communications Agency to run the routine military communications for all the Services, cutting out military duplications in leased telephone lines and message handling facilities. He started the studies that would eventually result in the establishment of the Defense Supply Agency to manage all military common-item procurement and supply—business that, conceivably, could encompass 60 per cent of the total annual Defense budget. He began the analysis that later led to creation of the Defense Intelligence Agency. "The Services need their own intelligence, certainly," he said, "but there is also a need for an overall view of objective, professional military intelligence coming directly to the Secretary."

The reason he started work on so many single manager agencies was, "We had such difficulty resolving Service points of view, I wanted to keep them out of things I felt they shouldn't be in."

Asked once which of the four top Defense jobs he enjoyed most, he answered, "I liked being Under Secretary of the Navy best. I wanted to leave Washington anonymous and even." Like Forrestal, he believed that Defense should stay out of politics. But in 1960, he found he not only couldn't avoid it, but he actually had to seek publicity.

"On the missile gap thing, I was faced with 'either you're going to have to fold or fight and I guess you better fight.' "

Since *Sputnik*, black predictions of impending disaster had become stock items in the repertoire of nearly every speech-maker in Washington who wasn't working for Eisenhower—and of some who were. As late as 1959, public estimates of the alleged "bomber gap" said Russia had at least 250 and possibly as many as 500 Soviet heavy bomber versions of the B-52. A year later, that estimate dropped to a more realistic 100 to 120, and budget experts quickly computed that, at a bare minimum, $150 million dollars had been spent on defensive hardware to stop each bomber that could attack the United States.

But by 1960, the public anxiety, in the midst of Presidential politicking, was that while the United States had been building bombers, Russia had been building missiles. Now, what about the "missile gap?"

Two years earlier, the Pentagon had known that, if Russia produced to capacity, she would have a three-to-one lead in ICBM's by 1960. But those 600 missiles were well short of being enough for the kind of salvo needed to knock out U.S. bombers and ICBM's so they could not retaliate. "However," said a McElroy aide, "it was murder politically and in the hearings to admit to a gap."

Pentagon experts didn't want a lot of *Atlas* missiles because: "(a) we don't need them; (b) we'd be cluttered up with obsolete weapons; and (c) it would take money away from other badly needed programs."

The "gap" argument persisted. *Life* magazine editorialized in 1959, "Neither *Polaris* nor *Minuteman* can be counted on as a significant addition to the national arsenal until well into 1964." Angrily, a Navy admiral countered, "This is categoric nonsense. Both *Polaris* and its submarine will be in the fleet next year. By then, we'll be able to pound out as many of these things as they want to give us money for."

Added an Army missile expert, "The defeatist psychosis running rampant through the country needs a good couch treatment. Our top-level military judgment is being quietly swept under the rug in favor of a popular catch phrase, 'Let's close the missile gap,' I might say parenthetically, a nonexistent missile gap." As it turned out, at the time Gates' critics contended the Soviet Union was pouring money into missiles, the Russians really were working on space vehicles.

Gates was dead set against putting up with misinformed arguments, but he searched unendingly for differences of opinion among his military advisers. "I sought a better unified Department but I didn't want it carried to where I received undivided military opinions, and I don't advocate a single chief of staff or a unified single service. I would be suspicious as hell if I ever got a single, nondissenting position out of the Services, and God help the country if we ever have a single strategy."

By November, 1960, Gates had served in the Pentagon nearly eight years, and "I didn't think I would be around even if Richard Nixon was elected, which I thought he would be."

Gates's being wrong on that prediction didn't bother him particularly. He had learned long ago about his Defense problems, "The only thing I know for sure is that you don't have any 'for sure' answers. Only history will record how well any of us did because we deal entirely in futures. Any way you go, who knows, you may be right."

Gates toyed with the idea of writing a "look-ahead" guideline for his successor as Lovett had done in 1952. He gave it up, did his briefing in person, instead. The man who listened to it had told President-elect John F. Kennedy he didn't think he had the talent to be a good Secretary of Defense. Kennedy, he said, would be much better advised just to keep Gates in office.

XI

Robert S. McNamara

[JANUARY, 1961–]

SHORTLY AFTER THE nation voted John F. Kennedy its thirty-fifth President, Kennedy invited Robert Lovett to his Georgetown home in Washington, D.C. Lovett was offered his choice of being either Secretary of State or Secretary of Defense or Secretary of the Treasury in the new Kennedy Cabinet. He declined all three jobs. He had already served four tours of duty in Government, he said, "and it seemed every time I left, I had to go have some of my insides taken out. I just can't afford to lose any more of my insides." Allowed by his doctors to work only half days, he added, more seriously, "It would be a disservice to the nation for me to accept a position calling for an eighteen-hour day."

However, one major problem he warned Kennedy about was "the foul-up factor," as he called it. Government machinery, he said, was rusting in its channel, taking too long to make up its mind. Conflicts of interest, deliberately injected to keep any one agency from becoming too powerful, had spawned far too many committees and an excessive layering of staffs. Too many people with too little work in their own fields were spilling over into others, provoked by curiosity, envy, and fear of losing authority.

For example, he elaborated, if Venezuela wants to buy six second hand interceptor aircraft, and the military wants to sell them, the State Department must be consulted on whether the sale fits U.S. foreign policy, and State will have to check further with the Organization of American States, which will determine how the sale will affect Trinidad and Mexico and Guatemala, etc. The

Central Intelligence Agency will want to know what Venezuela intends doing with these planes. The Labor Department will protest that new planes should be ordered, to create more jobs for U.S. workers. Commerce will have to determine the export licensing details, and Treasury examine the effect of the sale on the balance of payments. And so on. "Generally," said Lovett, "a minimum of seven agencies must approve before anything is done."

Of all the agencies of Government, Defense was most important to the nation, Lovett concluded. What Kennedy needed there, he advised, was "an analytical statistician who can get into this stuff and tear out the overlap, the empire building." And Lovett had a man in mind: forty-four-year-old Robert S. (for Strange) McNamara.

Kennedy investigated. Roosevelt had had his "New Deal" and Eisenhower his "New Look." Kennedy was shaping his "New Frontier." To push toward it, he intended placing a premium on brainpower and the ability to act in the people he hired to support him. Judging from the report of his talent hunters, McNamara seemed to fit.

With his old-style rimless spectacles and conservative suits, and his style of combing his hair straight back and parted slightly to the left of center, Bob McNamara looked like a man who had been too preoccupied with business to keep up on the latest men's fashions. San Francisco-born, only son of a shoe company sales manager, he grew up too thin and asthmatic to be much of an athlete, too self-contained to be much of a socialite. Though not entirely a bookworm (the year before college he had worked as an ordinary seaman on a freighter plying the Pacific and Caribbean), he concentrated most of his notable drive and a wide-ranging interest in reading and arithmetic and on building a facility in these subjects.

The first impressive payoff came when he was elected to Phi Beta Kappa at the end of his sophomore year at the University of California. Graduated in 1937, he earned a master's degree from Harvard's famed School of Business Administration two years later. After working briefly for a San Francisco accounting firm, he returned to Harvard in 1940 as an assistant professor.

In Cambridge, he became a disciple of the then new theories on applying the principles of statistical analysis to business management problems. Classified 4-F because of eye trouble, he took a leave of absence from Harvard when war started, and went to work as a civilian consultant to the War Department helping set up statistical controls for the vast Army Air Corps supply complex. After a short time in Army Assistant Secretary for Air Lovett's office, he was sent to England in 1943. Commissioned a captain, he served in England, India, China, and the Pacific, eventually becoming a lieutenant colonel and holder of the Legion of Merit.

At war's end, both he—for one month—and his wife, Marge—for five months—were hospitalized with mild attacks of polio. He had gone into debt during his earlier Washington civilian service. The illnesses added new financial problems. While he was recovering, he was asked to join nine other "stat control" experts who intended to hire themselves out as a team to the highest bidder from U.S. industry. McNamara agreed, planning to work just long enough to get out of debt before returning to teach at Harvard.

Of half a dozen offers the team got, the one from Henry Ford, backed by a strong recommendation from Lovett, was most attractive. The group went to Detroit to rejuvenate the antiquely managed and economically ailing Ford Motor Company. Soon labeled "the Quiz Kids" for their incessant probing after facts and figures, they later became known as "the Whiz Kids" for their impressive individual leaps to business success.

Of them all, said one reporter, "McNamara whizzed the fastest. In only fourteen years, he went from manager of the planning and financial analysis office to comptroller, to assistant general manager of the Ford division, vice president and general manager of the same division, head of all car and truck divisions, and finally (just one day after Kennedy became President of the United States), the first non-Ford-family president of the company."

In the process, he became something of an automotive maverick. Instead of buying a house where most other Detroit car-building executives lived, in fashionable Grosse Point Shores or Bloomfield Hills north of town, he bought a modest (by executive standards) $50,000 home thirty-seven miles west in suburban Ann Arbor, near the University of Michigan campus. He rarely asked the auto magnates to visit and avoided their almost continual round of back-slapping cocktail parties. His idea of entertainment was to invite some university professors over for a discussion, after a scotch and soda or two, of anything from new books to popular art movements to Oriental philosophy. An evening out was, more often than not, a trip with his family to the symphony. Intellectual exercise was the way, said his wife, that "he winds his clock."

During his eleven-hour days, he drove himself and the rest of the organization on a relentless pursuit of facts. There isn't anything in this business, he told the staff, that "we can't put some kind of measure on and operate better because of it." He made decisions with what one Ford man called "a ruthless determination."

"Almost any decision," McNamara answered, "is better than no decision at all. No decision *is* a decision, a decision to maintain the *status quo*, and that is nearly always a mistake."

Ford executives were impressed with his approach when he turned the classic two-seater Thunderbird sports car into a four-seater and watched sales quadruple. They were just as impressed when he led the industry in offering auto buyers such safety features as seat belts, collapsible steering wheels, and padded dashboards.

They turned a little skeptical of his techniques when his blueprints produced Ford's small-sized car, the Falcon. Although it outsold Chevrolet's compact two to one, most sales were to former owners of standard-size Fords who switched to the cheaper compact. The net result was a loss in revenue. (Anticipating similar undesired results, in 1947, General Motors had canceled its plans to build a compact.)

Many Ford men became dubious of the whole statistical analysis approach when the company halted production of an Edsel automobile. "It was killed," insisted one executive, "not because of its repulsive front grill or because we were slow building a strong sales team but because McNamara's charts showed there was no more market for a medium-priced car—something General Motors promptly disproved."

"Those charts," the executive dryly noted, "give you funny answers sometimes."

On December 7, 1960, Kennedy's brother-in-law and chief talent scout Sargent Shriver invited McNamara to visit Kennedy and discuss a Cabinet appointment. In Washington the next evening, avid reader McNamara's first question of the President-elect had nothing to do with Defense. Having heard gossip that Kennedy's book *Profiles in Courage* had been ghost-written, McNamara asked, "Did you really write that book yourself?" (The answer: others had helped on the research, but the final draft had been Kennedy's own.)

Offered the post of Secretary of Defense, McNamara said he thought he was poorly qualified and asked for five days to think about it. The new Ford president went backtracking over a list of people Kennedy said had endorsed him.

He also checked with Tom Gates. At the time, Ford was being criticized heavily in public for having invested huge sums in an English automobile factory. "When Mr. McNamara called," said Gates's secretary, "I gave him a hard time, asked him if he was in town to mend fences over that investment messing up our gold-flow problem." A sergeant in the office got on the phone and said he would arrange a lift for McNamara to the Pentagon, "but you'll have to ride in a Chevrolet. We don't have any Fords."

McNamara spent two hours with Gates the next day. The Pentagon office began to suspect what was going on. Said the sergeant that evening. "I knew he must think we ran a pretty casual, flippant office around here. I figured I'd be the first guy fired."

At the end of his five days, with his endorsers checked and the Department sized up, McNamara answered Kennedy with a crisp, "I'm confident I can handle it." He then exiled himself in a Washington hotel for almost four weeks. On the telephone from twelve to fifteen hours a day, he winnowed a roster of some 125 possible candidates for subordinate Defense appointive posts, looking not only for sharp people but ones who would agree to stay a full four-year term. "No individual coming in here can be effective unless he stays several years," he said.

With his staff arranged, McNamara was sworn in on January 21, 1961. It cost him a $410,000-a-year salary, and more. In order to head Defense, he unloaded some 24,000 shares of Ford stock and gave up options on another 30,000 shares. His personal financial sacrifice was estimated at $3 million.

Under Wilson, McElroy, and even Gates, the Pentagon's main subordinate offices had operated with a good deal of permissive autonomy, in much the same manner that Wilson's decentralized

General Motors was run. Just days after taking office, McNamara revealed that the operation was going to be different from then on, and patterned after his management method at Ford. "It's quite apparent decisions are not being made as fast as they could be," he said. "The Defense establishment could do everything twice as fast as presently."

In textbook phrases, he continued, "An administrator can follow either one of the two alternative approaches. One I call the judicial process. In this instance, the administrator waits for the problems to be brought to him, along with proposed solutions, which he either accepts or rejects. In the alternative, a man plays an active role as leader, probing for problems, seeking to develop solutions, accepting suggestions, requesting the advice of experienced personnel. He then acts decisively and effectively to accomplish the solution. This is the approach we'll try to take in Defense."

When he began turning that philosophy into practice, old Pentagon hands—particularly in the military departments—were stunned. Younger by far than any previous Defense Secretary, he filled out his immediate staff with men even younger. Some, like Kennedy's own White House people, had been children when the generals and admirals they were arguing against had already fought two wars. To Defense veterans, their aggressive probing for information smacked of impulsive intrusion by amateurs into sacrosanct fields.

McNamara continued the Forrestal-Gates practice of attending Joint Chiefs meetings. "It is inconceivable to me," he said, "that I would not have met with my five division managers at Ford." And he warned the military, "I want decisions to be made based on fact, not emotion."

A catch-all phrase, "cost-effectiveness," was soon common in Pentagon corridors. Applied to any military request, the commonsense translation of the arithmetical language of the analytical statistician, was simply, "Is it worth the cost?"

Backed by their charts and slide rule figures, his bright, tireless assistants challenged almost every past military assumption about proper weapons, proper organization, proper procedures. Nonplussed, sometimes embarrassed by their own now unacceptable generalities, often denied the approvals they sought, the military vented their frustration on these newcomers personally, sarcastically labeling them "the new Whiz Kids" and "McNamara's Band."

"It was tough," said one admiral, "having these kids prove you wrong all the time."

Highly pleased with his new team, McNamara considered it "one of the most competent ever put together, in or out of Government." Typical of the talent, though much older than most of them, was his Deputy Secretary, polished New York lawyer Roswell Gilpatric. A member of President-elect Kennedy's committee to develop a reorganization plan for Defense, Gilpatric had been stirring up controversy over the way the Pentagon was run since he had first worked there in 1951, as an Assistant Secretary and then as Under Secretary of the Air Force. ("They used to draw lots in the Joint Chiefs of Staff to determine the relative combat importance of airplanes, ammunition, and warships.")

Once an advocate of forming a single military staff at the Pentagon level, he had been considered briefly for the top Defense post. McNamara had called him at five o'clock one morning to ask, "Will you work for me?" After less than a year with McNamara, he had softened his single-Service stand, which had advocated eliminating the three separate Service Secretaries. Instead of being the divisive obstacle to progress he had considered them earlier, he felt that the Secretaries had been turned into something quite different under McNamara. "He is using them as operating vice presidents," said Gilpatric, "rather than having them just represent Service viewpoints."

In a pattern set as far back as the Marshall era, Gilpatric operated as McNamara's alter ego, acting without hesitation in McNamara's name when "the Boss" was on a trip, and concentrating most on internal administration when McNamara was in town. "In the early months," said one staff man, "McNamara was inclined to jump on his horse, point his saber at the hilltop and yell, 'Charge!' That rattled and aggravated a lot of people, particularly in Congress, who'd gotten pretty comfortable in their old age. Ros Gilpatric, smooth, poised, would come along in the aftermath and in his soothing, soft-spoken way, allow as how they had all best do what this young man wanted." Though he was about the only McNamara appointee brought on board in spite of his insistence that he would stay only two years (he actually ended up staying three), Gilpatric was one of the reasons McNamara said, in 1961, "I like to have people smarter than I am working for me."

Washington thought that was a nice bouquet for him to toss. But, after the Secretary's first few months in office, most people were convinced there probably just wasn't anybody smarter than McNamara. None of the new brain trust asked more questions than he. No military proposal escaped his double-barreled challenge of, "How does that improve combat effectiveness?" and "Why?" And he always seemed to know more facts about the answer than did the people he questioned. The staff was a bit overwhelmed by this new Defense Secretary. "He's certainly a speed reader, and I sometimes think he has a photographic memory. He never seems to forget anything," his secretary said.

Around the Pentagon the story was told about a colonel rushing into the Secretary's office and shoving a full-page cablegram in front of him. After a slight pause, McNamara said, "Thank you very much."

"Don't you want to read it?" asked the colonel.

"I already have."

After a few weeks, McNamara was being touted as Kennedy's best Cabinet selection by far among a group of new Government leaders considered generally top-notch. "He's the best walking proof," said an aide, "of what Kennedy meant when he said, 'We must move swiftly or while we wait the world will collapse.' "

McNamara's fifteen-minute ride each day between home and the office was spent working on documents or reading several newspapers. In the office shortly after 7:00 A.M., he usually left about 7:30 in the evening with some homework, came in again on Saturday about 8:30 in the morning and left around 4:00. "He's always pressed for time," said his secretary, "and just when we're starting to relax after finishing one job, he's already looking ahead to the next problem. Fortunately for us, he doesn't expect everyone to be as smart as he is."

In the office, he was surrounded by reminders of the past. On the wall behind him hung an oil portrait of Forrestal. His giant walnut desk had first belonged to General John J. Pershing, had been used by Army Chief of Staff Marshall in World War II, had been dug out of storage and put back in service by Louis Johnson. His secretary, Peg Stroud, had worked first for Gates.

In addition, he had inherited from his predecessors assets less tangible: rules, regulations, successful and unsuccessful patterns of operation by which he could profit. "Two people," he said, "with essentially the same objectives will arrive at essentially the same decisions." He was continually handing credit for much of what he did in his first few months to those in Defense before him—especially Gates.

Congress' venerable dean of military affairs, Carl Vinson, nearing completion of a half century of service on Capitol Hill, lauded McNamara in 1964 for "making changes without the chaos which is the almost inevitable consequence of radical reform." Vinson reminded the Nation of his House Armed Services Committee's years of hearings and reports "showing the need for the very actions which now have been taken within the Department of Defense."

What set McNamara apart was that he did what others had only talked about. Shortly after taking office, he drew up a list of 131 problems to be analyzed and solved, in compliance with Kennedy's simple-to-state but tough-to-implement instruction that McNamara was "to determine the military force necessary to support our foreign policy and, having done that, to procure and operate it at the lowest possible cost."

Calling together all his top staff executives, including the heads of the military departments, he asked for volunteers to tackle whatever items on the list they wanted. Some 112 of the 131 problems were dealt with by the end of 1961. McNamara drew up another long list in 1962, another in 1963, and another each spring after that. As months rolled by and decisions snapped out of Room 3E880, the length of the list gradually diminished.

McNamara put together a small staff just down the hall from his office. The staff's sole function was to analyze Defense organization and business management problems and answer for him the question "How did we get to here?" Its members culled Congressional reports (some of them dated decades earlier), critical studies by the General Accounting Office of the way Defense had worked, and suggestions from an advisory commission organized in Forrestal's time and headed by former President Herbert Hoover. "We started with this information," said McNamara, "and added a certain amount of determination and single-minded purpose."

As a result of the intensive study, many steps were taken. A list of only a few of them indicates the range and depth of McNamara's leadership. The Defense Intelligence Agency was set up. A Defense Supply Agency was organized to eliminate overlapping Service activities in the procurement of common supplies. The Air Force put development and first-production-run purchase of new weapons under a single command, replacing the two that had formerly divided these responsibilities. The Army finally took Lovett's advice and combined the duplicated functions and organizations of a number of specialized technical services into a single Army Matériel Command to buy and supply combat forces with hardware. Army's Strategic Army Corps and Air Force's Tactical Air Command combined some units to form a new Strike Command.

A single agency was set up to handle, for all three Services, the administration of contracts with industry, and another single agency established to audit the results. During the missile crisis, even some military programs that had nothing to do with missiles had sometimes ended up by costing 400, 500, even 1,000 per cent more than original price estimates—and they were almost always late going into operation. McNamara borrowed from the Navy's *Polaris* project a Program Evaluation and Review Technique (PERT) that the Navy said had been the key management control mechanism in keeping the program on time within budget. He made it mandatory for all complex, high-cost Service projects. He borrowed the Air Force's source selection procedure for picking suppliers and, in general terms, put it to work in all the Services. His "Whiz Kids" standardized reports and paperwork handling. They cleaned out mountains of duplicated and contradictory rules and regulations.

"Except in rare circumstances," McNamara said, "committees are of value only for exchanging ideas." Like Forrestal, he preferred holding individuals by name, rather than offices blocked out on an organization chart, responsible for solving problems. The Services, partly in self-defense, set up project officers with a good deal of lateral authority to run the key programs. Army Matériel Command, for instance, named more than thirty such men, mostly colonels and lieutenant colonels. "But," the head of Army Matériel Command told his generals, "when they ask you for something, they're wearing my four stars." Gloomy objections that "over-emphasis on expediters was contrary to organizational routine and won't work," were heard. The new management procedures not only worked but also gave the top Pentagon levels something they'd never had before: continuously current, detailed knowledge on how well the Army was utilizing more than half its annual expenditure for new hardware.

McNamara also launched a three-part Cost Reduction Program of "reducing operating costs, buying only what we need," and "buying it at the lowest sound price." By 1965, the program had created an annual savings rate of over $6 billion in the business side of Defense activity. Said one long-time Pentagon employee, "Except in the Forrestal era when we had so little money, military people always had individual programs designed to cut expenses. But with McNamara we set goals, we organized, and we started keeping score on the results."

Like everything else, Cost Reduction had project managers. Not a post, camp, or station in Defense was without some man assigned by name to see that the program worked. And each individual was known personally by McNamara's own Cost Reduction project officer in the Pentagon. Criticized because the Defense budget didn't drop, in spite of all these well-publicized savings, McNamara's man answered, "What these gripers conveniently ignore is that without the Cost Reduction Program we would have needed $6 billion more than we actually asked from the taxpayers this year to carry out the same Defense plan."

McNamara's logic hit old routines the hardest through the change he made in the way Defense's fighting strength was assessed. The new system had been suggested first by an Army comptroller in 1952 and was in the throes of Air Force implementation in 1959. In simplest terms, it was a fiscal identification of the military force structure according to what role a weapon was intended to perform. Air Force bombers, for instance, were no longer part of an inventory total called just "aircraft." Instead, along with long-range missiles and the Navy's *Polaris,* they were tagged the Strategic Offensive Forces.

Until this new look at exactly where resources were allocated, Congress had appropriated funds to the Army, Navy, and Air Force, to (a) pay personnel, (b) do research and development, (c) buy weapons, (d) finance operating and maintenance costs. The fault in this kind of scrutiny was that, although Congress could enthusiastically endorse buying more bombers, it also could, and often did, cut Defense requests for maintenance money—a lump-sum statistic in the old budget to cover everything from keeping bombers flying to keeping warehouses painted. As one budget expert explained, "It was like buying part of a car but not the rest. They'd accept the design and approve the engine, but they'd give us only enough money for three wheels and not enough to keep it lubricated."

Under McNamara's Program Packages, costs of research and development, personnel, hardware, and operating were earmarked according to the kind of Force they belonged to. There were Strategic Offensive Forces and Strategic Defensive Forces, General Purpose Forces, Airlift and Sealift Forces, Reserve and National Guard Forces—plus a handful of difficult-to-categorize activities, such as civil defense work and overseas military assistance.

The sum benefit of all this was that McNamara had a more specific, sensible dollar gauge on the kinds of forces in being and on what was being done to improve them in the future. "The budget," said Gilpatric, "has been changed from an oppressive document into a creative and dynamic one." Knowing what bombers and missiles could do and knowing how much was being spent on payroll, operating costs, maintenance, and outright purchase, McNamara had a valid basis for making choices.

"Almost instinctively," said one observer, "the Services resisted this, partly because the clarity and logic of program-packaging made it all too evident that some projects already in existence or in the planning stage actually were surplus to the Nation's needs."

With all packages in the force structure planned five years ahead (though with less firmness as the projections got further into the future), McNamara cut here and added there. His whirlwind performance in his first four years alone was both exciting and controversial. Either characteristic would have been enough to guarantee that his every move would be highly publicized. The two together earned him more attention than anyone in Washington except the President.

Underlying his program package analysis and most talked about was McNamara's awesome ability to rattle off figures like a human electronic computer. Complained one general, "He can absorb facts and separate the wheat from the chaff so rapidly he makes even bright people look dumb."

Very little got by him. Handed a thick tabulation of the force structure during his sixth month in office, he skimmed through the document. Suddenly, he stopped on page forty, pointed to a figure, and asked the assistant secretary who had put it together, "How come this total doesn't agree with the one on page two?"

Bored with stereotyped briefings, McNamara habitually asked for the background document to read before an oral presentation was scheduled. In the briefing itself, instead of just listening, he would fire questions: "How much is it costing?" "What are the alternatives?" "How much do they cost?" "How did you arrive at the figures?"

Among other things, his approach forced the Services to work together on the whole of a problem rather than its parts. (In the past, each Service had studied to death its piece of the puzzle, while discounting the others.) In his first year, particularly, the military was regularly disconcerted when McNamara "ran into such things as one Service proposing procurement of twice as many of a certain type of weapon as would be necessary to knock out all estimated aircraft of all potential enemies with only that weapon, not taking into account other available anti-air weapons and aircraft."

Moreover, related one officer, "Say he'd ask on a Friday for a Joint Chief's answer on some problem the following Monday. Even if the Joint Staff worked all weekend, they'd have a chance to brief the Chiefs for only about twenty minutes. Meanwhile, McNamara had all his civilian chart boys studying the same problem. The generals would get up in front of him and find themselves out-knowledged."

Although Defense spending jumped from $41.2 billion in 1960 to a plateau of around $50 billion by 1965, the result was not simply an opportunity for the military to buy more of everything. Probably McNamara's most significant contribution to military strength, said one veteran, was that "He forced the Services to get at the heart of their own basic logic on why they want things."

Typically, in 1963, when the Navy submitted a recommendation that the aircraft carrier due to be started that year have nuclear rather than conventional engines in it, McNamara fired back a biting note. "You state that nuclear propulsion permits a significant increase in beneficial military results for a given expenditure and you note that the benefits may be taken in the form of either reductions in carrier task forces or increased effectiveness, but you have failed to identify the magnitude of the increase in effectiveness or the possible reduction in force. Thus, I am asked to consider a course of action which would, among other things, add at least $600 million to the five-year shipbuilding program without knowledge of the ultimate effect of these outlays."

An admiral grumbled about the "use of computers versus military judgment." When he couldn't, or wouldn't, adjust to McNamara's cost-effectiveness system, he was gotten rid of. Others who didn't measure up were either eased out or not given any more important assignments.

Eventually, his cost-effective-based decisions got him accused of downgrading military experience in favor of civilian statistics. Answered McNamara, "I would not, even if I could, attempt to substitute analytical techniques for judgment based upon experience; (but) the better the factual basis for reflective judgment, the better the judgment is likely to be."

He never decided against a unanimous Joint Chiefs opinion. And when his advice to Kennedy was based on a split Joint Chief's opinion, he always indicated the degree of difference. Yet, he was accused of playing soldier and leaving the generals out of it. "The real point of issue," he countered, "is, 'Does the Secretary run the Department?' " It reminded many of Johnson's remark fourteen years earlier that, "Whether they vote two-to-one or unanimously, the Joint Chiefs are only advisers to the Secretary of Defense and the President who do the deciding."

"This idea of civilian-military rivalries is as outdated as inter-Service rivalries," summed up one Pentagon executive. "Everybody must face a perilous future together."

In 1962, Gilpatric philosophized, "When he arrived, Mr. McNamara felt we had to move quickly. Unfortunately, the system just couldn't move that quickly. During the period before we were all geared up to the new tempo, the new philosophy, there was bound to be confusion and complaining."

After he had reached a decision, McNamara didn't bother, as Gates had, to let the Services "have their innings." The military did not take kindly to such brusque treatment of their status.

Said one critic, "McNamara developed an 'Emily Post' problem. His difficulty was this nebulous matter of how things are done rather than what is done."

He told the military that he wanted to hear their differing views, but, once a decision was made, he expected them to fall in behind him and not rehash the problem in public. For that statement, he was accused of muzzling the military. He spent the equivalent of over three months out of each work year either testifying or preparing to speak before Congressional committees—"often," said an assistant, "before one that called him just because they had heard what a great witness he was." Although he was as open and honest as any Secretary had ever been, his tendency to plant some needling question under an avalanche of factual refutation both hypnotized and angered Congress. Their shortcomings exposed, in effect, as never before, Congressmen accused him of "not showing the proper respect."

He went to greater lengths than had any of his predecessors in helping to soften the local economic blow when he was about to close a base somewhere. As a result, Pentagon mail usually ran about four to one in favor of his shutdown decisions. But the mere fact that he announced closing or consolidation of some 660 bases during his first four years in office got him accused of callousness and of being "lacking in political judgment."

The combination of a closer look at war plans with the absence of any obvious revolutions such as the missile development in weaponry, led McNamara to move carefully in picking new hardware for production. As the market changed, companies that were slow to adjust lost business and blamed McNamara. "No new starts!" they demanded. They got madder when McNamara pointed out that it takes about six years on the average for a weapon to move from idea to production line and that there were, in fact, over 200 new weapons being worked on in the laboratory. And their frame of mind didn't improve when McNamara decided to quit shoveling out dollars, now that the missile crisis was over, and increase competition for Defense contracts.

To help combat the gold flow, McNamara turned the military assistance program in a new direction. The Pentagon continued to supply arms free to underdeveloped countries that could not afford to buy them. But much of the huge $100 billion in U.S. aid sent overseas since World War II had gone to Western Europe, which, by the 1960's, was obviously back on its economic feet. McNamara therefore began selling European countries U.S. military hardware. This step angered their home-grown munitions industries.

Kennedy had said that the United States could afford to spend whatever was necessary for her own security but *only* what was necessary. McNamara punctuated that by canceling some pet Service projects, and the military staffs in the Pentagon smarted because his perfunctory announcements had not been preceded by any ambassadorial work preparing them for the loss.

Among the most publicized storms were those over halting development of a nuclear-powered aircraft engine, after the Air Force had spent $511.6 million on it, and cancellation of a Navy missile in which $53 million had been invested. Work was also stopped on an Air Force airplane-missile, the *Snark*, which had already cost $677.4 million, and a $407.6 million Air Force combination aircraft-space ship.

Congress bitterly challenged McNamara's judgment when he ordered development for use by both Navy and Air Force of a single tactical fighter. The Services wanted their own, individual aircraft. He said that one plane for both would save the Government $1 billion. Congress griped that his cost-effective charts had overlooked military expertise, which can't be put in a graph.

Hard-nosed facts about the merits of long-range missiles led him to push ICBM procurement on *Minuteman* and *Polaris*, to level off support of bombers, and to relegate a favorite project of Air Force bomber pilots, the supersonic B-70, to the position of a research program only. Emphasis on ICBM defense became a political issue in the 1964 Presidential campaign—fostered in part by bomber advocates reluctant to leave "the tried and true for something untested in combat" and in part by industry, which makes its money off production runs, not research. The critics grew silent, however, when the B-70 program ran into "horrible technical problems," and it became clear that McNamara's decision had saved them from buying a white elephant and the nation from wasting literally millions of dollars.

He canceled the *Skybolt* missile, on which the Air Force had spent $417.1 million. Designed to be fired by a bomber from outside the target area's air defenses, it was counted on by both U.S. and British Air Forces to maintain the bomber's diminishing role in strategic warfare. He had spent "a tremendous amount of time" studying the weapon's value, its mission, its relation to other weapons designed for the same work, and said, "I was certain my decision was in the best national interest." The decision got him accused of ignoring the nation's defense needs, not listening to the military, and being insensitive to Allied requirements.

"Producing it would have misdirected the spending of $2 billion in the taxpayers' dollars," he said. "What our critics really ought to do is charge us for wasting the first $400 million."

For all the allegations that he was a cold, inhuman computer, McNamara was not insensitive to criticism. When Republican Presidential candidate Barry Goldwater accused him of "deliberately phasing out 90 per cent of our nuclear delivery capability," he quickly summoned a press conference. Goldwater's assertion, he said, "is so completely misleading, so politically irresponsible and so damaging to our national security, that it cannot be allowed to stand on the record." He then rattled off a set of facts to refute it. Asked later why he moved so fast, he commented dryly, "When a charge involves a basic error in fact, we like to be in the same edition of the newspapers with the correction."

The sporadic Congressional lambasting of his decision on the single tactical fighter cut him even deeper. When investigation degenerated to within a short breath of charging McNamara with stupidity, lack of character, and near-collusion with the industry winner of the contract, Washington officials were startled by McNamara's slashing rebuttal. One agency executive, who had worked for Forrestal in 1948, even called Kennedy and said he thought that McNamara's behavior had all the signs of massive irritation and mental fatigue demonstrated by Forrestal just before his suicide. Snapped a McNamara friend, "I don't know what Bob's breaking point is, but it's a lot farther north than anyone else's." Kennedy did order him to take a short vacation, however. (McNamara went with his family to the Colorado mountains for the outdoor relaxations he likes probably better than any others—hiking and skiing.)

McNamara's close staff assistants and top officials rallied to defend him. He is not heartless at all, they said. In truth, "he is very friendly and considerate." They began circulating anecdotes like the one about McNamara shipping an aide who took sick on a work-filled weekend to Walter Reed hospital. Visiting the man next day, McNamara issued orders: "From now on, I want you out of that building every night by eight o'clock." And there was the time he stopped in the middle of a busy schedule, after keeping two assistants working around the clock for days, to send their wives notes praising their work and saying how much he appreciated the wives' patience and understanding.

Nor, said the staff, was he a tyrant about work. "You'd think," said one general, "if you made a mistake around Bob McNamara, you'd get your head sliced off. He doesn't do that." Resigned to the fact that people will make mistakes, McNamara himself had once quoted a business expert saying any executive right 51 per cent of the time was a success. "My standards are somewhat higher than that," he added, "but that's the right philosophy."

Early in the compilation of the five-year force structure, for instance, his budget people made a $300 million error on one item. They discovered it only after they had given McNamara the wrong figure. "When I went to his office to correct it," said his Comptroller, "I expected a good chewing out. He just shrugged his shoulders and made a note of the change."

McNamara didn't expect the staff to be all business, either, even if he was. One day he walked into the Pentagon barbershop with a sheaf of work papers. He sat next to a deputy assistant secretary who quickly hid a copy of *Playboy* magazine under his barber cape. But the move was so hasty, he lost hold of the magazine. It slid to the floor in front of McNamara. Smiling, McNamara laid aside his work, picked up and handed back the magazine without a word.

For factual proof of McNamara's concern about people, his aides pointed to the $2.8 billion salary increase he had gotten for the military in his first four years in office—much more of an achievement than any other Defense Secretary had managed. In addition, extra pay for higher-skilled specialists had nearly doubled between 1961 and 1965. And there was McNamara's major boost in Government-furnished family housing for military personnel. "No other group in our society is paid less per unit of ability than our military leaders," he had said in typical McNamara phraseology. "We cannot compensate the man in uniform for the unique hazards of the military profession, but we can and we should see to it that he at least shares with the civilian population the rising American standard of living."

About the only qualification his close assistants put on him was, "We're happy when Mrs. McNamara is in town because he's calmer around here, and there's not quite so much drive and pressure."

McNamara worried about the angry, unhappy people in the military who objected to his decisions, primarily because Defense would be in dire trouble if their unhappiness was resulting from a conviction that basic military strength was being weakened. If the discontent was simply a normal, human reaction to all his changes, then he knew it was only temporary. He dug into a thorough analysis of it and decided it was not bedrock panic.

Later, he said, "There's a big difference between the life-and-death matters here and selling a few automobiles at Ford. But the problems in dealing with people are the same in any large organization. Even at the Catholic Ecumenical Council, the Pope put in closed circuit television to watch for crises. He actually had to hurry down to the hall once to prevent disagreement from breaking the meeting up."

"The more far-reaching a decision," he added, "the longer the time it takes for people to accept the change. The great interest of our total public is never focused on you in this position, only the pressures of the group immediately affected. There is a great temptation to yield to that pressure. But if you have the backing of the White House, you can make these decisions. Once you decide you intend to do what you think best for total national security, the rest is relatively easy."

Added a friend, "He came down here to get results. If the people liked the system and the policies, I think that's all he would ask. If they liked him and questioned his results, he'd probably feel he was a failure."

Besides the courage to withstand emotional upheavals around him, McNamara had another asset. Never before had a Defense Secretary enjoyed such rapport with and unqualified backing from the White House. "I couldn't accomplish anything over here without Presidential support," he had once said. "It is absolutely fundamental. I wouldn't and couldn't stay here one minute without it."

So high was White House regard for McNamara that he found himself being assigned outside chores. He was named head of a committee to study a proposal for developing supersonic passenger aircraft, to study Appalachian area problems, and to look into building a nuclear-powered merchant ship. He was heavily involved in finding talent to fill vacated posts elsewhere in the executive branch.

For all the squabbles surrounding his decisions, his performance "in the public interest" was impressive enough by 1963 to create agitation in the Republican Party for him to run for President. (Kennedy was asked in a press conference what he thought of the idea. He laughed and said, "I have too high a regard for him to launch his candidacy right now.") Although he was nominally an independent Republican, McNamara was considered as a vice presidential running mate for Johnson in 1964. Vetoed by regular Democratic Party leaders and by the heads of organized labor, he nevertheless was called on in the last two weeks of the campaign to rally all executive branches of Government and state the administration's case to the nation.

In this effort, he put the Defense case so strongly that it marred his budding friendship with Gates. McNamara told a Democratic forum that before 1961 the United States had but a single strategy, and it was stepchild to a predetermined budget; that planning was not coordinated between the Services; and that the weapons inventory was almost completely lacking in certain "major elements required for combat readiness." Gates bit back in a letter: "If the conditions actually had been as you have described them, then I could not conscientiously have remained in office—nor would I have been allowed to." He also reminded McNamara that in 1961 he had been forced to defend the Pentagon against a Democratic charge of a "missile gap" that had turned out to be phony, too.

In claiming that shortages in military strength had been corrected, McNamara was right. In implying that the Pentagon's previous leaders had not already been planning to take some of the same steps he had taken, he was unfair—or so many past Defense executives, in addition to Gates, felt.

Military soul-searching over strategy, similar to the bulk of McNamara's early moves to streamline the Pentagon's business efficiency, had begun before he arrived. At least as early as 1958, a growing number of strategists were insisting that it was untenable, and probably fatal, to try stopping a Communist-led revolution in Laos by threatening Russia with the mutual annihilation of Moscow and Washington, D.C. Such a promise to commit suicide was not credible in the first place, they felt, and, in the second place, was implausible as a guarantee because it counted on there being no error in Kremlin judgment about U.S. resolve. Finally, it unrealistically presumed that Russia had tight control over every warlike insurrectionist in the world.

But, whatever the long-range planners may have been thinking, it was true that Kennedy believed there had been almost complete reliance on massive nuclear retaliation, and that he had asked McNamara to see that there was more room to maneuver in foreign policy. The force to support what was labeled his "strategy of flexible response" had not fallen easily into place.

"Forces tailored to an arbitrary financial ceiling were given up," said McNamara, "in favor of forces tailored to various anticipated challenges. It is much tougher to tailor forces to a rational judgment of need than it is to merely squeeze as much as you can under an arbitrary budget ceiling. In a sense, you forget all about this roles-and-missions business. The emphasis needs to start with foreign policy."

The clue to what Kennedy wanted was housed in his Inaugural Address: "Let us never negotiate out of fear, but let us never fear to negotiate." Thus, while his diplomatic left hand sought platforms for bargaining with Communism, his military right hand was to develop strength to stop any form of Red aggression.

In one context, this strategy amounted to a vindication of Maxwell Taylor's insistent demands, until he retired in 1959, for conventional as well as atomic build-ups. In fact, Taylor was put back in service, first as Kennedy's special military adviser, then, in 1962, as Chairman of the Joint Chiefs of Staff. Probably the best summation of what Defense needed was spelled out by Cyrus Vance, former Pentagon General Counsel and Secretary of the Army, who replaced Gilpatric as Deputy Secretary of Defense in January, 1964. Said Vance later that year: "We are confronted by both missiles and machine guns, by nuclear forces and guerrilla bands, by a whole range of threats. No one answer, no one weapon, no one force suffices. We can afford no gaps through which we might be attacked. And we can afford no chance that peace might be lost, or a conflict escalated to fearful dimensions, because we were unprepared for any contingency."

Kennedy had only sporadic and generally unrewarding success with the left hand of his policy. The high mark came in 1963 when a treaty was concluded with Russia (later signed by several score other nations), agreeing to discontinue nuclear testing that might poison the atmosphere. Other than that, as events proved following Kennedy's personal talk with Khrushchev in Vienna, Austria, in 1961, the Communist word was not to be trusted even when delivered in unmonitored private. The Russian Government's refusal to start any discussions except on its own terms finally forced Kennedy's public comment, "We cannot negotiate with those who say, 'What's mine is mine and what's yours is negotiable.' "

McNamara had more success in building up the punch Kennedy wanted for the right hand. Manpower strength went from 2.5 million men (not counting about 1 million civilians working for the armed services) in 1960 to almost 2.7 million by the end of 1964. The Army streamlined its combat division structure with enough built-in flexibility so it could be shaped larger or smaller in a hurry, depending on whether it was fighting insurrection or battlefield war. The number of aircraft assigned a division doubled, and the division received more powerful weapons. (The Pentagon agreed with Maxwell Taylor's general philosophy about strengthening conventional war forces, but the bulk of the build-up came exactly as the other Joint Chiefs told Taylor it should in 1957—by boosting firepower and mobility.)

By 1964, programs to pre-position some Army, Navy, and Air Force units along with their combat supplies on location in or near various world trouble spots were maturing. So were programs to maintain forces in the United States on a "ready alert" status with huge air transports that could haul them to some brushfire flare-up in a matter of hours. In mid-1964, McNamara ticked off for the President (among other things): "a 150 per cent increase in the number of nuclear warheads in the strategic alert forces; a 60 per cent increase in the tactical nuclear forces deployed in Western Europe; a 45 per cent increase in the number of combat-ready Army divisions; a 44 per cent increase in the number of tactical fighter squadrons; a 75 per cent increase in airlift capability (with a 300–400 per cent increase to come); a 100 per cent increase in general ship construction and conversion to modernize the fleet; an 800 per cent increase in the Special Forces trained to deal with counterinsurgency threats."

And, he noted afterward, "We ought to have it. We spent $7.5 billion more per year, on the average, than the previous Administration's Defense expenditures to get it."

One wrinkle McNamara added in these public presentations was to reveal the heretofore classified figures on just how many nuclear bombs, bombers, and missiles the United States had marked directly to fight a nuclear world war—1,100 bombers, 800 ICBM's ready to fire, 260 *Polaris* IRBM's on station at sea. He reasoned that, if deterrence to nuclear war was enemy knowledge of the certainty of incineration, then he ought to use every communications means available to let possible enemies know what they were up against. "These forces have the ability to survive a surprise attack," he said, "and still deliver on target enough nuclear weapons to obliterate the Communist world as an organized society."

The Communists had not been idle all this time. After Khrushchev had once again threatened chaos in Berlin, Kennedy went to the beleagured city and summed up the conflict by telling its citizens: "There are many people in the world who really don't understand, or say they don't, what is the great issue between the Free World and the Communist world. Let them come to Berlin." His words might have been said of Laos or the Congo, of Viet-Nam or Cuba, or of any one of a half-dozen other places.

The first test of the Administration's "flexible response" ended in disastrous failure, although if it had been tried when originally scheduled, it might have been highly successful. In the spring of 1960, Eisenhower had given approval for the Central Intelligence Agency, with military advice, to train Cuban refugees who had fled from dictator Fidel Castro's version of Communism in their homeland. The plan, scheduled for midsummer, was to help them land an invasion force on Cuba to drive Castro out. The selected beachhead was a then unguarded strip of land known as the "Bay of Pigs." Training and supply problems forced delay of the mission until November.

In November, the attack was postponed again until the following spring. By then, Castro had fortified the landing area. That, plus some militarily poor decisions, plus what all later public reports indicated was appallingly poor communication between the new Administration and officials running the operation, botched it. Kennedy took full blame, and refused to discuss the personalities involved, "to avoid the people losing faith in constituted authority," said one official.

In 1962, when the United States discovered missiles and launch sites being put together in Cuba, Kennedy moved much more swiftly. He threw up a tight blockade around the island. B-52's were sent far enough north to be picked up on Russian radar screens. Carrier aircraft in the Caribbean fanned out on patrol as far away as Gibraltar. Russia backed down and pulled the missiles out.

But that flare-up had shown that the Pentagon had a long way to go in building its flexible force. To prepare for a possible invasion of Cuba, McNamara pulled fighter aircraft away from all over the country, into the Southeast, "and we were still short. . . . We needed escort vessels. We needed patrol craft, transport aircraft, and air defense." (During the crisis, McNamara packed a bag and, except for a couple of brief trips home, stayed in the Pentagon around the clock. The staff reported later, "He seems to thrive on trouble." And the staff was a little disconcerted at 10:30 on the Saturday night before events calmed down when he came out of his inner office and told them, "Well, I think I'll go to bed. Why don't you all go home?")

In the spring of 1965, Defense readiness was much better. Although the United States had 100,000 men on duty in the Dominican Republic and in South Viet-Nam, basic U.S. forces were still largely untouched. Just 10 per cent of the Navy's ships and men were embroiled in the support of the two battlegrounds. The Army's sixteen active divisions were still in place, five in Europe, two in South Korea, one in Hawaii, and the other eight on "strategic reserve" duty in the United States. Only about half the Marine Corps strength was in the two shooting areas, and only 10 per cent of the Air Force's tactical fighters and fighter bombers.

The previous fall, President Lyndon B. Johnson had announced that the force necessary to back up the strategy of flexible response had been built. McNamara had added cautiously that there were still some "loose ends." He stated: "An increase in mobility and in combat readiness are the two major headings under which they fall. In mobility, we must tailor the forces more closely to the challenges and there is still much pre-positioning to do of combat hardware overseas in readily available areas. In combat readiness, we have greatly increased the procurement of equipment. All of this needs to be brought up to a greater state of readiness by training and testing exercises."

By the summer of 1965, as it turned out, an important part of the training ground was the "small war" in South Viet-Nam—growing larger daily. Few people care to hear combat called "a training ground." Yet, in one sense, that is what the fighting in Viet-Nam had become: a test of untested troops, of untried operations concepts, of new hardware barely off the drawing boards, of previously unchallenged supply lines. As in any test, mistakes were made.

The strategy had not changed. Said Johnson, in August, 1965: "I told McNamara that he's my right-hand punch. I told him to take the power of this country and with it keep our word and our honor and protect the lives of our boys to the maximum extent possible. I told Rusk and Goldberg that they're my left-hand punch and to try to get us out of this war."

U.S. military experts would have preferred another battleground. Tucked away on the other side of the globe in an underdeveloped area, South Viet-Nam presented an extremely difficult problem in logistics. Moreover, the people of the small nation were weary of war. Desertions from the military sometimes ran almost as high as the number of new recruits drafted into the forces. Once drafted, every man wanted to become an officer because, by tradition, officers did not have to lead men into battle, but merely ordered them out. Worst of all from a military viewpoint, Communist guerrillas roamed almost at will through the countryside and even in the streets of Saigon. Nor would they stand and fight for long. Their goal was not to capture ground (the traditional military target) but to demoralize the people and undermine the non-Communist government. Thus, they attacked anything that symbolized the South Vietnamese Government, assassinating local village officials or ambushing troops sent to relieve a besieged Government-controlled hamlet; afterwards, disappearing safely into the jungle.

For the United States, it was a different kind of war and it looked like one that might already have been lost. To many, the idea of pulling U.S. forces out of South Viet-Nam seemed the proper course of action. To McNamara and his military-civilian staff, most State Department analysts, and the White House, the implications of the U.S. commitment meant that to give up in Viet-Nam would seriously, probably disastrously, expose all the rest of Southeast Asia to Communist domination and would raise considerable doubts among other underdeveloped nations in the world about just how strong an ally they had in the United States.

By June, 1965, U.S. military strength in Viet-Nam had already been built up to 51,000 men. Within four months, the numbers jumped to 139,670 and, instead of acting only as advisers to Vietnamese troops, U.S. military men were now in combat units. By the end of 1965, U.S. forces in Viet-Nam totaled 181,392 men. The numbers continued to increase in 1966.

The price paid for such escalation was high. And one man who was vilified back in Washington every time U.S. troops were killed or a supply line fouled up was McNamara. One Pentagon veteran said: "Reread the account of Louis Johnson and Korea. Wherever it says 'Johnson' substitute 'McNamara,' and wherever it says 'Korea' substitute 'Viet-Nam.' The cast changes but the plot is almost the same."

McNamara set up a high-priority team of Army, Navy, Air Force, and Marine Corps logistics experts with "expedite" authority to keep the right hardware moving in the right quantity to the right place. Yet even when mistakes were rapidly corrected, they were inevitably used as an excuse by his many critics to challenge the whole scheme of cost-effectiveness and the insistence on economy in running Defense. The big U.S. build-up in Viet-Nam still left approximately 75 per cent of all U.S. military forces free to support other U.S. commitments around the world. But critics in Congress and elsewhere charged and charged again that McNamara's past economy moves in Defense had left the nation ill prepared for the fighting in Viet-Nam, which, one of them said, was "shortsightedly draining all our military strength away from the rest of the world and into Southeast Asia."

Opposition to U.S. involvement in Viet-Nam was widespread, and much of it was focused on McNamara, both in his capacity as boss of the Department of Defense and as a leading foreign policy maker of the Johnson Administration. When he received honorary degrees during graduation ceremonies at two U.S. universities in 1966, altogether some 150 students walked out of the presentations in protest—although at one, New York University, the remaining 6,000 students gave him a standing ovation.

Speaking at his daughter's graduation from Chatham College, Pennsylvania, on May 22, 1966, McNamara commented:

> The era in which we live has been called the Age of Protest. Judging from the pickets out on the sidewalk, that does not seem an altogether inappropriate title. . . . But whatever comfort some of the extremist protest may be giving our enemies—and it is clear from Hanoi's own statements that it is—let us be perfectly clear about our principles and our priorities. This is a nation in which the freedom of dissent is absolutely fundamental.

Generally speaking, McNamara and his Defense Department found nothing in the dissent and criticism to shake their convictions about the correctness of what they had done and were doing in Viet-Nam. Quite the contrary. The tempo of U.S. battlefield success increased, and U.S. military experts pointed to growing evidence that the Communists were being thrown on the defensive. Deputy Secretary Cyrus Vance observed, in mid-1966: "I think it has been an extraordinary achievement to send 350,000 men to Southeast Asia in such a short period of time and to keep them supplied. We read comments from time to time about alleged shortages. [The Chairman of the Joint Chiefs] has said to me there was no shortage affecting either the campaign or the welfare of the troops."

Indicating that he had had this view confirmed in talks with commanders in the field as well as with the "scores of Congressmen and other visitors" who went to the area in late 1965 and early 1966, Vance added: "Everybody comments on the outstanding morale of our troops. I'm sure if people were suffering from shortages, we wouldn't have the morale we do.

"I might just add one thing. In a sense, this past year has been a test of the practices and some of the innovations which Mr. McNamara has introduced. The ability to support our forces in Southeast Asia and have them perform in such magnificent fashion is the acid test of what has been done the past few years. Against this test, it has come out damn well.

"That is not to say we are right 100 per cent of the time. You never are in this business. [But] looking at it over-all, it's a superb achievement—and it is a debt we owe to the scores of thousands of fighting men and their leaders, and those in the United States and elsewhere supporting them at every level, who have made this possible."

However, as McNamara and every one of his predecessors in office had learned, there is no end to the things that need doing in Defense. The Secretary himself had pointed this out just as the tide of war began to turn. The forum he chose was not one he routinely exploited.

Because for some time he has been considered one of the Administration's most important spokesmen, McNamara has often been asked to give speeches. He has accepted invitations only about two or three times a year, believing, as he once said, that he shouldn't spend the time unless he has something he feels needs to be said. On May 18, 1966, he felt he did when he addressed the American Society of Newspaper Editors meeting in Montreal, Canada.

Subsequent press write-ups and comments by people in and out of Government led many on his staff to ponder the hazards of trying to communicate to the nation from a public forum. A number of analysts hinted that the speech marked a break with the Administration—or, at best, that McNamara had usurped the Secretary of State's right to speak on foreign policy. Actually, and as a matter of routine, McNamara's speech had been previously approved by the Secretary of State and the White House. Both had received copies fully two weeks before the planned delivery.

McNamara noted:

> There is still among us an almost ineradicable tendency to think of our *security* problem as being exclusively a military problem—and to think of the *military* problem as being exclusively a *weapons-system* or hardware problem.
>
> The plain, blunt truth is that contemporary man still conceives of war and peace in much the same stereotyped terms that his ancestors did. The fact that these ancestors, both recent and remote, were conspicuously unsuccessful at avoiding war, and enlarging peace, doesn't seem to dampen our capacity for clichés.
>
> We still tend to conceive of national security almost solely as a state of armed readiness: a vast, awesome arsenal of weaponry. We still tend to assume that it is primarily this military ingredient

> that creates security. We are still haunted by this concept of military hardware. . . .
>
> From the point of view of combat readiness, the United States has never been militarily stronger. . . . But if we think profoundly about the matter, it is clear that this purely military posture is not the central element in our security. A nation can reach the point at which it does not buy more security for itself simply by buying more military hardware—we are at that point. The decisive factor for a powerful nation, already adequately armed, is the *character of its relationships with the world* [author's italics].

McNamara then pointed out that there had been 164 significant outbreaks of violence around the world in the previous eight years alone, involving 82 different governments, but that only 15 were military conflicts between two nations and that in not one of the 164—nor, for that matter, in any conflict since World War II—had there been a formal declaration of war. "The planet is becoming a more dangerous place to live on," he added, "not merely because of a potential nuclear holocaust." He recited statistics to show that "there can be no question but that there is an *irrefutable relationship between violence and economic backwardness. And the trend of such violence is up, not down* [author's italics]." Noting that most of the poor live in the southern half of the globe, he said:

> The conclusion to all of this is blunt and inescapable; given the certain connection between economic stagnation and the incidence of violence, the years that lie ahead for [poor] nations . . . are pregnant with violence. This would be true even if no threat of Communist subversion existed—as it clearly does. What is often misunderstood is that Communists are capable of subverting, manipulating, and finally directing for their own ends the wholly legitimate grievances of a developing society.
>
> But it would be a gross oversimplification to regard Communism as the central factor in every conflict throughout the underdeveloped world. Of the 149 serious internal insurgencies in the past eight years, Communists have been involved in only 58 of them, 38 per cent of the total, and this includes seven instances in which a Communist regime itself was the target of the uprising.
>
> Whether Communists are involved or not, violence anywhere in a taut world transmits sharp signals through the complex ganglia of international relations; and the security of the United States is related to the security and stability of nations half a globe away.

> And our role must be . . . to help provide security to those developing nations which genuinely need and request our help, and which demonstrably are willing and able to help themselves.
>
> The rub comes in this: we do not always grasp the meaning of the word *security* in this context. In a modernizing society, *security means development*. Security is not military hardware, though it may include it. Security is not military force, though it may involve it. Security is not traditional military activity, though it may encompass it.
>
> Security is development. Without development, there can be no security. A developing nation that does not develop simply cannot remain 'secure' [author's italics].

By 1966, McNamara had served in the Pentagon longer than any other Defense Secretary. There was general approbation of his cost-effective methods and his program packages. But he still suffered from what one aide had called his "Emily Post problem." And the build-up in Viet-Nam had increased the opportunity for human error within the Defense system to the point where there were more than enough excuses for those critics who wanted to imply (sometimes viciously impugning McNamara's motives) that if he could be got rid of, Defense would be much the better for it. There was still malice heaped on some of his decisions by citizens immediately affected. For instance, when he announced the closing of the Springfield, Massachusetts, arsenal, the Springfield paper ran his picture on its front page alongside one of Adolf Hitler and accused McNamara of anti-Semitism.

But any student of history, as McNamara clearly is, soon learns that a Defense Secretary hasn't much chance of refuting any such charges against himself. What bothered those who knew him well was that the public preoccupation with analyzing the McNamara personality tended to obscure many of the important issues that he raised. Many people considered him to be the leading exponent of certain positions that he had questioned, if not attacked. Among them were two he had mentioned in his Chatham College speech. Of one, he said:

> . . . it seems a little premature to worry that the computer is on the verge of replacing the human brain. Quite apart from everything else, that brain is an utterly incredible computer itself; probably the most magnificent bit of miniaturization in the entire universe. Though it weighs only about three pounds, it contains some

> 10 billion nerve cells, each of which has some 25 thousand possible interconnections with other nerve cells. It has been calculated that to build an electronic computer large enough to have that range of choice would require an area equal to the entire surface of the earth.

The second issue he discussed was management control:

> It is easy enough to wring one's hands over the complicated issues of meaning and value that an era of radical change involves. It is much tougher to tackle these issues honestly and humbly, and work tirelessly toward wise solutions. We sometimes do not even state the problem in a wholly realistic way. . . . We fear that organization in modern society is growing too big and too complex—and that we are establishing management controls that are too massive. . . . But it is possible that exactly the reverse is the case. It is possible that some of our gravest problems in society arise not out of overmanagement; but precisely out of undermanagement. . . . Exploding urbanization, to take a cogent example, has been a fact in the western world for more than two hundred years. . . . But there is no evidence whatsoever that man has overmanaged this problem. There is every evidence that he has undermanaged it.

Whatever public opinion may have been, by 1966, there was general approbation in the Pentagon of McNamara's cost-effective methods and his program packages. There were still disagreements, as there always will be, but much of the disharmony was gone. War spurred the building of civilian-military and inter-Service teamwork.

However the problems of the future are to be met, probably the best advice for one of the men who will have to handle those problems—the next Secretary of Defense—was contained in another public statement by McNamara. On November 11, 1962, long before Viet-Nam became a full-scale test of U.S. capability and resolution, while speaking at a Veteran's Day ceremony in Arlington National Cemetery, McNamara warned that the lessons of modern existence, "like the lessons of the soldiers, are easy to forget in the heat of battle. They must be learned in advance, and deeply understood. . . . The margin for error is shrinking."